CD 1 2/56

Publications on Russia and Eastern Europe of the
Institute for Comparative and Foreign Area Studies
Number 4

This book is sponsored by the Russian and East European Program of the Institute for Comparative and Foreign Area Studies (formerly Far Eastern and Russian Institute), University of Washington, Seattle.

The Octobrists in the Third Duma, 1907—1912

Ben-Cion Pinchuk

University of Washington Press

Seattle and London

Library of Congress Cataloging in Publication Data
Pints'uk, B
    The Octobrists in the Third Duma, 1907–1912.
    (Publications on Russia and Eastern Europe of the Institute
for Comparative and Foreign Area Studies, no. 4)
        Bibliography: p.
        1. Soŭiz Semnadt͡satogo okti͡abri͡a. 2. Russia.
Gosudarstvennai͡a Duma. 3d, 1907–1912. 3. Russia—
Politics and government—1904–1914. I. Title.
II. Series: Washington (State). University.
Institute for Comparative and Foreign Area Studies.
Publications on Russia and Eastern Europe, no. 4.
DK262.P52   320.9'47'08   74–2176
ISBN 0–295–95324–1

*Publications on Russia and Eastern Europe of the Institute for
Comparative and Foreign Area Studies is a continuation of the
series formerly entitled Far Eastern and Russian Institute Publications on Russia and Eastern Europe.*

To Miri

Acknowledgments

I owe thanks to many people for aiding the progress of this study from its beginning as a doctoral dissertation to that of a published book. I wish to acknowledge my intellectual debt to my teachers and colleagues in the history departments of the Tel-Aviv University and the University of Washington. I owe particular thanks to Professor Michael Confino, Director of the Soviet and East European Institute of the University of Tel-Aviv, who first introduced me to the intricacies and fascinations of Russian history as well as to historical research. At the University of Washington I was very fortunate to have the guidance and advice of Professor Donald W. Treadgold during the conception and progress of both the research and the writing of this study. Many scholars have offered constructive criticism as well as friendly encouragement, but I would like to particularly thank my good colleague Professor Zvi Yavetz of the University of Tel-Aviv, as well as Professors Peter Sugar and John Reshetar of the University of Washington. Finally, I am deeply indebted to Margery Lang, editor for the Institute for Comparative and Foreign Area Studies whose careful, intelligent, and untiring attention were of the utmost importance in helping me produce this book. All errors and interpretations are, of course, my responsibility.

Ben-Cion Pinchuk

Soviet and East European Institute
University of Tel-Aviv
1973

Contents

The Octobrists in the Third Duma,
1907—1912

Introduction

The Third Duma period, 1907–12, was one of crucial testing of the Russian constitutional monarchy, as established in the wake of the revolution of 1905–7. This period deserves much more atten⁀tion than hitherto given it by Soviet and Western historiography, for the establishment of a representative institution, despite its limited franchise and powers, represented a new epoch in Russian political life. For the first time in modern history, Russian auto⁀cracy had to share its power with the elected representatives of the people. To some Russian liberals it looked as if a start could be made in moving the country toward reform: the constitutional monarchy presented a third choice, one lying between the present alternatives of revolution or absolutism.

This study is devoted to the institution and the party that tried to make the constitutional monarchy a living reality: the Third Duma and the Union of October 17 (or the Octobrists, the largest party in those crucial years). The attitude of the tsar toward the Octobrists affected his attitude toward the Duma and thus consti⁀tutes part of the story; another part is the relationship of the Octo⁀brists with Peter Stolypin, the outstanding prime minister of imperial Russia, who in his own way tried to achieve much the same objec⁀tives as his Duma sympathizers. The Union hoped to clear a pas⁀sage between the extremes of reaction and revolution. An exami⁀nation of its relations with the leaders of the Third Duma, the court, and the government may contribute to a better understanding

3

of the political alternatives and dilemmas faced by imperial Russia on the eve of its demise.

As the largest faction in the Third Duma, the only Duma that served its full five-year term, the Octobrists tried to establish a working relationship between the representative institutions and tsarism. They tried to cooperate with the historically established authorities in an effort to implement the principles and promises of the October Manifesto and move Russia along the road of "peaceful renovation."

The Union was founded at the height of a revolution and after a humiliating defeat in war. As a political movement, Octobrism carried the imprint of both events.

From the turn of the twentieth century, powerful forces were preparing Russia for revolution and change. Chief among these forces were the increased impoverishment of the peasantry, the emergence of an industrial proletariat following the rapid industrialization, the formation of an organized opposition to the tsar on a broader scale than ever before that included both revolutionary and liberal groups, and, overriding all, the continuing reactionary policies of the government.

There were tangible manifestations of unrest and disaffection that preceded the revolution of 1905 and by the turn of the century the deteriorating conditions in the villages could no longer be ignored. A long series of famines preceded the outbreak of agrarian disturbances in 1901–2 in the provinces of Poltava and Kharkov. The number of strikes among the workers increased steadily, beginning in 1901, and the attempt by the authorities to combat subversive influences among the workers by setting up police-controlled labor organizations failed. Acts of terrorism against government officials, culminating with the assassination of V. K. Plehve, minister of the interior, in July 1904 were becoming more frequent and daring. The authorities remained adamant in their opposition to proposals of reform coming from the various liberal organizations and groups, yet these suggestions increased in militancy. From February 1901, the zemstvo, or county council, leaders were meeting at frequent intervals in "private" conferences that were becoming a quasi-permanent institution and the chief organ of liberal opinion. In September 1903, the Union of Liberation was founded, which, for the first time in Russian history, raised liberalism to the status of an organized political force.

The authorities retaliated with their customary reprisals, which were particularly oppressive under Plehve, who became minister of the interior in 1902. He was one of several persons who deserve the principal blame for the outbreak of the Russo-Japanese War in January 1904: Plehve thought that a "small victorious war" would help tsarism to stem the tide of disaffection and revolutionary activity. He was gravely mistaken. The war against Japan turned out to be an uninterrupted series of disasters for Russia's military and naval forces. The defeat was particularly painful for Russian nationalist feelings, since it was the first time in many years that an Asian country had bested a major European power. The Peace Treaty of Portsmouth officially ended the war on September 5, 1905, but not only were the weaknesses of the higher command and the army in general revealed, but there was also a humiliating revelation of the country's backwardness. The war became a lever for revolution rather than a diversion of public opinion from internal problems.

For a short while the Russo-Japanese War had eased internal tensions, but the continuing defeats brought an upsurge of discontent and revolutionary activities. A conference of left liberals, Social Revolutionaries, and delegates of national minorities held in Paris in September 1904 decided to work for the overthrow of absolutism and the establishment of a representative government. In November a conference of zemstvo leaders adopted an eleven-point resolution that called for, among other things, the granting of civil liberties, democratization and expansion of local self-government, and the summoning of a representative legislative assembly. The resolution was the starting point of a country-wide campaign.

Early in the year 1905 the leadership of the struggle against absolutism began to pass from the hands of the moderates into those of the revolutionary parties. The "Bloody Sunday" of January 9, 1905, when more than one hundred demonstrating workers were killed during a peaceful demonstration, crystallized the new turn in the opposition movement. A wave of demonstrations, protests, strikes, and acts of terrorism followed that flooded the empire.

Agrarian disturbances broke out in many areas and disaffection spread to the armed forces. During the second half of September a widespread strike movement began, culminating in a general strike that brought large sections of the country's economy to a halt. Soviets of workers' deputies appeared in several cities and threatened to replace the established authorities.

The government's reaction to those developments was a confused mixture of repression and concession. A rescript addressed to A. G. Bulygin, minister of the interior, in February 1905, announced the tsar's intention to convoke a consultative representative assembly, and in April he issued a decree proclaiming the principles of religious tolerance. The general strike thus resulted in the proclamation of the October Manifesto, which went beyond the promises of previous proclamations and decrees in meeting the demands of public opinion. S. Iu. Witte, the new prime minister, was the main influence behind the manifesto, a manifesto that did not stop the revolutionary parties, but did split the nonrevolutionary opposition.

The revolutionary events of 1905 dramatically demonstrated to this nonrevolutionary opposition the need for a way to adapt Russia to the twentieth century without a bloody revolution. Its left wing was willing to cooperate with the revolutionary parties until the final overthrow of the absolutist regime. The right wing, whose nucleus was the minority of the zemstvo congresses, reluctantly followed the more articulate Left most of the time, but with the spread of strikes and agrarian disturbances became increasingly willing to cooperate with the authorities in order to stop the deterioration of the established social and political order. After the publication of the October Manifesto, the right wing rallied to the support of the authorities. The left wing of the liberal movement founded the Kadet party; the right wing founded the Union of October 17.

The Union, established as a coalition of individuals and groups to help the authorities quench revolutionary chaos and redress the nation's honor, attempted to find an alternative to both autocracy and revolution while trying to cooperate with tsarism, whose monopoly of ultimate political power the Octobrists never contested.

The basic ideological orientation, political program, and tactics of the Union of October 17 had been determined during the period preceding the Third Duma. The history of the Union in the Third Duma, where it emerged as the leading political force, was one of continued effort to implement its basic assumption that Russia could be renovated by peaceful means and her national prestige could be restored without changing the ultimate source of political power. This assumption had yet to be tested.

The purpose of this study is to investigate the role played by the Octobrist faction in the Third Duma, its internal relationships, and its efforts to create a "workable" majority that would cooperate with tsarism in the "renovation of Russia." The period of 1907–12 was of crucial importance for Octobrism as a political movement and influenced the Union's attitude toward tsarism in the years preceding the revolution of February 1917. The fate of the Union of October 17 in the Third Duma was directly tied to the fate of constitutional monarchy and to its alternatives—autocracy and revolution—in imperial Russia.

1

The Union of October 17

The revolutionary year of 1905 became a turning point in the Russian liberal movement that had been active since the beginning of the twentieth century. The left wing of that movement, representing the majority in the zemstvo congresses,[1] founded a relatively well-disciplined and very articulate party, the Constitutional Democrats, or Kadets. The right wing founded the Union of October 17, the Octobrists.[2]

Although the Union became an ill-defined coalition of individuals and organizations, two groups initially founded it: landowning gentry who followed D. N. Shipov's neo-Slavophile liberalism and representatives of the higher rank of the Russian capitalistic class.

D. N. Shipov, who had been instrumental while chairman of the Executive Board of the Moscow zemstvo in making it a model for other zemstva, believed that the people, through its elected representatives, should be listened to by the tsar. Unlike the Slavophiles, Shipov did not believe autocracy was God-given, nor should it be absolute. Further, he did not feel that the Russian people had a universal mission to perform. These reservations put Shipov closer to liberalism, yet not in its legalistic-constitutional Western form. His emphasis on religious and moral ideals rather than rational and juridical formulas, and his strong support of independent local self-government, greater freedom, and personal liberties placed Shipov toward the liberal wing in Russian politics.

In addition to Shipov among the founding group were P. A.

Geiden, N. A. Stakhovich, Prince G. M. Volkonskii, N. A. Khomiakov, and M. V. Rodzianko, all of whom agreed with Shipov in principle. They all had well-established political attitudes and world views as well as considerable political experience. The capitalist group included prominent bankers, industrialists and such commercial entrepreneurs as G. A. Krestovnikov, P. A. Chestiakov, and the brothers Guchkov.[3] Most of them were newcomers to the political arena and except for A. I. Guchkov, played a secondary role in the Union.

Alexander Guchkov was eventually the most prominent leader of the Union. The bourgeois, a phenomenon new to Russian politics, was exemplified in this third-generation descendant of a Moscow textile industrialist who had served as the director of a Moscow discount bank since 1901. He was "flesh and blood of the Moscow merchant intelligentsia," as his long-standing rival and leader of the Kadets, Paul N. Miliukov, characterized him. Pragmatic, impatient with theory, action-oriented, he carried the imprint of his origin, and like other Great Russians, was intolerant of efforts by other ethnic groups within the empire toward some measure of autonomy. With other major business leaders, Guchkov was drawn into political action by the events of 1904–5. Together with his brother Nikolai, Alexander Guchkov was elected to the zemstvo and town congresses as a representative of the Moscow duma, where from the beginning he was a major spokesman of the right wing of the zemstvo congresses.

The Union, founded by these two groups near the end of 1905, reflected the character of its founders, their fears and aspirations. The military defeat with Japan and the revolution still raging in the country gave a peculiar twist to the composition and tactics of the Union, and its name, derived from the tsar's Manifesto of October 17, 1905, was indicative of the special connection between the Union and the policies pursued by the authorities. The Octobrists were anxious for reform, but reform within the established structure of the Russian Empire.

The two founding groups of the Octobrists, the liberal gentry landowners and the bourgeois, were joined by a third—the "scared" —an amorphous mass of middle-class people with no specific political convictions but who were frightened by the revolution and its economic and social consequences. The presence of the "scared" element in the Union became evident during its first convention in February 1906. Contrary to other rightist parties that mushroomed at the time, the Union had its chapters all over the empire,[4] and its regulations allowed any party or organization that accepted the major premises of its proclamation to become part of the Union.[5] The result was an influx of people from the middle or lower middle class, whose main concern was to stop the revolution. They joined the Union because it was considered a "respectable" antirevolutionary party. This "grey public," as they were called by Prince E. N. Trubetskoi,[6] had an important influence on the political tactics of the Union.

These disparate elements had one characteristic in common, a traditional, intimate connection with tsarism. It was not bond enough, however, to overcome the diversity of economic and social interests, and the result was a lack of internal ideological and political cohesion. The Union was not an organic development, but groups brought together by such external factors as the social radicalism of the revolutionary movement, the attitude of the future Kadets toward that movement, and finally, the tsar's October Manifesto that precipitated the Union's creation.

When it became apparent in the fall of 1905 that the revolutionary movement was moving from political toward social goals, the majority of the propertied elements rallied to support the established authorities. The specter of the new *pugachevshchina* (peasant uprising) frightened increasing numbers of landowners; strikes, demonstrations, and riots in the cities elicited a similar fear in the bourgeoisie. The political reforms that these same people had previously demanded became secondary to the preservation of the social-economic order—by any means deemed necessary. Their insistence on the preservation of the Russian Empire as a united and centralized state showed their alarm at the disintegrating effects of the revolution: a cohesive bond of fear became the basis of political cooperation. Where the lines were drawn became evident during the September and November 1905 congresses of zemstva and city dumas. The majority of the latter congress, already organized in the Kadet party, refused to dissociate itself from the revolutionary movement and supported a proposition to grant broad autonomy to Poland.[7] From the right wing remaining the Octobrists drew most of their future support.

The October Manifesto that gave the Union a name and a political banner promised the creation of a political system in which a popular representative body would assume a key position, implying thereby the legitimate existence of political parties. The forthcoming elections to the First Duma caused the creation of tens of political organizations. It was at this point that the right wing of the zemstva and city dumas movement established an organization, the Union of October 17, a political entity resembling more an ad hoc coalition of individuals and organizations than a full-fledged political party. Even its name, *Union*, indicates a reluctance on the part of the founders to engage in political strife and to gain political power. The organizational form has clearly the imprint of one of its chief founders, D. N. Shipov.

The Union's "statute" (*ustav*) invited willing groups and individuals to cooperate with the authorities in the realization of the premises and promises of the October Manifesto. Even independent political parties that shared the basic tenets of the manifesto and wished to promote the "peaceful renovation" of the country were invited to join, although nothing was said in the statute about their exact status in the Union.[8] The founders created a very loose organizational structure, and were not only ready to accommodate different political organizations but also to give the local "assemblies and conferences" the right to "determine their program and activities."[9] An attempt by A. I. Guchkov to pass a new statute, one that would have given the Union a tighter and more cohesive structure, was opposed by the second party convention. The only propositions adopted were those regulating the composition and functions of the Central Committee.[10] This looseness of organization was one of the more lasting features of the Union.

There was no all-embracing ideology in the Union. It had been established to promote the "peaceful renovation" of the Russian Empire, a vague goal that in its details meant different things to each of the various groups that joined. During its entire existence, Octobrism showed an almost inherent resistance to the development of a definitive philosophy. "What is the Union of October 17?" was asked again and again by friends and foes alike, many years after the Union became a permanent feature of Russia's political life.

Yet some underlying theoretical assumptions can be isolated —ideals and goals that were shared by most Octobrists. The desired regime was some kind of a constitutional government in which the ultimate political power would rest with the tsar, but in which the representatives of the people would participate in shaping the destiny of the country. It would be a regime that would guarantee peace and law, and create the proper atmosphere for the gradual resolution of the country's most urgent social and economic problems. Beyond differences in phraseology between the zemstvo-Shipovite and the bourgeois element, both hoped to live in a monarchy ruled by law, a Russia where the individual would be free from terror and administrative abuse and where his rights would be guaranteed. They wanted a government responsive to the people and responsible to the tsar, but primarily the founders of the Union wanted a government capable of maintaining internal peace and of restoring the damaged national pride. The pre-October regime had shown signs of internal and external collapse, and to avert a catastrophe, the Octobrists demanded at least a minimum of political and social reform.

The zemstvo liberals of Shipov's persuasion and the capitalist entrepreneurs of Guchkov's background used different terms, yet strived in 1905 to achieve very similar goals. Shipov had the Slavophile idea of a state welded by mutual trust between the tsar and the people; a state where the "power of authority" would belong to the tsar, and the "power of opinion" to the people. This would destroy the wall of bureaucracy separating the tsar from the country. Shipov wanted to combine broad self-government on the local level with a responsive tsarism at the center.[11] Although he was suspicious of formalistic Western constitutionalism, in 1905 he accepted the idea of a constitutional monarchy. Shipov and his followers in the Union "became 'constitutionalists by imperial decree' because they were loyal, not because the October Manifesto agreed with their teaching."[12] Yet when they became constitutionalists they followed their convictions with great moral and intellectual integrity.

For Guchkov, Shipov's "power of authority to the tsar and power

of opinion to the people"meant a constitutional monarchy ruled by
the tsar, responsive and to some extent accountable to the representatives of the people, but independent of the political parties.
Hence Guchkov's opposition to a parliamentary regime.

> I am a convinced adherent of the constitutional-mon-
> archist system . . but by no means of a parliamentary
> system. I cannot conceive the peaceful development of
> contemporary Russia with all the peculiarities be-
> queathed by Russian history and rooted in Russian exis-
> tence, with the peoples' representatives invested with
> the broad rights of legislation and supervision over the
> administration, but also with a strong government respon-
> sible only to the monarch and not to political parties.[13]

This was Guchkov's summary of his political ideology. A pragmatist in politics, he considered a constitutional monarchy the
most suitable for contemporary Russia.

The founders of the Union, in accepting the idea of a constitutional regime that implied some kind of limitation on the formerly
unlimited powers of the tsar, defined their basic difference from
the rightist parties established at the same time.[14] The Octobrists
differed from their former allies, the Kadets, mainly in tactics and
priorities. They abhorred the Kadets' fascination with the revolutionary movement; they rejected the Kadets' lack of faith in the
sincerity of tsarism. The Octobrists espoused gradual and peaceful change promoted by a "renovated" tsarism; the Kadets were
impatient and demanded radical and immediate reforms in the social
and political structure of the empire. The October Manifesto signified for the Octobrists the end of the revolution and a cornerstone for "peaceful renovation"; for the Kadets it meant only the
end of the first phase in the struggle with autocracy. For the one
it meant a new phase in the national tradition, for the other, a
springboard for the final break with that tradition.

Although nationalism emerged early as the major ideological
banner of Octobrism, it is much easier to establish its concrete
manifestations than its theoretical formulations. It rose from a variety of sources: Slavophile notions on the peculiarities of the
Russian Empire were blended inharmoniously with the instinctive

nationalistic feelings of Moscow's commercial class; the "official nationalism" of the bureaucracy coincided with the industrialists' fears of foreign competition and the frustrations and jealousies of the landowners from the western provinces. At its inception, the Union's founders emphasized the need to preserve the "unity of the Russian Empire," establishing at that point an opposition to separatism even while it was still part of the general zemstvo movement.[15] The Union's proclamation in November 1905 promised equal rights to all national minorities.[16] This form of nationalism signified the reluctance of the Union to sever its emotional ties with Russia's past and with tsarism; it represented a continuity of Russia's national tradition. Tsarism was thus made an instrument of the Union's nationalism, a tool to preserve or, rather, renovate the greatness of Russia. The image of the tsar as a benevolent sovereign had deep roots in Russia's national consciousness: the broad masses of the peasantry had always made a distinction between the tsar and the bureaucracy that distorted his good intentions. It was this view that received its ideological formulation by the Slavophiles, and was accepted by the Union and incorporated in its nationalistic ideology.

> We cannot relate ourselves negatively to what was created by old Russia. We thought that the greatness of Russia, her glorious name, which had been disgraced in Manchuria, had to be restored, renewed, and carried over to the new Russia. We thought that the monarchic principle, which played such a tremendous role in Russia, had also to be carried over to the new Russia. *The doctrinairism of the extremist parties, their alienation from the entire historical life of Russia,* repelled us from them.[17]

This was the political credo of Octobrism, as it had been presented before the first party congress on February 8, 1906, by Guchkov. Here we find an integrated statement on nationalism, on a renovated monarchy, and on the organic links with Russia's national history. The idea that a strong monarchy was a pledge for a strong Russia, and an instrument of unity for all the nationalities in a *Russian* Empire, was quite prevalent in the Union.

Nationalism meant for the Octobrists historical continuity, and

the manifesto was a call to support the historical regime to renovate the country. The Union's opposition to national autonomy for
the non-Russian nationalities was also an expression of protest
against the excesses of revolution that had reached their highest
peaks in the borderlands. Therefore the two major expressions of
the Union's national ideology were its opposition to separatism
and its effort to strengthen the military might of the empire. A
strong Russia became for the Octobrists a guarantee to preserve
a united empire and to block radical changes in its political and
social structure. Nationalism thus became a link between the past
and the future as well as a means to reconcile and bind the tsar
and the people together.

The manifesto issued by Nicholas II on October 17, 1905, gave
Octobrism its first and basic political program as well as its
name. "In the strict execution of the Manifesto of October 17 by
the government are included all the principles of our aims, activities, and propaganda," explained M. A. Stakhovich, one of the founders of the Union. "On it depends the salvation of our country, the
end of sedition and disorder." [18]

In its subsequent political programs, the Union tried to give
its interpretation of the manifesto, but it never went beyond its
basic premises. The realization of the promises and principles
through public support became the Union's goal.

This landmark in Russia's political history, the October Manifesto, read:

> By the grace of God, We, Nicholas II, Emperor and
> Autocrat of All the Russias, Tsar of Poland, Grand Duke
> of Finland, etc., etc., etc., declare to all Our loyal
> subjects:
>
> Disturbances and unrest in the capitals and in many
> places of Our Empire fill Our heart with a great and
> painful grief. The welfare of the Russian Sovereign is
> indissolubly bound to the welfare of the people, and
> their grief is His grief. Out of the present disturbances
> there may grow a serious disorder and a threat to the
> integrity and unity of Our Empire.
>
> The great oath of Imperial service requires that, with
> all the force of Our intelligence and authority, and as

quickly as possible, We bring to an end disturbances perilous to the state. Having ordered the appropriate authorities to take steps against open acts of disorder, riot, and violence, so as to protect peaceful persons who seek quietly to perform their duty, We, in order to carry out the general policies outlined by Us for quieting the life of the nation, have found it necessary to unify the activities of the central government.

We make it the duty of the government to execute Our firm will:

1) to grant the people the unshakable foundations of civic freedom on the basis of genuine personal inviolability, freedom of conscience, speech, assembly, and association;

2) to admit immediately to participation in the State Duma, without suspending the scheduled elections and in so far as it is feasible in the brief period remaining before the convening of the Duma, those classes of the population that are now completely deprived of electoral rights, leaving the further development of the principle of universal suffrage to the new legislative order;

and 3) to establish as an inviolable rule that no law may go into force without the consent of the State Duma and that the representatives of the people must be guaranteed the opportunity of effective participation in the supervision of the legality of the actions performed by Our appointed officials.

We call on all faithful sons of Russia to remember their duty to their Fatherland, to assist in putting an end to these unprecedented disturbances, and to exert with Us all their power to restore quiet and peace to Our native land.

Issued at Peterhof on October 17th, in the year of Our Lord 1905, and in the eleventh year of Our Reign.

The original text signed in His Imperial Majesty's own hand. [19]

Nicholas

The manifesto certainly introduced new elements into the political structure of the empire. It promised to grant the people
unshakable foundations of civic freedom; to broaden suffrage to
include "those classes of the population that are now completely
deprived of electoral rights" (by the Bulygin Duma law). The most
important clause promised "to establish a rule that no law may go
into force without the consent of the State Duma." It included an
explicit promise to grant "the representatives of the people" the
opportunity of "effective participation in the supervision" of the
administration. Did the manifesto establish a constitutional monarchy in Russia? It is difficult to give an unqualified answer to
this question. Although quite explicit in some points, it had been
phrased in general terms, and had the air of a promise. Whether it
would serve as a basis for a constitutional monarchy or a temporary concession depended on the interpretation and execution of
its principles and promises, as well as on the new Fundamental
Laws, which would be published in March 1906. The tsar remained
the ultimate source of political power, and it all depended on him
and on the people who had wielded absolute power in Russia before the manifesto.

The founders of the Union chose to interpret the manifesto as
having established a constitutional monarchy. This was the basic
premise of the Union's proclamation, the first and most detailed
political program of Octobrism, published in Moscow on November
10, 1905. Within its introduction and four chapters,[20] long-standing aspirations of Russia's liberal movement were expressed, as
well as an interpretation of the principles of the October Manifesto. The general approach was rather pragmatic; its authors
stressed the need to implement the general principles into positive laws and actions.

It dealt first with "The Preservation of the Unity and Indivisibility of the Russian State," expressing the Union's opposition to
the separatist tendencies in the borderlands. Yet with the rejection
of any idea of federation, the authors of the proclamation promised
to create conditions that would encourage the development of the
native cultures of the national minorities. They even envisioned
the creation of self-governing regional associations intended to

solve local problems. Only Finland was recognized as entitled to
certain autonomous rights, provided it kept its political ties with
the empire.

The chapted entitled "The Development and Strengthening of
the Principles of Constitutional Monarchy . . ." gave the Union's
interpretation of the manifesto. The founders stressed their com-
mitment to "the principle of universal suffrage," thus making the
Duma truly representative of the nation that would participate with
the monarch "in legislative work and in the government of the
country."[21] The tsar, according to the authors of the proclamation,
represented a unifying principle that stood above any particular
interest. Nicholas's view of his role was probably far from the
Octobrists' interpretation.

The "Guarantee of Civil Rights" contained a detailed list of
civil rights and freedoms, which corresponded to the classical
principles of liberalism: the freedom of worship, speech, association, equality before the law, and so forth.

These general principles and premises were covered in the
preamble and the first three chapters; the fourth chapter on
"The Nondeferrability of the Convocation of the State Duma,"
outlined the concrete actions and bills that the Union promised
to pass through the legislature. The peasant question ranked
first in urgency, and the Octobrists promised to act in the Duma
to abolish all legal discriminations from which the peasantry suffered. It promised to encourage the government to take measures
to improve agricultural methods, to regulate small-scale rent, to
reorganize the Peasant Bank, to assist in resettlement, and so on.
Further, the Union could not avoid the long-standing demand of
Russia's peasantry for more land. They proposed the creation of a
fund from state and appanage lands to satisfy the land hunger of
the peasant. They went a step beyond, adding that "in case all
these measures prove inadequate, it is permissible, given conditions of national necessity, to confiscate parts of private lands
on terms of just compensation set by the legislature."[22] In essence, this was a more moderate version of the Kadets' agrarian
program. In the proclamation, there was no reference to any need
to dismember the peasant commune.

The treatment of the labor question carried the imprint of the capitalist element in the Union. They stipulated that the solution of the problem "cannot be decided in the interests of the worker himself without the support of industry in general; only a soundly developing industry can safeguard the welfare of the worker."[23] The authors promised to promote in the Duma labor legislation similar to that existing in the most advanced industrial countries. They recognized the workers' right to establish trade unions, and to use strikes as a means to achieve economic goals.

The proclamation included a series of traditional demands of Russian liberalism in the spheres of local self-government such as its extension to new areas and spheres of activity, democratization of its institutions, and so forth. Among the reforms proposed by the Octobrists, the most important were in education, responsibility of the administration, a "truly" independent judiciary, and the introduction of a progressive income tax.

The proclamation remained the principal policy statement of the Union for many years; later political programs changed only slightly the Union's basic aims. The fear of alienating potential voters and causing internal divisions became a major obstacle in the formulation of clearer political attitudes than those contained in the proclamation.

The second convention of the Union on May 6, 1907, did make some changes and clarifications. The clause on the nature of the post-October regime defined what the Union meant by a constitutional monarchy. It read: "The Russian Empire is a unified and indivisible hereditary constitutional monarchy, where the emperor, the carrier of the supreme authority, is *limited* [italics mine] by the representatives of the people and the personal rights of the citizens."[24] The program also included demands to increase the number of elected deputies in the State Council, the upper chamber of the legislative body, which in 1905 had been liberalized to include not only the usual imperial appointees, but an equal number of deputies elected from such higher institutions as the universities, the stock exchanges, the zemstva. The Union also demanded superiority of the Duma over the council in financial matters; disagreement between the two chambers over the budget left the government free to choose which figures it preferred. The Octobrists were sensitive to these limited budgetary rights and made a general request to "review and extend the budgetary rights of the Duma."[25]

The most important departure from the proclamation was the new agrarian program in which the Octobrists maintained that the "peasant question" was the outcome of low productivity and over-population, not the scarcity of land. The emphasis now was on increasing productivity of available land rather than the allocation of more land. They supported Stolypin's agrarian policy and urged the creation of "small freeholding land units, thus creating *otrubs* or *khutors* (different kinds of consolidated farms) and the adoption of land regulation measures."[26]

The Union was evasive on the "Jewish problem," calling for a review of existing legislation, but carefully avoiding a clear stand. The resolution did not satisfy the Union's critics to the left, yet raised some suspicions among its potential allies to the right.

It is of interest to note that the second convention adopted a resolution asking the authorities for a more democratic franchise.[27] Less than a month later, on June 3, 1907, Stolypin published the new electoral laws and the Octobrists could hardly hide their satisfaction.

The Union's early history set the pattern, establishing certain attitudes and commitments that became crucial for its role in the Third Duma. With the avowed goal of bringing together all elements in Russian society whose aim was the "peaceful renovation" of the country, two premises were implied in the Union's policy: an end to revolutionary unrest and the government's desire to take a new course. But the revolution was not yet over in November 1905 and its specter continued to lurk ominously in the years to come. Tsarism was far from interpreting the manifesto as establishing a constitutional monarchy. Autocracy was not yet prepared to follow a new course, nor was it clear as to what course it would follow at all. The Union faced the vexing dilemma of how to bring about the desired changes without a revolutionary upheaval.

Of utmost importance was the choice of allies to reach "peaceful renovation," to realize the promises of the manifesto, to stop revolutionary terror and the arbitrariness of the central and provincial administration. The Union's overriding concern was to stop the revolution. The majority of the Octobrists had no doubt as to whom to support in the struggle between the established authorities and the revolutionary movement; they would always prefer law and order to reform and change. This determined the Union's positive attitude towards the government, particularly after Stolypin became prime minister, yet in spite of that support the Union frequently criticized the government and expressed its reservations over many of its actions. Striving to achieve internal peace and raise the national prestige, the Octobrists realized that suppression alone would not suffice. Many understood that Russia needed basic reforms, but at the same time they feared the chain reactions that might result from rapid change. Their problem was how to strike a balance between stability and change, and to do so they tried fruitlessly to push the authorities in the direction of definite changes and reforms.

At the beginning of 1906, revolutionary violence was only one of many factors contributing to the fear and insecurity in the country. The government's actions became more and more a threat to the peaceful citizen. Punitive detachments combed the country-side, burning villages and executing hundreds without trial. Whole provinces were put under martial law or other forms of emergency jurisdiction. The local administrations abused their power as in the days of the "preconstitutional monarchy." Repression and administrative arbitrariness went on, its victims very often the peaceful citizen. Autocracy regained its shaken confidence and showed signs of regression to previous methods in an effort to diminish the meaning of its concessions.

The Union supported without reservation the suppression of revolutionary chaos but as early as February 1906 at its first national convention, its leadership criticized the authorities for relying on repression alone and demanded a realization of the promises of the manifesto. Yet even within the Union, there was strong opposition to the proposition requiring the authorities to rescind martial law when there was no need for it. The opposition came from the "scared" element, largely from the provinces. [28]

The Union's faction in the First Duma was small and its leaders, Geiden and Stakhovich, came very close to the Kadets on many issues. They were a great deal more liberal than the bulk of the Union's leadership and members.

The dissolution of the First Duma and the subsequent proclamation of the new martial laws of August 24, 1906, brought about
a split in the Union. The leaders of the faction in the Duma and
Shipov opposed these actions and refused to join the new government formed by Stolypin.[29] Guchkov and the majority of the Central
Committee gradually, but eventually in unequivocal terms, came
out in support of Stolypin's policy. The more liberal wing, joined
later by Shipov, left the Union and formed the Peaceful Renovation
(Partiya Mirnogo Obnovleniya) party.[30] Guchkov made it clear that
uppermost in Octobrist minds at that time was the need to repress
the revolution and that Stolypin was the man who could achieve it.[31]
    The split did not affect the basic ideological orientations or
tactics of Octobrism. Shorn of its left wing, the Union became a
more purposeful political organization with Guchkov as its major
leader, and he, more than anyone else, determined its future policy. Nationalism and a strong stand against the revolution formed
its main elements. On October 5, 1906, Guchkov emphasized that
he opposed the anticonstitutionalism of the extreme Right, but
considered them possible allies in the struggle against the revolution: "When the attack on the monarch's prerogatives begins we
will be allies." He maintained that the Union shared the rightists'
devotion to the "fatherland," their position on the nationalities
problem, and their support of a strong reformed army.[32] The publication on November 9, 1906, of the ukase on Stolypin's agrarian
policy brought the Union even closer to the government and the
rightist organizations.
    It was in the interest of the Union, and fitted their basic polit-
ical orientation, when the Second Duma was dissolved and new
election laws were published that strongly favored the propertied
class, particularly the landowners. The June 3, 1907, election laws
were designed to elect a "trustworthy and workable" Duma. To
accomplish this purpose, a majority was assigned to those segments
of the population on which Stolypin could depend for cooperation
in realizing his reform program and one which would not, at the
same time, insist on rapid change in the constitution or on radical
social and economic legislation. The representation of the peasants and the national minorities was drastically reduced. The re-
arrangement of voting power was designed to affect the leftist

parties and the mechanics of the elections enabled the government, more than before, to manipulate their outcome.[33] The Octobrists became its main beneficiaries. They, with their rather pragmatic approach, considered the new election laws befitting Russia's stage of development. The first two dumas were really "unworkable." The dissolution of the Second Duma and the new election laws signified an unwritten alliance between Octobrism and Stolypin. The Union became the major nongovernment proponent of Stolypin's policies in the time to come.

2

The Third Duma

The regime established by the October Manifesto presented a curious combination that baffled the foreigner and confused the native. A German almanac defined the post-October regime as a "constitutional-autocracy," which appears to be a contradiction in terms. A constitutional regime of sorts was established by the manifesto, by the two houses of the Duma, and by the revised Fundamental Laws, but no alteration was made in the ultimate seat of sovereignty and the tsar remained in theory and in practice the source of political power. Even though the manifesto contained elements that could lead to the development of a constitutional regime, the institutions that were supposed to implement them were ill-defined and precarious. The government was responsible only to the tsar; the bureaucracy retained its arbitrary and unresponsive character; and the armed forces remained under the tsar's sole control. The new institutions could, theoretically, use their budgetary powers to influence the government, but even in this sphere, autocracy could get the necessary resources. There were special provisions in the Fundamental Laws that gave the administration the means to circumvent the houses even in their specific field—legislation. Autocracy remained in complete control of the real sources of power.

The political history of the period could be described as an

24

attempt to establish some balance between the constitutional and the autocratic elements in the Russian regime, a struggle in which the autocratic was usually more successful.

Nicholas II has been described as conservative, chauvinistic, and extremely possessive of his autocratic power. Even after the publication of the October Manifesto and the convocation of the chambers, he considered himself a *samoderzhets,* the unlimited ruler of "all the Russias" and not a king bound by a constitution. The last tsar assumed that the normal situation was the loyalty of the Russian nation to its ruler. In spite of the establishment of "representative legislation," Nicholas still refused to share his power with the parliament; he never conceded that there was any question about the ultimate location of authority.[1]

Nicholas considered the convocation of the Duma an expression of ill will toward his regime and the people's representatives a threat and encroachment upon his prerogatives, not his partners in a common effort to "renovate Russia." The first two Dumas justified his suspicions. He saw their revolutionary oratory as a threat to peace and the Duma's forum as an arena of revolutionary propaganda.[2] Writing to Stolypin, he remarked that the house of representatives was a hotbed of sedition that had yet to prove its loyalty and usefulness.[3]

The influence of the various liberal groups in effecting the promulgation of the manifesto, and the behavior of the Kadets in the first two Dumas imbued the tsar with a deep mistrust towards the liberal "public men."[4] His suspicions about their motives and capabilities were carried over to the Octobrists and the Third Duma.[5]

Indecisive and malleable, Nicholas was greatly affected by extragovernmental forces in shaping the destiny of the country. His immediate family, close entourage, and favorites of the moment, all of whom had the common denominator of reactionary views, grew steadily in influence after the dissolution of the First Duma.[6] They had close personal connections with the right wing in the State Council, the provincial administration, and with the extreme rightist organizations in the country and, since Nicholas saw these people far more often than he saw his ministers, they could easily undermine the influence of the "visible" government.[7]

Of the government officials who labored against these odds of

influence, Petr Arkadevich Stolypin, prime minister and minister of
the interior from 1906 to 1911, was most effective, and his policies
and fate had a direct bearing on the Octobrists in the Third Duma.
Coming from the landed gentry who had served tsarism for genera-
tions, in many ways he was representing his class when he attempted to reconcile its interests with the changing social and
political circumstances. "Stolypin was the best representative of
the obsolete nobility's class structure," S. I. Shidlovskii, one of the
Union's Duma leaders, maintained. "He knew that the regime had
outlived itself, that it needed radical reforms and he tried to introduce a certain graduality in this process."[8] Despite his title of
prime minister, Stolypin was not head of the government in actuality, for each minister was individually selected by and accountable
to the tsar. Stolypin, deriving his power from the tsar, was very
much aware that to be able to carry out his policies he had to neutralize opposing forces close to the tsar. He underestimated their
power, however, and eventually succumbed to those who opposed
change and reforms.

Stolypin's aim was to preserve the authority of tsarism by introducing reforms that would strengthen its social and public base.
Convinced that the socioeconomic and educational advancement of
the nation had to precede major political reforms, he sought to
reconcile public opinion and government by minor reform and to
remove certain out-of-date practices that were incompatible with
the spirit of the times.[9] His political motto was "first pacification,
then reforms." The prime minister saw the function of government
as provision for the well-being of the people and maintenance of
order, a kind of enlightened-patriarchal central authority.

Stolypin's chief and immediate objective when he took office
was to strengthen the power of government for the purpose of restoring order at home and rebuilding Russia's prestige abroad.
His "message" to the first two Dumas was that order and the rule
of law must precede reforms, but he had no reverence for legalistic
forms himself, and when he thought that something was necessary
he ignored its legal aspects. This facet of his personality created
incidents and conflicts with his most loyal supporters, the Octobrists.

The extent of Stolypin's support of a constitutional regime is apparent in his actions and words. He accepted the Duma as a permanent feature of the regime. He realized that with a "suitable" composition, the Duma could be of help in achieving his goals; its abolition, he thought, could be fatal to tsarism. He certainly rejected the idea of returning to pre-1905 absolutism. "One should not even talk about a return to absolutism," he told Peter B. Struve in 1907.[10] To L. A. Tikhomirov's proposal to abrogate the Fundamental Laws he added the remark that it would have been a "wicked provocation and the beginning of a new revolution."[11] He accepted the changes brought about by the October Manifesto, but fought a losing battle against the reactionary elements of the old regime. They, more than the revolutionary parties, constituted the real obstacle to a constitutional regime.

The prime minister hoped to achieve at least partial cooperation of the educated classes through the Duma.[12] "Don't forget," Stolypin once said to P. G. Kurlov, assistant minister of the interior and the head of the Police Department, "that the sovereign granted the Russian people representative institutions. It is our sacred obligation to enable them to function."[13] He personally appeared many times in the Duma, participated in its debates, reported in committees, and read its reports. Although he established intimate relationships with the Duma leaders and briefed them privately on government policy, Stolypin considered the Duma as essentially only a peripheral institution, one to advise and help the administration but not direct it. He thought that Russia lacked the educational and social basis for a more active representative institution, but he was ready to tolerate the Duma as long as it fit in with his scheme for rebuilding Russia. Stolypin soon realized that it was possible to circumvent the constitutional arrangements when he deemed it necessary without endangering his position. He found it hard to understand complaints about illegal actions of his government, particularly in its use of Article 87 of the Fundamental Laws. Stolypin maintained that the constitutional elements came, not to replace the old order, but rather to renew and strengthen it. He asked the Third Duma in one of his speeches "not to destroy the historical structure of Russia, but to help in recreating, rebuilding,

and strengthening it."[14] Reserving the right to support autocracy in
his own way, he manipulated elections, and enacted legislation
outside the Duma.

Although Stolypin considered the first two Dumas as centers
of revolutionary propaganda, there is evidence to prove that he
was reluctant to dissolve the second. P. N. Miliukov admitted that
Stolypin did his utmost to prevent this action,[15] despite the strong
pressure from organized nobility and the court to abolish the Duma
altogether.[16] By changing the suffrage Stolypin probably secured
the continued existence of the representative institutions. The
June 3 law was designed to elect a "workable" and "cooperative"
Duma. The composition of the Third Duma came close to what he
desired.[17]

Stolypin shared many of the political attitudes and goals of the
Union of October 17. "Stolypin arrived in St. Petersburg without
any program. In his convictions he was close to Octobrism," S. E.
Kryzhanovskii, the general director of the Ministry of the Interior,
maintained.[18] A mutual understanding developed gradually between
Stolypin and the Union that became a working alliance after the
publication of the June 3 election laws, and lasted, in spite of
frictions and disagreements, throughout Stolypin's premiership.
The Union and Stolypin differed sometimes on the methods of pacification or the speed of reforms, but both strove to renovate Russia
and retain its historical regime.

Guchkov praised Stolypin's determined struggle against revolution and supported his program of economic and social reforms.
Stolypin was impressed in turn by Guchkov's stand on the issue of
the field courts-martial and invited him to join his government after
the dissolution of the Second Duma. The negotiations failed when
Stolypin refused to draft an agreed program for the government.[19]
In spite of this failure Stolypin and the Union continued to work
together to strengthen and revitalize tsarism rather than destroy it.
While they did not always agree, Guchkov found Stolypin close to
the Union's "ideas, aspirations and political aims."[20] Stolypin
considered the Octobrists "a group that was concerned with the
future of Russia and could appreciate the efforts the government
made to heal Russia's wounds and cure her diseases."[21]

On the eve of the Third Duma there existed between the Union

and Stolypin at least a tacit understanding that many of their conflicts were the result of their different roles. The Octobrists who
had won election as Duma deputies were relatively less inhibited
in expressing their views and in pressing for reforms. Stolypin had
to account to the tsar and appraise, as well, the various influences
shaping his will. As prime minister, Stolypin was naturally more
sensitive than the Octobrists were to the influences of the traditional power structure and even though the ideas and aims of the
Union were close to his own, his public concurrence would compromise his position with the tsar.

The friendship and cooperation between Stolypin and the Union
fluctuated mainly because of objective factors unrelated to the
partners. Although Stolypin succeeded in restoring a semblance of
peace, unrest and dissatisfaction threatened to engulf the country
in a new revolution. In spite of Stolypin's policy of avoiding military confrontations abroad while Russia was recovering from defeat
and revolution, the international situation remained dangerous, reminding the Russian nationalists of the weaknesses of their country. But serious efforts for reforms had been repeatedly thwarted
by the reactionary elements entrenched in the imperial administration and in the court. Stolypin's achievements and failures in many
ways reflected and were sometimes intimately related to those of
the Union and the Duma.

The Party Composition of the Third Duma

The election laws of June 3 gave the government a potentially
workable and cooperative duma. Because of increased requirements
for voting, the changes in regional allocation of electors, and manipulation of the elections, the Third Duma contained only a small
contingent of the "untrustworthy" elements, the peasant and national minority deputies. Thus out of 442 members, only 68 were
peasants, 27 were workers, and 27 came from national minorities.[22]
The "trustworthy" element included 173 members who had the title
of "hereditary nobleman" (*potomstvennyi dvorianin*), 53 orthodox
clergy, 12 government officials, and 17 Cossacks; 194—or more
than 40 percent—described themselves as landowners (peasants
not included).[23]

On its convocation the Third Duma had ten parties represented

and a small group of unaffiliated deputies. The numerical strength
of the various parties changed during the five years, but the fluc-
tuations were almost exclusively limited to the parties standing to
the right of the Kadets. The national minorities, the two socialist
groups, and the Kadets remained almost the same. The Progressists
grew from 25 in 1907 to 39 in 1912, the extreme Right from 40 to 52.
The main losers were the Octobrists, whose strength fell from 148
to 122.[24] There are wide discrepancies among the various sources
as to the numerical strength of each group. While the Duma *Ukazatel*
has the official list of membership, it cannot serve as the sole
source for determining party affiliation because of loose party discipline and alliances, particularly in the center and Right.

The deputies could be divided, roughly, into four major group-
ings: the extreme Right—49; the right wing of the center (moderate
rightists and the nationalistic group)—89; the Octobrists—148;
the opposition, composed of the national minorities, the two socialist factions, the Kadets, and the Progressists—137.[25] Each
group exercised its special influence on the Union and its policies in the Duma.

The major party in the "opposition" in the Third Duma was the
Kadets, whose influence outweighed its number. With the high intellectual level of their members, their party discipline, and their
influence among the educated class of the country, the fifty-three
Kadets were able to push the Union to more liberal positions.[26]
The Kadets lost much of their zeal in the first two Dumas, but
even in the third continued to criticize the government and on
several occasions gave a more liberal slant to the Duma legislation, becoming thereby major targets of the Union's nationalistic
and antirevolutionary attacks. In spite of the acute rivalry between
the Union and the Kadets, many attempts were made to coordinate
the actions of the two and even to establish some kind of an alliance. The Progressists, who developed out of the party of Peaceful
Renovation, numbered twenty-five at the first session and thirty-
nine at the fifth. This rather amorphous group considered its major
function the bringing together of all moderate-liberal factions,
mainly the Kadets and the Octobrists, to create a liberal-constitu-
tional center. Old animosities, as well as genuine differences of

orientation, repeatedly foiled their efforts, but their presence, together with the Kadets, were a constant spur to the Octobrists to live up to their own principles. They often forced the Union to justify itself, and on many occasions the Union followed a more parties also competed for the same votes in many by-elections. The national minorities group, composed largely of the Polish Koło, the Poles representing the Lithuanian, Polish, and Belorussian groups, and the Muslim factions, usually voted with the opposition after their repeated attempts to reach an agreement with the Octobrists failed. The two socialist factions, fourteen Trudoviks (Laborites) and fifteen Social-Democrats, had negligible participation in the Duma's work; most of their energies were devoted to predictable attacks and interpellations and were one of the major causes of disruptions and tensions during the Third Duma. Occasionally the extreme Left joined the Kadets and the Octobrists against the Right.[27]

The Moderate Right, which later merged officially with the nationalistic group to form the Nationalist party, had altogether eighty-nine deputies. This faction was created by Stolypin and Guchkov in their efforts to form a stable majority that would support the government. "After discussing the situation with Stolypin we decided to try to split the right wing of the Duma and from its more moderate members form a group that would support Stolypin's cabinet," recalled Guchkov.[28] They contacted P. N. Balashov and P. B. Sinadino, who formed the Moderate Right and the nationalistic factions, which usually voted and behaved as one. Coming from the mass of unaffiliated deputies that stood to the right of the Octobrists and formed when the chamber was already in session, the Moderate Right had no real ideology or political program. The majority of the faction belonged to the landed gentry, many from the western provinces, who supported the authorities out of habit and their fear of peasant disorders. With the passage of time the group developed a strong nationalistic outlook, trying to appear as the defenders of Great Russian nationalism and the Orthodox church. Their thirteen-point program was a rather poor amalgam of nationalistic and antirevolutionary slogans.[29] The group had never

nourished strong constitutional convictions, yet supported the kind
of representative regime that granted their class some influence
and material benefits.

The Moderate Right, later the Nationalist party, were the closest
allies of the Union in an uneasy partnership that lasted throughout
the Third Duma. At the outset of the Third Duma, the Nationalists
and some of the Moderate Rights broke from the Right to form, in
October 1909, the Russian Nationalist faction. In April 1911 members of the former Moderate Right separated again to form the independent Nationalist faction. A nationalistic ideology, a similar
social background, and Stolypin's manipulations were the basis of
their close cooperation. From the very beginning the group influenced the policies of the Union, pushing it to the right, increasing
the internal frictions within the Union and counteracting the Kadets' influence. The cooperation between the Union and the Moderate Right constituted the basis for the government coalition in
the Duma.

The rightist faction of forty-nine deputies was essentially anticonstitutional in outlook, accepting the Duma only because it was
the will of the tsar, but opposing any interpretation of the manifesto
or the Fundamental Laws that would imply a limitation of his absolute power. A strident anti-Semitic and antiminorities nationalism
characterized their political credo. Most of the rightist deputies
and constituency came from the so-called monarchistic organizations that mushroomed after the publication of the October Manifesto. They gained considerable support in the western provinces,
where they established close relations with the local administration. The government, in its search for popular support, encouraged
these organizations and financed most of their activities.[30] The
rightist Duma faction was composed mainly of deputies from the
western provinces and included a large proportion of government
officials, landowners, and Orthodox clergy, who comprised about a
third of the entire group. They usually supported Stolypin because
he was the prime minister chosen by the tsar, yet they considered
Stolypin's policies too liberal and a potential threat to the regime.
The rightists added a peculiar tone of crude Great Russian chauvinism and anti-Semitism to the Third Duma. Their demagogical

and obstructionist tactics created an atmosphere of tension and acrimony and on many occasions disrupted the regular functioning of the house. They had a disproportionate influence, through connections with the administration and the court, on Stolypin's policies. Although the rightist faction usually voted with the Octobrists on government proposals, their tactics had an important influence on the ability of the leading party to achieve its goals.

The Octobrist Faction

The Union of October 17, the major beneficiary of the new election law, emerged as the largest faction in the Third Duma. Officially the faction numbered 148 representatives at the beginning of the first session, but this is only one of the numbers that one finds concerning its numerical strength. Guchkov, in his memoirs thirty years later, estimated that 170 deputies were affiliated with the Union.[31] S. I. Shidlovskii, another leading figure in the faction, recalled that soon after the convocation of the Duma, it numbered over 200 men.[32] But even Guchkov (who was overly optimistic concerning the total number of Octobrists in all sessions of the Third Duma) admitted that only 100 to 110 were "true" Octobrists. "Those who did not want to be Kadets or members of the 'Union of the Russian People' unavoidably joined the Octobrists," the Duma correspondent of *Novoe vremia* remarked.[33] This casual identification with Octobrism rose out of the lack of political experience and clear ideological orientation within the large group to the right of the Kadets, presenting the Octobrist leadership with the opportunity to form a large faction without undue concern for the political orientation and motivation of the "adherents" (*primykaiushchikh*). "The attitude to the party program of those who joined was not clarified. Everyone who so desired could register as a member of the Octobrist faction without any investigation," Shidlovskii complained.[34] Because the Union was ready to cooperate with the government, it attracted many who by habit looked to the government for direction and followed one policy—always remaining on the side of those in authority.[35] This made for a larger Union but increased internal tensions and division.

The Octobrists in the Third Duma were following the organizational pattern that characterized the Union from its very beginning. The heterogeneous composition[36] and rather vague commitments to commonly held beliefs led to a greater decrease in their number than in any of the other factions in the Third Duma. There were 148 Octobrists in the first session, 138 in the second, 125 in the third and fourth, and 122 in the fifth.[37] The artificial inflation and subsequent falling away of membership was one of the major weaknesses of the Octobrists and was responsible, at least in part, for the Union's failure to pursue a consistent policy and accomplish its established aims.

All the socioeconomic groups except labor were represented in the faction;[38] ninety-nine deputies were landowning gentry and only ten were peasants.[39] Although the Octobrists were described by their opponents as a "bourgeois" party, only fifteen deputies were industrialists or engaged in commercial and banking occupations.[40] The majority came from the same milieu as the Moderate Right. It is also important that many of the Union's Duma deputies were, at some time, in the service, either with the central or with the local administration. Thus while V. K. Fon-Anrep or G. G. Lerkhe were elected as houseowners and M. V. Rodzianko as a landowner, "they are yesterday's functionaries (*chinovniki*) and officers—functionaries of diverse 'skills,' but by training and life experience they are closer to 'service' than to houseowning or to the land."[41] Experience and training imbued them with a feeling of respect for established authority, as well as with the desire to support and cooperate with it.

The Octobrist group in the Third Duma had the appearance of a coalition of conflicting factions and orientations, but lack of party discipline served sometimes as a safeguard against major splits. On almost any issue one could find Octobrists voting against the "party line," which, in many respects was a meaningless term in the Union. However, this "voter's freedom" immobilized the Union as a political force. Rumors of impending splits and intensive friction within the Octobrist faction provided a recurring theme in the political commentaries of the period.[42]

The extreme right wing of the Union was composed mainly of landowners and zemstvo men who joined the Union during the agrarian disturbances in 1905–6. Many of them were government functionaries of dubious constitutional convictions, who became Octobrists because it looked as if the Union was in line with the government policy and who eventually left the faction. Among their leaders were Ia. G. Gololobov and L. V. Polovtsov. The left wing included the Union's most articulate members, many of them zemstvo liberals with strong constitutional convictions. On many issues they voted with the Kadets, yet differences of opinion concerning social reforms and the structure of the empire prevented a permanent alliance between the Kadets and the left Octobrists. Shidlovskii, A. F. Meyendorff, and Lerkhe were among the leaders of the group.[43] The majority of the faction belonged to the center; they occasionally voted according to the prevailing mood, pressured by the faction's leadership, but usually followed the government line, frequently changing views and votes overnight. These internal divisions delineated here were not institutionalized nor rigid: there were no well-defined factions within the Union; people changed their allegiances frequently, giving rise to unexpected combinations. The Union was united by its fear of revolution and by its support of Stolypin's policies of repression. Nationalism expressed in terms of restoration of Russia's military might, internal unity, and security, were the other main unifying principles.

Much of the lack of party discipline could be attributed to the faction's leadership, particularly Guchkov. He was responsible for the policy to increase the numerical strength of the faction regardless of ideological background. It could well be that even a more consistent organizational effort on his part would have failed to produce more cohesion in the faction, but Guchkov, who enjoyed great personal prestige, did not really try. "Guchkov, the head of the Octobrist party in the Duma, paid no attention to its organizational problems. He immersed himself entirely in military affairs," Shidlovskii, a member of the faction's secretariat, complained. "It looked as if the party had become a tool in the hands of its leader."[44] Guchkov was also the man who established the close cooperation between the Union and Stolypin and he persisted in this policy even when it became detrimental to the image of the Union as an independent and principled political organization, Shidlovskii

averred.[45] On many occasions this intensified the internal tensions
of the faction.

As the largest faction in the Third Duma, the Octobrists seemed
to be in a position to make an effective effort to realize their goals.
In the most general terms they were united in a desire to achieve
internal peace and security, gradual but not far-reaching reforms,
and the restoration of national military power and international
prestige. In the minds of many Octobrists these goals amounted to
the restoration of their pride in belonging to the Russian Empire.
This pride had been shattered by defeat, revolution, and the rule
of an arbitrary bureaucracy. For the majority of the Octobrists
neither the Right nor the Kadets offered an appealing program to
achieve these goals.

To understand the goals as well as the behavior of the Octobrists in the Third Duma one has to bear in mind that the latter
were impressed by what had happened to Russia in the years from
1904 to 1907. They had lived through the traumatic experiences of
the 1905–7 revolution and the defeat in the Russo-Japanese War of
1904–5. The revolution had undermined their confidence in autocracy's ability to maintain internal order and it had imbued them
with an ever-present fear of the renewal of terror and consequent
destruction of a social order from which many of them had benefited. Octobrism's antagonism toward the Kadets and its support
of Stolypin, a "strong man," was nurtured by this fear. Yet the
Octobrists were afraid of an "official" anarchy, one created by an
arbitrary administration in a country ruled by emergency and martial law.

The defeat in the Russo-Japanese War was considered by the
Octobrists a national disgrace, a wound to national consciousness.
The desire to prevent such a humiliation in the future resulted in
the Union's preoccupation with military matters. The trauma of
defeat and the fear of revolution had antithetical effects on the
Union's course in the Duma. This fear of a new revolution brought
many Octobrists to conservatism as an attempt to check change
and reform; only the more intelligent thought that reform might avert
a new revolution, and even they were not sure how much should
be implemented. The defeat had a more dynamic effect, prompting

many conservative Octobrists to espouse change and reform. They understood that the causes of the humiliation were not limited to the army, but included an inadequate educational system, a corrupt higher command, and poor communication and industry. Thus reforms were needed in order to regain and maintain Russia's international prestige.

The years from 1907 to 1912 were charged with keen international competition, tensions, and crises. They were also years of social and economic tensions within the country itself; revolution, or at least revolutionary outbursts, was always near the surface and the traumatic experiences of 1906–7 could not be forgotten nor dismissed. The dilemma between conservatism and change continued to agitate the Union.

Recalling his expectations after the defeat in the war, Guchkov said that the October Manifesto and the convocation of the Duma

> gave hope that we would follow the road of unavoidable evolution, the road of wide, daring, and courageous reforms, that would lead us to those avenues of social and political development traversed by all our West European neighbors. . . . I thought that we too would follow the economic, political, and social road followed by other nations.[46]

To accomplish those goals, Guchkov prepared a detailed legislative program of ninety-nine articles, yet he did not dare to present it before the faction's plenum. He knew the divergent opinions of the Union membership and feared splits.[47] Instead, the general assembly of the Union's Duma faction adopted on October 29, 1907, a seventeen-point "statement" of goals and principles that would guide it in the future.[48] More concrete and detailed than its original proclamation on only a few points, the statement promised that the Union would strive to create a constitutional center that would try to implement the promises of the manifesto without infringing upon the rights of the tsar and at the same time defend the rights of the legislative houses. The statement referred vaguely to the need to "broaden the budgetary rights of the Duma and its supervisory power over the administration appointed by the sovereign." The

statement was more concrete than the proclamation with regard to
the status of the national minorities. Local self-government in the
borderlands was to be encouraged only to the extent that would
guarantee the "unity and indivisibility of the empire" as well as the
interests of the Russian population. The Octobrists opposed any
suggestion that would have granted immediate equality to the Jewish population; they recommended only a "review" of the existing
laws. A clear effort was made by the Union in this statement to
placate their allies to the right.

The Union's faction included in its statement the almost ritual
condemnation of revolutionary violence and a demand to guarantee
by proper legislation and an independent judiciary the "promised
freedoms." The statement was now a little more detailed and concrete than previously: that extensive parts of the empire were ruled
by various kinds of emergency laws and extraordinary regulations
could not escape the attention of the Octobrists. They required a
review of the need for such regulations as well as a clear definition
of when and for how long the ordinary legal procedures should be
suspended.

The chapters on self-government and education repeated the
demands of the proclamation. These were also to be the more impressive fields of achievements of the Union in the Third Duma.
The Octobrists' solution to the "peasant problem" had by now almost
completely coincided with Stolypin's agrarian policy, whether already enacted or just planned. "The major aim of the agrarian legislation in the Duma should be the creation of such conditions that
will facilitate the transition to more intensive and improved economic methods by the peasantry." The Union's proposed legislation
in the field of labor-employer relations included shorter work hours,
establishment of arbitration committees, legalization of unions,
and economic, not political, strikes. To improve the status of the
lower classes, the Octobrists promised to reform the tax structure
and introduce a progressive income tax.

This was the most detailed and comprehensive program adopted
by the Union during the Third Duma period. Although vague and too
general in certain points, it was more specific than before and reflected the Union's aspirations and basic attitudes. The Union

emphatically denied any intention to compete with the tsar's authority; it asked only to act within the rights prescribed by the Fundamental Laws. In spite of the Union's realization that the Duma's rights were ill-defined, their request to broaden the budgetary right was equally so as was their demand to broaden suffrage. The clauses on local self-government and for the realization of civil rights were concrete and detailed, for these areas were of immediate personal concern for the Octobrists and their constituency. The chapters on the peasant and labor problems were also specific: the agrarian policy was designed to avert confiscation of private lands—while the proposed labor reforms were the minimum required, according to the authors, to secure a docile and stable working force. The program for national minorities and for Jews showed the Octobrists' efforts to establish a workable coalition with the groups to their right.

The Union was ready to cooperate with the government in an effort to renovate Russia by peaceful means. Its success or failure depended to a large extent on the Octobrists' ability to create a workable Duma majority and on the authorities' willingness to live up to their promises.

3

The Antirevolutionary Coalition

The Union became the center of the "government majority" in the Third Duma. Since there was no parliamentary regime in Russia, the term "government majority" referred to a coalition of groups in the Duma that accepted the basic policies of the authorities, usually supported the government's initiatives and bills, and passed proposed budgets. There were no formal alliances nor mutually binding obligations on either side. As far as the government was concerned there was no "government party" nor "government majority" in the formal sense and when it did not get the support of a majority of deputies, it had means to circumvent the Duma. After the dissolution of the first two Dumas, the real danger of an oppositional majority was another dissolution, or even the abolition of the Duma itself. Since the Union accepted the basic power relations in the empire, its members tried their best to be the center of a pro-government coalition.

The terms "Duma majority," "government coalition," and "opposition" had only limited meaning in the Third Duma. The looseness of party affiliation and lack of political and parliamentary experience created great flexibility in voting. One could find occasionally an ad hoc combination of a surprising nature, frequently one that crossed official faction lines.

The June 3 electoral law was designed to elect a "trustworthy" and "workable" lower chamber. The actual composition of the Third Duma justified, to a large extent, Stolypin's expectations for a majority that accepted the basic premises of the regime and was willing to cooperate with the authorities.

Theoretically, two coalitions could be formed in the Third Duma: an Octobrist-liberal-Left and an Octobrist-Right. The first could muster approximately 260 votes, the second 300. On several occasions the Octobrist-liberal coalition dominated the scene, especially when Stolypin used it to promote certain political reforms that raised strong opposition from the reactionary Right. In many ways the majority of the educated public preferred this coalition. Yet the more usual majority was that of the Union and the parties to its right—one more to the liking of the court and the administration. The two majorities corresponded, in a way, to Stolypin's policy of "first pacification, then reforms." That the Octobrist-Right coalition prevailed was indicative of the stress put by the authorities on pacification and on strengthening the regime.

The social composition and the basic political orientation of the majority of the Union's deputies made a coalition with the factions to their right more attractive than with those to the left. Stolypin and Guchkov formed the Moderate Right and Nationalist groups so those groups would cooperate with the Union and provide the premier with a cooperative majority. Guchkov recalled that the purpose of the Moderate Right was to vote for Stolypin's initiatives in the Duma, but the Union leader added "since the Union too considered Stolypin the best choice to head the government, in spite of occasional differences of opinion, the cooperation between the Octobrists and the Nationalists was, in general, a successful one."[1] The rightist group usually voted for the government's policies, thus constituting part of the dominant majority.

Many of the causes that brought together the various elements composing the Union operated in forming the government majority. Above all, it was an antirevolutionary coalition that supported the established authorities in their struggle to preserve the socioeconomic order and the unity of the empire. In 1907 they were united in a common hatred of the Kadets and the revolutionary Left. The majority, with a few exceptions among the rightists, supported Stolypin's agrarian policy. As the major ideological basis for cooperation, nationalism provided a common plank of strengthening

Russia's military might, of suppressing internal chaos, and of restoring international prestige. Yet the coalition, like the Union, was composed of groups that held conflicting views about the methods for achieving those goals. They had different interpretations of the character of the post-October regime and the meaning of "peaceful renovation." The coalition not only contained contradictory groups but frictions and divergent views within each faction as well. Since it was an artificial creation of the government, its internal cohesion and policies were largely determined by the government.

The Union's participation in either of the combinations of which they were a large part was decided by its composition and the prevailing mood in the Duma and the country. It usually followed the authorities' line, but its support was neither automatic nor unqualified. There were periods of close cooperation within the coalition and with the government as well as periods of opposition and internal tensions, but even at times of united opposition to the government the Union made no concrete nor decisive effort to affect government policy.

The election of the Duma's presidium brought together for the first time the various elements that comprised the government majority. The formation of the coalition took place only a few days before the opening of the first session.

In a series of meetings between the Octobrists and representatives from the yet undifferentiated mass of deputies that stood to the right of the Union, an effort was made to work out a common program and to reach an agreement on the composition of the presidium.[2] The Union refused to merge with the various rightist groups or to agree to a common program, although both sides emphasized their loyalty to the tsar, the necessity of strengthening the military might of the country, and their support of the government in its struggle against anarchy and sedition.[3]

An agreement was finally reached not to elect to the presidium any members from the factions to the left of the Octobrists, and N. A. Khomiakov was proposed as Duma president. He was a veteran of the zemstvo movement and one of the founders of the Union.

Khomiakov, an amiable man with great integrity, was elected by a vote of 371 to 9. The three vice-presidents belonged to the Octobrists, the Moderate Right, and the Right. The election of the Duma's secretary, who belonged to the presidium, created a stormy debate in the Duma and inside the Octobrist faction. The candidature of the rightist G. G. Zamyslovskii was opposed by the leftist Octobrists F. N. Plevako and M. Ia. Kapustin,[4] and despite the agreement with the Right, a sizable group of Octobrists voted for V. A. Maklakov.[5] The presidium was composed of two Octobrists, one moderate rightist, and two rightists. Thus the anticonstitutional elements had a decisive voice in procedural matters in the Third Duma.

In a lackluster acceptance speech, Khomiakov expressed his sincere hope that the Duma would contribute its share in "bringing peace to Russia," in "ending the hostility and malice of partisanship, healing the wounds of the suffering homeland, and realizing the sovereign will of the tsar."[6] The speech was in the best tradition of Slavophile liberalism, expressing a sincere desire to work in a fraternal way in the Duma and with the government to restore peace to the country. This was a vain hope; the spirit of the Duma was not one of a loving family, nor was peace in the country around the corner.

The Debates Over the Address and Declaration

The debate that followed the tsar's message opening the Third Duma revealed the fragility of the government coalition and its internal contradictions. Only Stolypin's declaration of his government's policy brought the coalition together again, in spite of the obvious disagreement within its ranks.

The Duma selected a committee of eighteen to draft a declaration in response to the tsar's greetings. The resolution that was eventually presented before the plenum was drafted by the Octobrists Guchkov and Kapustin.[7]

The debate in the plenum centered mainly on the inclusion of the term *Autocrat*, as demanded by the rightist faction, and *constitution*, as the Kadets demanded. It developed into an acrimonious debate over the desired regime and the interpretation of "peaceful renovation." Not surprisingly, the Octobrists were closer in their views to the Kadets than to their coalition allies.

P. N. Balashov, the leader of the Moderate Right, made it clear, to the great embarrassment of the Union, that his group "does not and will not recognize the term 'the renewed state structure' as meaning a western European constitution."[8] Count V. A. Bobrinskii, another leader of the same group, was even more explicit: "By the act of June 3 the Autocratic Sovereign revealed his unlimited power."[9] The Moderate Right demanded the inclusion of *Autocratic* in the tsar's title. The rightist group stressed that the tsar was all-powerful in practice and theory and V. M. Purishkevich's and N. E. Markov's speeches contained undisguised threats to the representative institution.

The Kadets demanded the inclusion of the term *constitution*. Their speakers, P. N. Miliukov and A. I. Shingarev, maintained that the post-October regime was not a renovated autocracy but a new constitutional monarchy. The Kadets explained that the "coup of June 3" was only an aberration, not a return to former absolutism.

During the debate the Octobrists came out as convinced supporters of a constitutional regime. Guchkov spoke for most of them:

> I belong to the party that understands clearly that the
> Manifesto of October 17 implied a voluntary act of denial
> by the monarch of his unlimited rights. We have no doubt
> in our mind that by his own act our monarch had estab-
> lished a constitutional regime in the country. But, we do
> not think that we have the right to force our interpreta-
> tion on anybody.[10]

Guchkov's pronouncement on the new regime was reminiscent of Slavophile formulas. He assumed that after October the tsar would be free to communicate with his people, free from court cliques and favorites,[11] an interpretation of utmost importance to future positions taken by the Octobrists, particularly by Guchkov.

A realist and a pragmatist, Guchkov maintained that this was not the right time for lengthy constitutional debates:

> We must now only recognize the fact that the people
> were given extensive rights and the opportunity to par-

ticipate in the . . . reconstruction of our fatherland. We
are not using controversial terms to designate what was
given. Not by words will I convert into constitutionalists
those who are still fighting against the change. I will
not convince them by words but I believe that the peaceful and loyal work of the Third Duma will reconcile them
with the change.[12]

The same ideas were expressed by other Octobrists. Kapustin,
from the left wing, maintained that the address to the tsar had to
reflect the true aspirations and hopes of the country. Russia needed
neither a revolutionary utopia nor the return of the old regime. The
manifesto had established a constitutional regime that brought together tsar and people and there could be a constitutional regime
without mentioning the term.[13] Plevako argued against the Kadets:
"Our language is capable and strong, you can find in it expressions
for the broadest freedom feasible on earth."[14]

The virulent attacks by the Right against the idea of a constitutional regime pushed the Octobrists to a more determined defense
of the constitutional idea, an effect opposite to what the Right
expected. Count A. A. Uvarov admitted that for a while he had supported the inclusion of the term *Autocrat* in the address. But when

a series of speakers from the Right gave this historical
title . . . their interpretation . . . these men reminded
me of the medieval dark ages. . . . I am sorry, but I cannot share these medieval feelings. Therefore . . . my
attitude to the correction of his holiness Mitrofan [to
include the title Autocrat] has radically changed after
listening to what has been said.[15]

The amendment of the Right was defeated by a 212 to 146 vote.
The Octobrists' draft excluding the terms *constitutional* and *Autocratic* was finally adopted, with the Kadets retreating from their
demand to include the term *constitution*.[16] The Right, the Socialists, and the national minorities factions abstained.

The content and spirit of the address corresponded to the general ideology and aims of the Union. It included an expression of
gratitude and a promise to work diligently for the welfare of the

country.[17] The debate brought into the open some of the basic disagreements between the Octobrists and their allies to the right. It
is worth notice that the right wing of the faction did not participate
in the debate.

The debate on the address raised doubts as to the viability of
a united government majority, but these misgivings disappeared
after Stolypin's declaration, which outlined his policy in concrete
terms.

Ranking first on the prime minister's list of priorities was the
restoration of order and peace to the country. "First pacification"
was Stolypin's motto and he was ready to use any means to achieve
this goal.[18] Although the premier opposed the "addition of foreign
flowers to the Russian stem," referring to the post-October regime,
he explicitly stated that "the regime in which we live is a representative regime, granted by the Autocratic Monarch."[19] For Stolypin
the tsar remained the ultimate source of authority who summoned
representatives from the people to help him in his legislative tasks.
The prime minister outlined a brief reform program that could be
accomplished only with the restoration of internal peace. Stolypin
mentioned a few bills that his government intended to introduce in
the Duma, most of them corresponding with the Union's program:
broadening of local self-government, educational reforms, strengthening of the armed forces, and positive laws to guarantee the freedoms granted by the tsar.[20]

Stolypin emphasized that the major task of the government at
the time was the carrying out of its agrarian policy. His aim was
to raise substantially the living standards of the peasantry, not by
"bribing the village nor by the use of force and fomenting sedition,"
but by strengthening the concepts of private ownership, by encouraging the replacement of communal ownership by privately owned
farms, and by using improved agricultural methods.[21] The government called upon the Duma to support its legislative initiatives.

The Duma's response contained no surprises. The debate was
in many ways a reiteration of the one on the address. The opposition repeated its criticisms of the regime and the coalition again
demonstrated its devotion to the tsar. Count Bobrinskii, the spokesman for the Moderate Right, promised his faction's support of the

"ministry" that was selected by the sovereign, but added that it would not be an automatic or an uncritical support of all government actions.[22] The rightists concurred with Bobrinskii, Markov promising that his faction's program in the Duma was only one "to assist the Sovereign, the Emperor, in his legislative initiatives."[23]

For the Octobrists too the debate presented another chance to express their views on the regime and Stolypin's policies. Guchkov proposed acceptance of Stolypin's declaration by calling for the beginning of the legislative work that would accomplish the much-needed reforms.[24] A sincere desire to stop futile constitutional debates and prove themselves in their legislative capacity characterized most of the Union's speakers, for they were eager to prove that the Third Duma, contrary to its two predecessors, had the capacity and willingness to work. Although the general tone was one of support for Stolypin's basic policies, almost all the Octobrists expressed some reservations, doubts, and criticism concerning Stolypin's declaration. They made it clear that the Union would support the government, but reserved the right to criticize and to differ. Presaging their course in the future, there was no allusion to a possibility that the Union might try to oppose or change government policy by using the budgetary power given the Duma. Count Uvarov expressed the Octobrists' general mood when he said:

> There is no place in the present Duma for an opposition that objects to all government actions only because the government initiated them. . . . The Union of October 17 should not be considered the government's party that accepts all its actions. . . . We will reserve our freedom to criticize all the actions and bills proposed by the authorities. . . . We pray to God that the government's actions will be of a nature that we will be able to approve them and add our assistance to the extent that it would be required.[25]

M. Ia. Kapustin enlarged on the "warmer" welcome the Octobrists expected from the authorities: "The Union of October 17 is a nationalistic party, cherishing Russia's past and its history."[26] They had come to the Duma with a strong desire for a "creative cooperation" with the government, and intended to gain its favor by deeds. Kapustin expressed his hope that, together with a determined policy against revolutionary terror, the government would develop and guard civil freedoms.[27]

N. P. Shubinskii rejected the notion that the Octobrists came to the Duma to follow the government's line. "We have our own views, feelings, ideas. When we agree with the government, we will work together, when we disagree—too bad."[28] Shubinskii complained about the oppositional tone that was present in the speeches of other members of his party. He considered this "slip" of the center to the left a threat to the Duma, one that could disrupt the representative regime.[29]

To the great surprise of the coalition the Union's formula fell short by three votes of the necessary majority. No formula received the required votes.[30] The Union refused to vote for the Progressists' program, which included the request to implement the October Manifesto. The left wing in the Union grumbled, accusing Guchkov of yielding to pressures from the Right.[31] The failure to get a majority to vote for the Union's formula showed the Union's lack of parliamentary experience as well as the weakness of the government coalition. Many Octobrists were absent from the hall when the vote was taken. The rightists voted against the formula, protesting some of the Octobrist speeches, proof that when confronted with problems of basic political orientation, the coalition lacked internal cohesion, between its groups and inside each group as well. The coalition, whose bases were the Union and Moderate Right, was dependent to a large extent on votes from the Right or the moderate Left.

The vote on the formula in response to Stolypin's declaration prompted the coalition to consolidate its ranks. Two "whips" had been elected by the Union to impose party discipline. The Union and the Moderate Right factions decided to unite behind the government program as stated by Stolypin, and formed an "information" center, inviting the rightists and the Progressists to join in its activities.[32] The response was noncommittal. Yet after the theoretical debates that opened the Third Duma, the government coalition of the Union and the factions to its right became a working reality.

The Coalition in Action

The government coalition expressed itself mainly in its support of the initiatives and actions of those in authority and for the first time since the establishment of a representative regime in Russia, the Duma passed the budget as proposed by the government. The coalition acted harmoniously in defeating most of the attempts made by the oppositional factions to censure the administration's actions. From the dozens of interpellations concerning illegal actions by the authorities, only a few were recognized as deserving further consideration. By opposing reforms that would limit this repression, the antirevolutionary character of the government coalition expressed itself mainly in negative terms. Most of the repressive measures taken by the authorities were defended by the coalition, which meanwhile vehemently attacked the opposition. Yet, even though they acted in concert in defense of the government's actions, there were throughout the coalition signs of internal strain and dissension.

The opposition, particularly the largest group, the Kadets, was refused meaningful participation in the regular work of the Duma and its committees. They were given only minor roles in the committees and were excluded altogether from the Defense Committee, on Guchkov's initiative.[33] It was followed by the Duma's decision on January 29, 1908, to accept his request to give the head of the Defense Committee the right to close its sessions to nonmembers.[34]

The Octobrists made a united effort to demonstrate their patriotism and disapproval of some of the statements Miliukov made after he had been abroad, joining the Right in leaving the hall during his speech.[35] The antirevolutionary coalition rejected systematically interpellations that criticized Stolypin or his ministers. Requests to investigate the behavior of the local authorities came in an unending stream from the opposition, but most of them were rejected, or bogged down in committee. The only exception was the investigation of the illegal conduct of I. A. Dumbadze, the governor of the Crimea.

The debate on the bill providing proper compensation for the victims of revolutionary terror, a bill that included a strong condemnation of all revolutionary activities, became one of the high points

of the antirevolutionary campaign in the Third Duma. During the
debate, the coalition speakers attacked the entire opposition, particularly the Kadets, accusing it of fomenting sedition, rebellion,
and murder. The Kadets' role in the revolutionary period was criticized and sharply censured, but despite this attack, Guchkov,
speaking for the Union, asked the opposition to support the bill,
remarking that their opposition to terror as a means of political
action would add to the real value of the law.[36] Guchkov knew that
without the support of the Left, the bill would have only a declara-
tory meaning. He failed to enlist their support, understandably
enough: the attacks on the entire history and value of the liberation movement left the opposition with no alternative except a
negative response.

   Quite frequently the harmony between the Union and the administration was disrupted by incidents that had internal repercussions
in the coalition and in the Union. On April 29, 1908, V. N. Kokovtsov,
the finance minister, rejected a proposal to form an ad hoc Duma
committee to investigate the management of state-owned railways,
maintaining that only the tsar had the right to nominate such a
committee. "Thank God we do not have a parliament," remarked the
minister.[37] In the storm that followed the remark, the Duma had to
be adjourned. The Union's faction authorized Count Uvarov to respond and he, indicating the grave implications of Kokovtsov's
attitude, pointed out that the prime minister had, in political terms,
declared that a representative regime was established with the
convocation of the Duma. That meant, contended the Octobrist,
the existence of a parliament.[38]

   Khomiakov, the Duma president, expressed his discontent with
Kokovtsov's remark, characterizing it as rather "unfortunate."[39]
Kokovtsov threatened to resign, forcing Stolypin into an embarrassing position, for in the preceding few months friendly relations had
prevailed between the Duma and the government and no one wanted
to disrupt them. A meeting was arranged between Kokovtsov and
Khomiakov where both agreed that the entire thing was just a mis-
understanding.[40] At the next Duma meeting on April 26, Khomiakov
announced that Kokovtsov had retracted his remark. The incident
was resolved, but it left ill feeling in the Duma and showed the

precarious nature of the entire representative regime and the consistent effort needed to avoid a clash between the imperial government and the Duma on matters of principle.

The most important instance of internal tensions within the antirevolutionary coalition coming into the open was the debate on the budget of the Ministry of the Interior. It revealed some basic disagreements between the Union and the government about the course of the internal policy followed by the administration, but also intensified the struggle within the Union's Duma faction.

The division caused by the debate on the budget lay in one of the main objectives of the Union of October 17, support of the government in its struggle against revolution and anarchy. But the Union never espoused a policy of repression as an end in itself. The restoration of peace and order to the country relegated the repression of revolutionary terror to only one facet; the other was the establishment of a state in which the rights of the individual citizen would be protected by law and the courts. As time passed it became apparent that while revolutionary terror was on the decline, the arbitrary practices of the administration were not changing and the "promised freedoms" of the October Manifesto remained only promises. Whole provinces were ruled by various emergency regulations, but even more ominous was the slowly developing process of disintegration of the provincial governmental apparatus. The deliberations of the Third Duma provide ample evidence that Stolypin tried to stop this process, but with limited success.

The October Manifesto undermined the old order, but new laws to replace the old ones were slow in coming. A state of lawlessness or, as S. Ia. Elpatevskii called it, "between the laws" (*mezhduzakoniia*) reigned in the land.[41]

The old power structure remained. The tsar, most of his ministers, governors, gendarmes, and police were not replaced and still wielded their unlimited power. Those who forced them to grant the manifesto were punished by exile or courts-martial. But autocracy never regained the self-confidence that it had before the defeat in the war and the revolutionary upheaval, and the authority of the central government was damaged by its local agents more than by any real or imagined revolutionaries. Cracks appeared in the state mechanism from top to bottom. "In reality Autocracy ceased to exist," remarked Elpiatevskii.[42] In the central government the disintegration was caused by the increasing influence of the "irresponsible men" (*bezotvetstvennye liudi,* about whom more will be said later), who neutralized and eventually defeated Stolypin. By 1908, the process of disintegration of the state mechanism was visible in the provinces where the emergency laws had given unlimited powers to local administrators. The distance from St. Petersburg and personal connections with the court protected these administrators from effective supervision by the central government. The activities of the monarchistic groups, the most important being the Black Hundreds, undermined further the sense of security of the peaceful citizen. The police were preoccupied with their political functions. Externally the country was regaining peace and order, but the former tranquillity was not regained. The feeling that the government was able and willing to protect life and property had not returned to the countryside and provincial town. The average citizen and landowner had not become a revolutionary but rather watched helplessly the disintegration of his small world.

Most of the Octobrists in the Duma came from the social milieu that felt threatened by what was happening in the provinces. The outrageous behavior of some governors and the provincial administration in general reached such proportions that even "loyal" papers like *Novoe vremia,* the *Kievlianin,* and *Golos Moskvy* were full of complaints.[43]

The budget of the Ministry of the Interior was discussed after Easter vacation, when the deputies had just returned with fresh impressions and firsthand information on what was happening in the countryside. While many of the Octobrists were so deeply distressed that they voiced their protests and demanded change, there were others who defended the administration. The debate revealed again the split in the Union among those who demanded reforms and those who were afraid of change.

Baron Meyendorff, in an eloquent speech, expressed the hopes, fears, and frustrations of the Union: Stolypin had brought new hope and had rescued Russia from internal collapse, but the Union's expectations were not yet fulfilled; the "true" danger to Russia was the firmly entrenched state machinery.[44]

Behind the guise of state security there are personal vendettas and intrigues.[45] . . . The Union of October 17 thinks that the Russian people are not demanding too much from the authorities when they ask for a little fairness and justice for themselves.[46]

S. I. Shidlovskii, detailing and documenting what he said, contended that since 1880 the police were increasingly instrumental in determining the country's internal policies.[47] The use of emergency regulations, he maintained, gave impetus to that tendency and was responsible for the mounting fears and insecurity in the land.

Prince Gregory Golitsyn's scathing criticism of the administration created the strongest impression, for he was known to be, normally, a moderate and restrained man.[48] An unimpassioned analysis of the facts, the prince explained, brought him to the conclusion that while "at the center reigns the constitution, tyranny prevails in the provinces. The trouble is the result of the disintegration of the central and local administration."[49] The authorities could not justify the situation by the assertion that they had not yet prepared the proper laws: "From the assertion that certain bills were not yet prepared to the disregard of any law, there is a long distance."[50]

Golitsyn, like others, made the distinction between the government and its local agents, between center and province. The Octobrists had faith in Stolypin and his intentions, but what was happening in the country convinced them that the prime minister was thwarted by the entrenched servants of the old order who found powerful allies close to the throne. Golitsyn pointed out that "a whole set of *satrapies* developed in Russia. They are not subject to the law nor to the head of government. In their territories they run the courts, issue special regulations, govern solely at their own discretion."[51]

The Octobrist Uvarov was even more explicit. He maintained that the central government would have liked to change things for the better, but Stolypin did not have full control as minister of the

interior, "He has dispersed his authority; he himself, perhaps inadvertently, gave full power to local dictators." [52]

One of the primary reasons for the emergence of "local dictators"
was the use of various emergency regulations in many areas of the
empire. The Octobrists recognized the need of such regulations, but
refused to accept them as a permanent feature of Russian life. There
were warnings from Golitsyn and Uvarov that the use of extraordinary regulations over a long period would foster an atmosphere of
lawlessness and that they were unwarranted and dangerous for the
future of the country. [53]

Undersecretary of the Interior Makarov rejected the charges
brought by the Left and the Octobrists. [54] He held that the proper
way to air complaints was through interpellations, that the budget
of the Ministry of the Interior and not its policy was the subject on
the agenda. He argued that the government, too, was concerned with
the extended use of the emergency regulations and pointed out
several cases where there was a relaxation of their application.
The authorities did not consider the regulations permanent, yet
deemed it necessary to be careful in their abolition because the
time of peace had not yet arrived. As long as anarchy and sedition
could be detected, he continued, the government would not hesitate
to fulfill its duty, by any means, to tsar and country.

The tone of the Octobrists changed perceptibly after the government's statement. After Golitsyn's and Meyendorff's speeches,
Guchkov said to *Slovo*'s correspondent that their views were justified: "The speakers rightly pointed out the legalization of illegality in the provinces." [55] He even suggested adding to the formula
of acceptance of the budget specific demands for reforms of the
police, a clear definition of the competence of the local administration, and so forth. Makarov's speech had made him more cautious.
He refused to renew the debate, arguing that the Left was trying to
subvert the peaceful functioning of the Duma: "There is no doubt
that not all the parties are equally interested in making the Duma's
work successful and fruitful." [56] Eventually he joined Bobrinskii's
proposal to allow three speakers from each side to respond to
Makarov. Shubinskii, who was selected by Guchkov as the main
Octobrist speaker, accepted Makarov's argument that the subject

had to be "numbers" and not government policy.[57] He made a detailed defense of the government, accusing the revolutionaries of being responsible for the need to use emergency regulations and for the delay in the implementation of the freedoms promised in the manifesto.

In spite of the criticism and the obvious disagreements within the faction, it voted as a whole for the budget of the Ministry of the Interior. No real effort had been made to force the authorities to change their policy. The Octobrists, disappointed and outraged by the government, reacted in the same manner as their constituencies in the countryside. They continued to support those in authority, unwilling to look for an alternative course of action. The same pattern repeated itself throughout the period of the Third Duma.

The Agrarian Problem

One of the major issues that brought together the government majority in the Third Duma was its support of Stolypin's land reform, which he considered the cornerstone of his entire socioeconomic policy as well as a prerequisite for other reforms. The government majority and particularly the Octobrists supported Stolypin's agrarian policy out of class interest as well as out of conviction; they thought that it presented the only realistic approach to the solution of the agrarian crisis.

The Union of October 17 changed its agrarian policy between the time it was founded and the convocation of the Third Duma. The section dealing with the peasant problem in the Union's proclamation included a clear reference to the acceptability of partial confiscation of private lands, but the peasant commune was not mentioned—it was apparent that neo-Slavophile attitudes that glamorized the peasant commune influenced the authors. The first party convention almost split when the agrarian problem was raised. In the First Duma the agrarian proposal of the Octobrists, presented by P. A. Geiden, was only a more moderate variation of the Kadets' agrarian program. The crucial point was the acceptance of confiscation of private lands as the main solution to the agrarian crisis.[58] The threat of confiscation presented by the first two Dumas was one of the major causes of their dissolution and the change in the electoral law. Only a duma composed of a majority of "trustworthy elements" would tolerate the agrarian measures that were implemented by the use of emergency legislation.

The split with the *Mirno-Obnovlentsy*[59] after the dissolution of the First Duma made it easier for the Union to accept Stolypin's agrarian program. The First Duma was dissolved primarily because the government was determined to prevent the acceptance of an agrarian program that would mean the confiscation of private lands. During the period between the First and Second Dumas the authorities promulgated a series of laws concerning different aspects of the peasant's life. The major measure was the Ukase of November 9, 1906, which became the cornerstone of Stolypin's agrarian policy. The Central Committee of the Union issued the following statement after publication of the ukase: "Now the agrarian chapter in our program can be entirely dismissed. All our wishes in that field have been implemented by the government's laws." [60]

What was the agrarian policy that had been so eagerly received by the Union?

The goal of Stolypin's land policy reform was to replace the peasantry organized in the communes by a well-to-do class of peasant landowners. The events in the countryside in 1902–3 and particularly in 1905–6 convinced the authorities that the peasantry in the communes presented a threat to the established political and social order [61] and the people who planned and executed Stolypin's land policy tried to create in the village a large class of small freeholders that would provide a broader base for the regime. [62] They hoped, by strengthening the principles of private ownership, to divert the peasants' attention from the confiscation of private lands. Private enterprise was considered the best means of changing the lot of the peasantry and of solving the agrarian problem, but it was political rather than economic consideration that prompted the implementation of this policy. [63]

What became known as "Stolypin's Land Reform" was actually planned by S. Iu. Witte, V. I. Gurko, A. V. Krivoshein, and others before Stolypin even came to St. Petersburg, but Stolypin became its ardent supporter and the man who implemented it. [64] This series of laws and regulations covered various aspects of the peasants' life and agriculture. Its principal point, the reform of peasant tenure, was included in the Ukase of November 9, 1906, in the provision for an efficient legal machinery to help the creation of privately owned, consolidated farms instead of the communal lands. The ukase did not abolish the commune, but accelerated and encouraged its disintegration by providing that every householder in the commune could demand and get his lot in hereditary private ownership.[65]

In communes where there had not been a general redistribution of land in the preceding twenty-four years, the peasant household was entitled to all the land in its possession, regardless of the actual share due to the household. If a redistribution had taken place within the previous twenty-four years, the household had to pay for holdings exceeding its share but at the price of the time of the Emancipation. Any commune could pass to private ownership by a vote of two-thirds of its members. The rights in the communes of those who seceded were not impaired: the stipulation that the seceding household would get its actual holdings in private tenure at the very low price fixed for the excess land encouraged the well-to-do peasant to leave the commune.

The ukase included provisions that enabled the seceding peasant to demand his share in one consolidated plot. It should be emphasized that the transferring from communal to private tenure did not necessarily mean the creation of a consolidated farm, since a holding was often composed of widely scattered strips. This stipulation (*zemleustroistvo*) allowed for either consolidated lots or compensation to the peasants who demanded it—an important facet of Stolypin's land reform, since only on a consolidated plot could the freeholding peasant introduce advanced agricultural methods, and only on a consolidated farm could the enterprising peasant use his labor and resources to change radically the traditional agricultural routine of the commune. In addition, the ukase included provisions that enabled the head of the household to become the sole owner of the family plot.

The government coalition, with a few exceptions on the extreme Right, considered Stolypin's agrarian policy the only safeguard of the established socioeconomic order. The ratification of Stolypin's bills became one of the main unifying elements of the coalition.

The majority of gentry landowners in the coalition, anxious to avoid confiscation of their land, were its enthusiastic proponents. The capitalist element in the Union considered the encouragement of private enterprise in the village and the outflow of the impoverished peasants into the industrial centers beneficial to the development of the national economy.

The Union's enthusiastic reception of the Ukase of November 9 incurred a hostility from the Kadets that hindered future cooperation on other matters. Guchkov considered the ukase Stolypin's most important achievement as prime minister. Stolypin,

> by transforming the peasants into small landowners gave promise of laying a firm foundation for Russia. . . . He realized that Russia could not become a strong power until the majority of her population—the peasants—became interested in the safeguarding of individual property and, therefore, the state order which guaranteed them this property.[66]

The Third Duma devoted much of its time to the agrarian problem, passing hundreds of bills legalizing Stolypin's initiatives and allocating financial resources to implement his policy. Their aim was to raise the standard of living of the peasantry and encourage private enterprise in the village. The *zemleustroistvo* bill that supplemented the ukase passed the Duma almost without objection.

The debate preceding the passing of the ukase was the main occasion for discussing and clarifying the attitudes of the various factions towards the principles of Stolypin's agrarian policy. The debate started on October 28, 1908, with as many as 210 deputies registered to participate.[67] The Agrarian Committee of the Duma, dominated by the Octobrists Rodzianko and Shidlovskii, introduced only a few changes in the original government draft, but these amendments went further than the original bill in facilitating the disintegration of the commune. The committee broadened the authority of the arbitration committees, established to decide in cases of conflicts between the individual peasant and the commune.

Shidlovskii, the speaker and later head of the Duma's Agrarian Committee, was also the Union's major representative in the debate.

Unlike other participants in the debate, Shidlovskii presented Stolypin's policy in the general concept of the development of the country's economy. Against the project of confiscation presented by the
Kadets, Shidlovskii outlined a liberal's concept of an agrarian
policy that used a variety of means and methods to solve the crisis
in the village.[68]

He saw the causes of the agrarian crisis as lying in the general
backwardness of the national economy in low productivity, and in
obsolete farming methods. The dearth of land (*malozemele'*) was, he
felt, a symptom of overpopulation, not the cause of the crisis, for the
population had grown considerably since 1861, while the agricultural output lagged far behind. More intensive farming was needed
to change the situation, and the commune was an obstacle to progress in the village. His argument continued: the distribution of all
the available private lands would not solve the crisis, for problems
of overpopulation in other countries had been solved by the migration
of the surplus labor; those who could not find employment in agriculture should be encouraged to leave the village; confiscation of private land would not solve the crisis nor bring peace to the countryside, because even slight improvements in farming methods would
raise the peasants' income more than the addition of all the private
lands; the solution lay essentially in intensive development of industry, for no improvements in agriculture could abolish the crisis if
industry were not capable of absorbing the surplus labor from the
village.[69] However, Shidlovskii resumed, in addition to industrialization a variety of methods and reforms were needed and the government had to help those willing and capable of advancement and
improvement.

He elaborated: the basis of a sound peasantry was utilization
of the "creative" forces in the village. "We have to develop in the
village an environment that will educate the peasantry to be economically efficient and enterprising and therefore it has to be
educated to respect private property." [70]

Shidlovskii maintained that the peasants themselves wanted
to be free of the tutelage of the commune.

> The basis of a state of law is the free, energetic and
> independent individual. You will not get such an indi-

vidual without providing him the natural right of private
property. I think that those who really strive to make
our country a state of law cannot oppose private ownership of land.[71]

The majority of the Duma Agrarian Committee held that the
commune had a negative influence on the peasantry and the state.
This view had been the reason for the committee's favorable attitude toward the Ukase of November 9, Shidlovskii explained, for
the ukase facilitated the spread of private ownership in the village
and thus strengthened the cultural element among the peasantry.
It was a big step toward solving the agrarian crisis.

The majority of Octobrists participating in the debate supported
Stolypin's policy. Their main arguments were a less sophisticated
recapitulation of Shidlovskii's elaborate presentation. Count Uvarov[72] countered the Kadets' argument that the ukase had to be
rejected because it was passed as an emergency law, maintaining
that it was the Kadets' fault that the Second Duma did not give
due consideration to the ukase. Prince Golitsyn rejected Miliukov's
allegation that the ukase was designed to protect the selfish interests of 130,000 gentry landowners.[73] Golitsyn, accusing the Kadets
of conspiring with the revolutionary movement to spread chaos and
bloodshed, received a tumultuous and enthusiastic response from
the center and the Right of the Duma.

But even on this subject the Octobrists were not completely
united. Kapustin had strong reservations about the revisions introduced in the bill by the Agrarian Committee,[74] and expressed a
fear that a forced dissolution of the commune, as long as other
conditions affecting peasant life were not changed, might be a
doubtful blessing. He argued that the commune had been a regulator
of peasant life, and the development of an adequate educational
system, legal reforms, and a raising of the general cultural level
should precede its destruction.[75] As long as other urgently needed
reforms had not been implemented, the Duma should not hurry the
destruction of the mainstay of peasant life—the commune. Despite
this criticism, Kapustin promised to vote for adoption. V. V. Khvo-
shchinskii demanded the return of the bill to committee, arguing

that while it was a move in the right direction, it had to be dealt with along with other bills concerning the peasantry.[76]

Strong dissent came from the peasants in the faction. M. D. Chelyshev, from the Province of Vladimir, blamed the government for the lack of capital to help the peasant improve his farming methods.[77] Heavy taxes and alcoholism were the primary reasons for the impoverishment of the peasantry, he felt, and he strongly objected to the deliberate creation of mass unemployment. "Where will you throw those who know only to follow the plow, how will you feed them?"[78] he asked, adding that the government should provide additional cheap land for the peasant.

D. A. Leonov, a left-wing Octobrist, objected to the changes introduced by the Agrarian Committee[79] as negating the spirit of the ukase and forcing the dissolution of the commune when it was still a viable institution.

An interesting phenomenon in the Third Duma was revealed by the debate. On issues concerning the life of the peasantry, peasant deputies belonging to factions ranging from the extreme Left to the extreme Right adopted similar positions and brought almost identical arguments. Thus, as early as November 12, 1907, a group of peasants from different factions joined to propose a bill that would have allotted free land to the peasants. The proposal was never brought before the plenum and remained in the Agrarian Committee.[80]

Most peasant Octobrists voted eventually for the ukase, yet they expressed strong reservations concerning various aspects of the bill; all demanded additional land for the peasantry. The divergence of views between the landowning and capitalist leadership of the Octobrists and its peasant members was consistently apparent: the leadership supported Stolypin's policy, the peasants voiced reservation and demanded more land. P. E. Bazilevich, from the Province of Chernigov, argued that the commune had negative effects on the peasantry and its disintegration had to be encouraged,[81] yet he demanded more land be given in private ownership to the peasantry. "The peasants need land, and we, as men of the land, put our trust in the Duma that it will provide us peacefully and justly the land."[82] The roster of peasant Octobrists expressed their fears of what might happen with the forcible dissolution of the commune: N. K. Leus from the Province of Kharkov rejected the notion that all the ills of the peasantry could be attributed to the commune and felt that the peasants themselves should be given the right to decide their future; [83] A. E. Favorskii maintained that the entire "project" had not taken into account the reality of life in the village—the ukase was designed "in the tranquil offices at the center . . . and should be accepted on principle . . . only out of high policy considerations, but after the introduction of major changes in its details." [84] Favorskii voiced his apprehension about the creation of a small class of kulaks to the detriment of the majority in the village, and he, too, voiced the opinion that the government should provide more land for the needy. Similar fears were expressed by I. L. Spirin, [85] who added that the dispossessed would remain in the village, destitute and full of hatred. M. F. Barybin commented, "We peasants have to acknowledge with regret that this bill will not give land to those who do not have it or have very little. Consequently, the agrarian problem, the burning problem of the peasantry's life, will not be solved by this ukase." [86]

The debate dragged on until November 15, 1908, when the coalition passed a resolution limiting the speeches to ten minutes. Peasant deputies expressed dismay with "useless chatter." [87] The ukase was passed in the third reading on April 24, 1909, in the form drafted by the Duma's Agrarian Committee, thus confirming Stolypin's major piece of agrarian legislation.

In spite of strong opposition and delaying tactics by the Left, the Union passed all the bills that comprised Stolypin's agrarian policy. For the majority of the Octobrists, as for Stolypin, this new policy was the socioeconomic basis for national renovation.

With the first passage of the ukase at the end of 1908, the government coalition had exhausted much of the program that held it together. The country regained a state of relative tranquillity that diminished the antirevolutionary zeal of the coalition. The animosity toward the Kadets receded with time and new problems of internal and military policy created tensions within the coalition and the Union itself.

4

Problems of National Security

The "loyal" majority in the Third Duma expressed its patriotism
and nationalism by devoting much of its attention to matters concerning the military might of the nation. Defeat and revolution had
shaken their faith in tsarism's ability to secure the internal peace
and international prestige of Russia. The years from 1907 to 1912
were a period of almost continuous international tensions accompanied by an accelerated arms race and internally the specter of a
new revolution was ever present in the minds of many. Guchkov
recalled many years later that the Octobrists in the Duma lived
under the strong impression created by the 1905 military defeat and
were eager to help to remedy the situation.[1] To restore the feeling
of national pride and security by the renovation of Russia's military
might became a major preoccupation of the Octobrists in the Third
Duma and the most important manifestation of Octobrist nationalism.

The restoration of Russia's military was also one of Stolypin's
major objectives. He considered the reform of the armed forces a
prerequisite to and an expression of a strong government capable
of restoring order. Stolypin found in Guchkov a determined and
single-minded supporter. Cooperation between Stolypin and the
Union on military matters constituted one of the most important
bases of their friendly relations.

The field of national security was potentially the most fruitful
ground for cooperation among the Octobrists, their allies in the
coalition, and the government, but it was also a delicate area, for

the tsar was hypersensitive on all matters concerning his monopoly of the armed forces. Although the Union and the coalition were far from desiring to curtail the autocrat's prerogatives, the possibility of a clash was ever present. Thus, the problem of national security not only provided the closest and most intimate cooperation between Octobrism and tsarism, it was also the source of the most violent clashes between the two.

For many Octobrists the way the tsar handled the problems of the renewal of military prestige became a test of confidence in the viability of the regime. How to reform the armed forces without curtailing the tsar's prerogatives became a major issue for the Octobrists, their allies, and the government. The Union's goal was not to diminish the tsar's control, but rather to increase the competence of his officialdom and cleanse it of clique and court favoritism. In its efforts to achieve reforms in the armed forces, the Union used all the means at its disposal: behind-the-scenes influences, secret criticism in committee, and open criticism on the floor. They even tried to use the budgetary powers of the Duma, yet failed to effect any significant reforms. In many ways the Octobrists' preoccupation with military matters embarrassed their ally, Stolypin. The reactionary elements in the court used the tsar's fears to compromise the prime minister, the Union, and the Duma, and to weaken Stolypin's position. For many Octobrists it became gradually apparent that tsarism, as represented by Nicholas II, was incapable of restoring Russia's military might, a conclusion that had far-reaching consequences in the future attitude of many Octobrists to the regime.

On November 10, 1907, the Duma decided to form a thirty-three member committee for national defense. Composed entirely of "loyal" elements, the committee became the most important forum for the coalition, which treated the problems of national security as a kind of private preserve, to voice its patriotism. The Kadets and other opposition factions were excluded by a decision of the committee's head. It became the center of the coalition's cooperation with the regime.

The Defense Committee quickly attained elite status—special relations were established by its leadership with the government and the military. The war minister, A. F. Rediger, and leading members met regularly;[2] Stolypin provided the committee with necessary information and clarification.[3] "The most important Duma members" participated with Stolypin and other ministers in the planning of the re-equipment and renewal of Russian military forces at the end of 1907, A. A. Polivanov recalled.[4] St. Petersburg's high society, particularly the military, courted Duma leaders, and Guchkov's preoccupation with military matters gained him respect in the administration and "society" alike. V. A. Sukhomlinov, who replaced Rediger in 1909 as war minister, recalled that "in frivolous Petersburg the appearance of the people's representatives stirred social life. New cliques and new centers of gossip were formed."[5] What disturbed him most was the following the Duma leaders established among the higher ranks of the bureaucracy and even among the officers and officials of the War Ministry.[6] Sukhomlinov learned to his great amazement that "outside the military existed another commission, composed of military officials under the leadership of Guchkov and connected to the Duma" that included several members of the General Staff. On the minister's insistence the tsar dispersed this "underground institution."[7] Guchkov confirmed Sukhomlinov's testimony on the existence of close relations between the Octobrists and the military: "Strong ties were gradually established between me and my colleagues in the National Defense Committee and military-navy circles, thanks to which our work became more productive." General I. V. Gurko, together with other staff officers, agreed to meet informally with members of the Defense Committee and discuss problems of military organization and financing.[8]

The government coalition was more than eager to satisfy military budgets and throughout the Third Duma there was not a single case of refusal to allocate money to the military (the navy was an exception). When the first budget was presented, A. V. Eropkin, speaking for the Union, pledged unwavering support to any request presented by the authorities, for, as he put it, on the allocation of the necessary resources depended

> . . . the might and prestige of Russia as well as her development and international credit. In this field our expenditures have to be lavish; the resources have to be found and will be found. We know that our electors are behind us. [9]

This willingness to finance the military characterized the Third Duma: in 1908, it passed a bill increasing the salaries of the officer corps; in 1909, by its own initiative it added thirty-nine million rubles to increase the military equipment stock;[10] huge resources were allocated to build the Amur and other strategic railways. It must be noted, however, that except for the extreme Left, all the other factions also usually voted for the required military appropriations.

But the Octobrists, and particularly Guchkov, strove for more than military appropriations—they wanted fundamental reforms in the organization and command of Russia's military establishment. The weaknesses that were revealed in the war with Japan were basic—corruption in the highest ranks of the army and navy, the influence of favorites and "irresponsible" persons on military affairs, and the dominant role of the tsar's relatives in the military. While none of the Octobrists questioned the tsar's prerogatives and ultimate command of Russia's military forces, they objected to the nepotism and favoritism that corrupted her military might. The Union wanted to increase the role of the "visible" government in military affairs. Their clash with Nicholas was in a way inevitable; despite their good will they inadvertently touched an area that was most jealously guarded by the tsar as his exclusive domain. In their efforts to reform the military, the Octobrists eventually came into conflict with Stolypin and their allies to the right and at the same time heightened their own internal tensions.

Guchkov later recalled:

> In my first contacts with the higher authorities, I became convinced . . . that in our country's life the decisive role is not played by the visible government, that is only a facade, but by behind-the-scenes forces . . . concentrated mainly in the court, wherefrom they . . . decided the fate of Russia.[11]

Stolypin was powerless against the "irresponsible" circles, Guchkov maintained:

> The main obstacle to reforms were the so-called irresponsible men, the personal sympathies or dislikes, the whims and interests of the Supreme Authority, and in the strong representation of irresponsible persons in the War Ministry.[12] When we considered the necessary reforms in

the army, it soon became apparent that no serious reforms could be accomplished with the existing structure
of the War Ministry.[13]

The Octobrists wanted to abolish the Council of National Defense (Sovet Gosudarstvennoi Oborony), which was formed during
the war with Japan and headed by the Grand Duke Nikolai Nikolai-
evich, and to transfer its functions to the government. The Union
also hoped to remove many of the tsar's relatives from key positions in the armed forces. Together with War Minister Rediger, the
Duma's Defense Committee planned the introduction of modern
techniques in the armed forces, the destruction of obsolete for-
tresses, modernization of training, promotion according to talent,
and so on.[14] These reforms were designed to strengthen the government against the "irresponsible" forces.

The tsar watched the Duma's initiatives with apprehension,
considering even the existence of the Defense Committee a threat
to his prerogatives.[15] The possibility of a clash followed by a rift
between the Union and the government was ever present; it took
place gradually and where one might have expected the utmost
cooperation between the two—this field of the tsar's prerogatives.

Guchkov chose to attack the role of the grand dukes during the
debate on the military budget on May 27, 1908, explaining later that
he had concluded that without a thorough reorganization of the War
Ministry, no serious progress could be made. The grand dukes,
making arbitrary decisions apart from the ministry, were a major
obstacle to effective management by its official head. Since there
was no way to get the open support of the ministry or the military
for the removal of the princes, he decided to make it a public issue
by an open attack in the Duma. There is evidence that Stolypin might
have known about Guchkov's intentions: Polivanov recorded in his
diary on May 27, 1908, that Finance Minister Kokovtsov maintained
that Guchkov had Stolypin's approval.[16] Whether Stolypin knew the
content of Guchkov's speech or not, its aim was in line with what
Stolypin himself might have had in mind. He too was thwarted by
similar forces in his attempts to renew Russia.

Speaking for the Defense Committee, Guchkov analyzed in detail the proposed appropriations.[17] The major defect of the budget,
he said, had been the "weak participation of the legislative institutions" in its preparation.[18] The second half of the speech was

devoted to an analysis of the causes of the defeat in the Russo-Japanese War and the reforms that were necessary to prevent such a disaster in the future. Guchkov's words indicated how the defeat and the resulting national humiliation had become a point for criticism, how the lack of reforms in this sensitive area brought an oppositional tone. He accused the central authorities of being the primary cause of the defeat, of being responsible for its instigation while utterly unprepared to wage it successfully, and then of signing a disgraceful peace treaty.[19] The war proved that the structure of the War Ministry was obsolete and that the higher command was staffed with incompetent officers, the Octobrist leader said.

This accusation was particularly grave, since most of those responsible for the defeat still held key positions and Guchkov was thus not only condemning past failures but also present defects. Little had changed since the defeat, he continued, the old defects remained, the same nepotism, the same court connections determined the appointments to the higher staff.[20] The reforms planned by the War Ministry came to nought because of the intervention of the Council of National Defense, which had become the major obstacle to improvement. To achieve the necessary changes "the government has to separate itself unequivocally from the representatives of the past"[21] Guchkov said, while admitting that he had "grave doubts concerning its ability and willingness to carry through the required reforms."[22] Since the war, the organization of the military affairs had become even more chaotic. The presence in key positions of the grand dukes

> . . . who are by definition not responsible to anybody in the government, is an unnatural situation. . . . We have to admit . . . that while we recognize our impotence to fight this situation, we consider it our duty to call it the right name—irresponsibility.[23]

Guchkov portrayed the Duma and the people as ready to suffer great sacrifices for the cause of national defense, and therefore having the right to expect "at least a little self denial of some material benefits on their part."[24] The speech was greeted with long outbursts of clapping from the majority of the chamber.

Without precedent in Russia, the direct attack on the grand dukes created a sensation. Except for the extreme Right, all the factions hailed Guchkov's courage. He admitted, during a press conference, that his speech had been approved by the Union's faction.[25] Asked whether his speech represented a change in the relations between the Union and the government, Guchkov replied no, that contrary to the Kadets, the Union would cooperate with the government to implement the necessary changes and that all future requests by the military for appropriations would be granted by the Duma.[26]

Guchkov's criticism was applauded by the Left, the Kadets, and parts of the Right, but some dissent rose from the Moderate Right, who were afraid that Guchkov's attack boded ill for the future of the coalition. The Right expressed its reservations, in spite of its former support, opposing the direct criticism of the tsar's family as an attempt to curtail the monarch's prerogatives. V. M. Purishkevich announced that his faction considered it

> utterly impermissible to discuss on this forum subjects that constitute the prerogative of the autocratic leader of the Russian army. . . . It is our duty to protest in the strongest terms against this precedent. . . . It might lead the Duma on an undesirable and extremely dangerous road.[27]

The reaction of the government and the court were of greater concern than that of the other Duma factions. Rediger informed the Duma that many of the defects mentioned by Guchkov were known to his ministry and an effort was being made to correct them.[28] "I have to admit," the war minister said, "that to my regret, much of the criticism expressed here is justified." He asked for patience, since it required time and great effort to rectify the shortcomings. Nine years later Guchkov recalled that Stolypin, in reaction to the speech, told him that

> in essence I completely agree with you. Even the tsar considered the removal of the grand dukes from their posts. But after your speech I am afraid that their position has been strengthened, since the sovereign would not like to create the impression that he acts under your commands.[29]

It could well be that Stolypin actually said so privately. He probably shared many of Guchkov's views on the reforms of the

military and the obstacles in their way, but he could not make it
known publicly. His power emanated from the tsar, and he could
not associate himself with a public attack on the tsar's relatives.

Guchkov's criticism had some positive results. The Council of
National Defense was reorganized and the prime minister became
its head. Many of the tsar's relatives resigned or accepted posts
that gave them only titular responsibility. Although Guchkov's
criticism was not an attempt to intervene against the tsar's prerogatives, but rather a move to create public pressure for reform of the
military, he alienated the tsar and the court clique. Guchkov's subsequent activities on behalf of Russia's national security enhanced
the court's dislike of the Union and mistrust of the Duma. It created a most dangerous situation for Stolypin, for his close relations
with the Union presented a threat to his position in the court.

Criticism of the Naval Ministry

The Octobrists' attempts to reform Russia's military establishment were a concern to the navy. On this issue the Octobrists tried
to use not only constructive criticism but also the Duma's budgetary power. The failure of these attempts had far-reaching effects
on the course taken by Stolypin and on the internal relations of
both the Duma and the Union's faction.

The navy's defects had been glaringly revealed in the Battle
of Tsushima, where the greater part of Russia's high-seas fleet
suffered a crushing defeat that affected Russia's military prestige
and power throughout the globe. The years preceding the First
World War witnessed a headlong race in the construction of naval
armaments——all the major powers subscribed to Admiral Mahan's
theory that a large high-seas navy was a prerequisite of great power.
New kinds of battleships were being built—the dreadnoughts, heavily armored battleships, were the latest development. Russia's
Naval Ministry, which had scarcely changed its composition, refused to lag behind the other major powers. Without a clear plan of
Russia's real needs, without a clear definition of priorities between
the various branches of the armed forces, and without even a detailed construction plan, the Naval Ministry ordered the construction of four dreadnoughts. It asked the Duma for the allocation of
credits for the ships already in construction.

There is evidence that Stolypin, as well as other ministers, had strong reservations about the need for a high-seas fleet, but it became an obsession with Nicholas, and he used his authority to get one. Polivanov, recording one of the government's debates on the subject, quotes Stolypin, on January 11, 1908: "The Council of Ministers does not know of a construction program and is therefore in a difficult position. Moreover, even the sailors have not reached an understanding as to what their needs are." [30] Sukhomlinov, after he replaced Rediger as minister of war, also opposed the idea of a grand fleet, thinking that the navy was of secondary importance in the defense of the country. But the tsar, with the added weight of pressure from France, insisted on building one. [31]

The Octobrists were opposed from the very beginning. They considered the dreadnoughts of lower priority than the rebuilding of the land forces. As a prior condition to any future allocation they demanded basic reforms in the organization and personnel of the Naval Ministry. The memory of Tsushima was still fresh, the people responsible were still in command. [32]

The Naval Ministry was under fire for a long time. A series of articles published in *Novoe vremia* accused the department of corruption and possible treason in its highest ranks in the construction of the cruiser *Riurik* by the British company Vickers. Brut, a pseudonym of a former navy commander, accused the navy of negligence in security and manipulation of court connections in favor of the British company. The Octobrists N. V. Savich and A. I. Zvegintsev introduced an interpellation about the *Riurik*. [33] The navy's evasive explanations before the committee strengthened the existing suspicions [34] and the Duma adopted, on May 23, 1908, a resolution drafted by P. N. Balashov, of the Moderate Right, that expressed the Duma's dissatisfaction with the navy's explanations and its hope that proper measures would be taken by the government to punish those responsible. [35] This resolution was adopted on the eve of the review of the navy's budget in the Duma.

The regular budget was approved by the Budget Committee despite strong criticism. But the committee refused to allocate the required funds for the four dreadnoughts. An unprecedented unanimity was reached on that issue when deputies of the Right joined the Kadets and others in criticizing the conduct of the Naval Ministry. On May 17, 1908, Stolypin met with leaders of the Right in a last effort to change their minds, but failed. [36] They maintained that this

was the only way to force the navy to reform itself. Zvegintsev, the
speaker for the Budget Committee,[37] made a scathing attack on the
Naval Ministry, citing defects in almost all its branches, but particularly in the higher command and in the central administration.
He wondered why there was no institution that would coordinate and
plan the naval and land defense of the country. Such a council
would "have to be a responsible institution, and therefore would
have to be organized and headed by men who were personally accountable for their conduct."[38] Zvegintsev argued that the government was the proper institution to fulfill that function; a comprehensive and detailed plan for the defense of the country and
allocation of credits to the different branches had to precede any
new construction allocations for the navy.

Other speakers from the Right and the Left echoed Zvegintsev's
criticism. All received enthusiastic applause from the entire house.
D. A. Leonov[39] defended the committee's decision to deny the allocations as being the only effective weapon to force reforms on the
department, and he expressed his hope that it would not be needed
in the future. Savich, a leading member of the Defense Committee,
demanded top priority for the land forces,[40] arguing that the government did not present a convincing naval construction plan nor
accurate estimates.

Guchkov defended the Duma's right to refuse to appropriate the
required credits,[41] remarking that it was the Duma's duty to the
sovereign to expose the defects of the Naval Ministry.

> Had we not fulfilled that duty, I would have said that
> it was in vain that the October Manifesto was proclaimed;
> that we have been summoned here in vain. Our first duty
> is to tell the truth to our Supreme Leader. We have to
> remember that the old regime had died because it lived
> in falsehood.[42]

Guchkov continued, saying that it was only with great sorrow
that he and his friends refused to allocate the required credits,
but nothing had been done to reform the defects that brought the
navy to Tsushima, and as long as the government would not appoint
an investigation committee to expose those who were responsible
for the defeat, the Duma would not be convinced that the authorities
intended to open a new chapter in the history of the Russian navy.

The relics of the past might take over again, Guchkov warned, and he expressed his fears of the "irresponsible" forces behind the scenes.[43]

In a last effort to move the Duma to allocate the credits for the dreadnoughts, Stolypin himself appeared before its members.[44] He acknowledged that the refusal to allocate the credits stemmed from a genuine concern to reform the navy and not out of a lack of patriotism. He stressed that he did not come to defend the department for its defects, but that a government has to act, not just look for culprits. It had realized that a strong navy was needed to ensure Russia's security. Stolypin explained that the government accepted the need for a comprehensive defense plan, a clear and detailed naval construction plan, and fundamental reorganization of the Naval Ministry, as demanded by the Duma,[45] but that it took time to correct all the defects. If they stopped construction of new naval units, the future of the navy and the international status of Russia might be endangered. The allocation would be an act of confidence in the Russian navy, Stolypin pleaded.

But even Stolypin did not succeed in swaying the Duma to his side, possibly because the tenor of his remarks made them feel that he spoke more out of duty than conviction. The Duma adopted the regular budget of the Naval Ministry, without the allocation for dreadnoughts. It also attached a five-point resolution demanding that the government prepare an elaborate and comprehensive program of defense that would include the navy; the "radical reorganization of the Naval Ministry," the creation of a Naval General Staff, and a detailed long-range naval construction plan.[46]

The Duma's refusal had no real effect on the construction of the four dreadnoughts; that went on as before. The State Council, which had equal financial rights, appropriated the required sums, thus neutralizing the Duma's decision. In cases of disagreement between the chambers, the government had the option to decide.[47]

But the Duma's decision had important political repercussions. The court and the reactionary circles connected with it in the State Council regarded Guchkov's attack on the grand dukes and the Duma's refusal to allocate credits for the dreadnoughts as a challenge to tsarism's monopoly over the armed forces. Stolypin was quick to disassociate himself publicly from the Union's position. On June 13, 1908, in a speech before the State Council, Stolypin made it clear that the government would not accept any "dictates" from the Duma: in refusing to vote for the credits, the Duma had embarked on a dangerous path and established a dangerous precedent. In Russia, the prime minister stated unequivocally, the government was responsible only to the tsar.[48] The Union was disappointed in Stolypin's crude reminder of the realities of power in the Russian Empire. What hurt most, read a comment in the Union's paper *Golos Moskvy*, on June 2, 1908, was not Stolypin's objection to the decision taken by the Duma but that "in his speech he entirely left the constitutional ground and denied the Duma's right to refuse allocations for the dreadnoughts. His arguments were incomparably more insulting than his conclusions." [49]

The government thus foiled the Union's attempt to make effective use of the Duma's budgetary rights. Autocracy had at its disposal enough means to circumvent a reluctant Duma, while the Octobrists had little taste for an all-out struggle. The construction of the dreadnoughts continued in spite of repeated refusals to allocate the credits in the next sessions. The Duma passed resolutions calling for the establishment of a senatorial investigation committee, but without result. The problem of the construction of a high-seas fleet became again a major issue in 1912, and then Guchkov and his friends were defeated, even in the Duma.

The debate on the naval construction program was just a prelude to a crisis that threatened to wreck the entire political system established by Stolypin, the crisis over the allocation of funds for the establishment of a Naval General Staff.

The Crisis Over the Credits for the Naval General Staff

What became known as the first governmental crisis originated in the State Council. It had the appearance of a conflict between the Duma and the State Council, but in reality it was a concerted attempt by the reactionary forces to get rid of Stolypin and the weight of his cooperation with the Duma and, more particularly, with the Union.

The reactionary Right, concentrated mainly in the court, State Council, and the various monarchistic organizations in the country, had gradually become disenchanted with Stolypin. His severe repression of the revolutionary movement had restored the self-confidence of the old bureaucracy and his cooperation with the

Duma's center factions raised their suspicions about his devotion to autocracy. The reactionaries thought that he took too seriously the "constitutional game" and by his cooperation had strengthened the representative regime, which many of them had never accepted. The court clique considered Stolypin an outsider who had unexpectedly reached the peaks of power. The right wing in the State Council never considered itself a governmental party, but rather the guardian of tsarism's rights. It was largely composed of veteran bureaucrats; some like Witte, Dmitri F. Trepov, and P. N. Durnovo, had personal grudges against Stolypin and considered him a usurper.[50] Stolypin, in turn, had not shown too much consideration for the sensitivities of the veteran bureaucrats and was too liberal for such monarchist organizations as the Union of the Russian People (Soiuz Russkogo Naroda). In spite of the financial support given to these organizations by the government, they conducted a vicious campaign against its premier. Using their court connections they accused Stolypin of subverting the "Russian historical principles."[51]

With the achievement of relative peace in the country, the forces of reaction were afraid that Stolypin might move toward basic reforms. His cooperation with Guchkov and with the Duma in general raised the Right's fear that an attempt was being made to strengthen the government and Duma at the expense of the tsar's prerogatives, particularly in the field of national defense and foreign policy. Stolypin as well as the Octobrist Duma appeared to them as dangerous and superfluous.

The crisis of spring 1909 developed from a minor issue that was intentionally exaggerated and became a conflict of principles that threatened the entire constitutional system. On May 24, 1908, the Duma passed a bill that allocated the credits for the establishment of a Naval General Staff. The program was prepared by a group of young naval officers, including A. V. Kolchak.[52] The State Council rejected the bill in December 1908, claiming that the Duma encroached upon the tsar's prerogatives. According to Article 96 of the Fundamental Laws, all matters concerned with the organization of the military and naval forces were within the exclusive jurisdiction of the tsar. P. K. Shvanebakh, Durnovo, and Witte, who were the main speakers on the subject,[53] attacked Stolypin's Duma policy and his "agreement" with the Octobrists on matters concerning the military. Several council members insinuated that Stolypin and the Union were conspiring to curtail the tsar's prerogatives. The bill was introduced and passed again by the Duma on December 19, 1908. Savich, analyzing Article 96 of the Fundamental Laws, could find no infringement on the tsar's prerogatives in the bill. After strong pressure by Stolypin the State Council passed the bill by a vote of 87 to 75, but during the debate, Witte insinuated that Stolypin harmed the sovereign in order to gain favor with the Duma.[54] Stolypin considered the council's behavior an attack on himself and the Duma, rather than an expression of concern for the tsar's rights. Stolypin was ill during the debate, and Kokovtsov asked the approval of the council in order to avert an undesirable conflict with the Duma. The passage of the bill triggered an all-out attack by the Right. Using their influence in the court, the opponents of the bill convinced the tsar not to ratify it. Stolypin threatened to resign, and for a while it looked as if it was the end of his career. An empire-wide campaign, in the press, the Duma, and "society," was launched by the Right reactionary element against Stolypin and his Duma "allies," the Octobrists.[55]

Stolypin threatened to resign not because he thought the prestige of the Duma had been damaged, but because the strengthening of Russia and avoidance of a political reaction was foremost in his mind. He was a politician and a realist; he knew that to achieve his goals he needed the tsar's backing, since Russia was still primarily an autocracy. Stolypin made it clear a month later in the Duma when, during the debate on one of the bills, he said: "One should not forget that our government cannot turn to the right nor to the left. Our government can follow only one road, the straight road indicated by the sovereign."[56] The offering of his resignation when he thought he had lost the tsar's confidence was termed by his opponents as an "unprecedented scandalous action," but Nicholas refused the resignation. He would not allow his prime minister to withdraw because of a problem created by the house of representatives. "I have not created the Duma to command me, but only for advice," the tsar remarked to Sukhomlinov at the height of the crisis.[57]

In a letter to Stolypin on April 25, 1909, the tsar refused finally to ratify the bill and reminded his prime minister that "we are living in Russia and not abroad or in Finland. Therefore I would not even consider the idea of resignation. This will certainly be a subject for talk in Moscow and Petersburg, but the hysterical uproar will soon subside."[58] Nicholas commanded Stolypin to work out regulations that would define clearly the rights of the Duma in naval and military matters, ending his letter with: "I warn you that I reject in advance yours or anybody else's request of quitting the service."

On August 29, 1909, new regulations were published by the government further curtailing the Duma's budgetary rights on military matters. The "August regulations" did not pass through the legislative process as prescribed by the Fundamental Laws, and were later challenged in the Duma, yet their publication ended officially the governmental crisis.

The Octobrists, particularly Guchkov, were one of the major targets of the attack from the Right during the crisis within and outside the Duma. Guchkov was accused of plotting with Stolypin to encroach upon the tsar's prerogatives in foreign and military policy to divert more power to the government and the Duma. Guchkov and the Octobrists were called "Young Turks."[59]

When the conflict was shaping up, Guchkov inadvertently supplied more ammunition to his enemies. During the debate on the budget of the Foreign Ministry, he said that in spite of all efforts to exclude foreign policy from the competence of the house of representatives "those questions will undoubtedly become the subject if not of direction, at least of criticism, discussion and influence of the popular assembly."[60] Since the government would need the country's support and the Duma's credits, he declared, the people's representatives would have to be informed and consulted—a clear request to broaden the Duma's competence in the sphere of foreign policy. The right of free expression in the field of foreign relations was long overdue, Guchkov complained.[61] A. P. Izvolskii, the foreign minister, did not deign to reply to his demands.

The Budget Committee refused for the second time to allocate credits for the construction of the new naval units. Zvegintsev, speaking for the committee, explained that the committee was not convinced that a decisive effort had been made to reform the Naval Ministry.[62] The Octobrist Savich justified the refusal to grant the credits on the grounds that the navy had not made good use of the resources at its disposal, nor had it produced a detailed construction plan.[63] These accusations came at the height of the tensions between the State Council and Stolypin, and were used by the Union's enemies.

It was Guchkov again who, in his candid manner, supplied the best arguments to these enemies. Russia had just suffered a shameful diplomatic defeat after the annexation of Bosnia-Herzegovina by Austria-Hungary and had retreated after an undisguised threat from Germany to intervene militarily. Rediger had reported to the tsar that the army could not possibly defend the country.[64] Guchkov was familiar with the situation and knew the defects of the higher command. In a closed session of the Duma Defense Committee with the war minister he demanded the replacement of a large part of the Naval General Staff.[65] When the tsar learned about this demand he remarked that "the Octobrists try always to seize what does not belong to them. Therefore I prefer the Moderate Right."[66]

Guchkov made public his criticism of the War Ministry on March 19, 1909, in his speech on the military budget.[67] He asked finally whether the time had not yet come for a "radical reorganization of our entire military system." Guchkov insinuated that the government had not fulfilled its obligations the way the Duma had and had not prepared the country for an international crisis. The leader of the Union denounced

> the vain attempt of men of the past to try to undermine
> our great effort by raising secondary issues of rights
> and prerogatives (applause from the Left, hissings from
> the Right). We know that the goal of these men is to
> plant again the fatal seeds of discord [between the tsar
> and the people].[68]

Purishkevich retorted immediately by accusing the Octobrists of being responsible for the weakening of Russia's international position by their criticism of the armed forces.[69] Russia did not need new ways or new men; "We do not need any special cotton-patriotism" Purishkevich said, referring contemptuously to Guchkov's origin. N. E. Markov, joining his fellow rightist, accused Guchkov of sharing the aspirations of the Young Turks, and of being in alliance with the Social Democrats.[70] The meeting ended in general disorder.

The State Council's attacks on Stolypin were considered by the

Octobrists as an assault on the Duma and on Russia's chances to move forward and regain its prestige. N. A. Khomiakov, the Octobrist president of the Duma, accused the Right of plotting to overthrow Stolypin's government, to replace it by a reactionary cabinet, and even to dissolve the Duma. "I am convinced that neither of these gentlemen was truly concerned with the fate of Russia. The extreme Right has no program at all," Khomiakov charged.[71] The same views were expressed by N. P. Shubinskii, the right-wing Octobrist, who rejected the accusation voiced in the State Council that the Union intended to curtail the tsar's prerogatives. He remarked that those who made such accusations were the men who had brought defeat and misery to the country, and, since there was still danger of revolution, the man who had fought it successfully had to remain in his post.[72]

The Central Committee of the Union published an official statement concerning the governmental crisis.[73] The statement accused the extreme Right of conducting a smear campaign and repeated the Union's unconditional support of the monarchy and Stolypin. "The politically cautious, yet progressive, activity of the Duma, coinciding to a great extent with the no less cautious yet progressive activity of the government, presents a solid guarantee for the implementation of urgently needed reforms carried out by peaceful means." The Union's statement went on to express the Union's revulsion at the aims and methods of the extreme Right, which it accused of opposing the renovation of Russia.

The crisis over the allocation of credits for the establishment of a Naval General Staff had far-reaching political consequences. The assault on Stolypin failed, but it served as a warning to the prime minister to be extremely cautious with his reform plans. It was also an assault on the Octobrists and particularly on Guchkov. The Right tried to break the close cooperation between Stolypin and the Octobrists in the field of military reforms. Using the tsar's extreme sensitivity regarding his military prerogatives, the Right succeeded in stemming Guchkov's efforts to implement basic reforms in the military. Rediger, the war minister, who established close relations with the Duma's Defense Committee, was replaced by Sukhomlinov, whose main talent was his ability to please the court. Rediger's remark that Russia has to use for its military command "what is available" served as a pretext to get rid of the daring minister. This was in answer to Guchkov's criticism of incompetence and lack of training of the higher military command. On April 16, 1909, the tsar instructed Sukhomlinov, the new war minister, not to pay too much attention to the Duma: "You are my minister and there is nothing to discuss with them." He asked him to make it clear to Guchkov and others to be less critical of the army.[74]

The close relationship between Stolypin and Guchkov was based to a great extent on a mutual understanding of the need to strengthen the military might of the nation. After the crisis this "alliance" was shaken. For some time the relations between the government and the Union remained tense. Stolypin cautiously but perceptibly cooled his relations with the Union. The Octobrists' attempt to give the Duma a more decisive voice in military affairs had failed. The influence of the Duma and its Octobrist leaders on military matters had sharply decreased. Guchkov's later efforts to revive the Duma Defense Committee failed, too, and eventually he resigned as its head. Stolypin kept his post by abstaining from any concession to the Octobrists on military matters, and by encouraging the creation of a new central faction to replace the Union as his main supporters in the Duma. He was looking for less compromising allies. The conflict also had important repercussions on the political alignments and relations inside the Duma itself.

5
Strains in the Coalition and Union

The government crisis of spring 1909 was both an indication and a cause of increased tensions within the Duma coalition and the Union. Following the passage of the ukase at the end of 1908 amending the 1906 agrarian ukase, the Duma went through a period of disruption and disintegration that culminated with the resignation of N. A. Khomiakov in March 1910. It was a period of confusion, lack of direction, and unpredictability, yet disintegration of the government coalition was not total. It was never a harmonious combination and it became even less so during this time. The same combination of groups continued to support the government, pass its bills, and approve its budget, but it became less predictable and more erratic. The work of the Duma came to an almost complete standstill as a result of obstructional tactics used by the Right. The inherent contradictions within the coalition and the Union became more obvious, the artificiality of the combinations and factions more evident. The Union's faction went through great internal strains, conflicts, and splits that considerably diminished its numerical strength.

The causes for these developments lay both outside and within the Duma. The country was regaining a semblance of peace and order, there were no tangible manifestations of revolutionary activities, yet repression continued as before. The central political issue was whether and how Stolypin would move to implement the second half of his formula: "first pacification, and then reform."

The reactionary Right in its various forms regarded any move toward decisive reform as a possible inducement for new revolutionary upheaval. Some Union members were in agreement, but the majority of the Octobrists held an opposite view, contending that lack of reform and the continuation of repression would result in new outbreaks. In a way, both were right. Fundamental reforms, once started, could have had unpredictable consequences. On the other hand, repression alone was not enough to secure stability and permanent peace in the country. For diametrically opposite reasons, Stolypin's policy came under fire from both reactionaries and reformists. But the political initiative and power were with the reactionary camp, which used its influence in court to force Stolypin to move cautiously away from his devoted supporters—the Octobrists. Stolypin was trying to create a central faction that would not compromise his position in the court. When he failed to find a suitable substitute for the Union he tried to revive the cooperation on new grounds.

The period between the passage of the ukase and Khomiakov's resignation was one of great inconsistency and tension within the Duma's political alignments. In many ways the coalition that formed the "cooperative" majority had exhausted its common program. The ukase was passed in fall 1908. The revolution appeared to be over. The election campaign became a memory, and with it the hostility toward the Kadets among many Octobrists became less pronounced. The Kadets gradually became "respectable" by working hard in committees and on the floor. By toning down their criticism, they hoped to move the Octobrists toward a more liberal stand on constitutional issues. On many occasions the Octobrists found these neighbors to the left closer than their "allies" to the right.

Most of the tension and changes in the political combinations came from the factions to the right of the Octobrists. The Right, using its connections in the court, became more militant and demanding in and out of the Duma, systematically creating an atmosphere of conflict, appearing as the defenders of the monarch's prerogatives and Russia's "historical principles." By their outrageous behavior they had forced the resignation of Khomiakov. They led the assault on the "alliance" between Stolypin and the Octobrists, weakening the core of the government coalition. The Moderate Right and the nationalists, who eventually merged into one

Nationalist party, moved closer to the Right. The attempt of the Moderate Right to split the Union alienated the Octobrist leadership and jeopardized future cooperation in the coalition. The issues that were raised during the period revealed some of their basic differences with the coalition. The tactics and issues used by the Right also exposed some basic disagreements within the Union's faction.

It was no secret that the Union's faction included deputies with different and even opposing attitudes and views. Stolypin's actions, the concerted assault of the Right, and the change in attitudes toward the Kadets made the differences even more obvious. The worsening of relations with the government increased tensions within the faction, and party discipline, always a problem for the Union, became a farce. Union members took opposing stands on major issues, debating with each other on the Duma floor. A successful attempt was made to detach a small group of right-wing Octobrists from the Union. The Union did not disintegrate, and continued to exist as a separate political entity, with its internal tensions and differences, in spite of the efforts made from the Right and the Left. However, it was much weakened as an effective political force.

The passing of the bill on the credits for the Naval General Staff for the second time marked the beginning of the deterioration of relations between the Union and its allies to the right and growing cooperation between the Union and the Kadets. The gulf between the Union and the Right reached its widest distance during the government crisis in March-June of 1909 with the adoption of the three bills on religious freedom and the denunciation of the Union of the Russian People by the Octobrists and Kadets; the breach coincided with the governmental crisis.

The major battle against the Octobrists and Stolypin was waged and decided outside the Duma; its main manifestations in the Duma were the acrimonious debates over the three bills on religious freedom. The mood among the Octobrists was shown principally in criticism of certain government actions or defaults and in minor corrections of bills submitted by the administration. But there was no real attempt to force the government to fulfill the promised reforms and the budgets and credits were passed: Octobrism had not changed its basic orientation.

At the beginning of the second session, the Kadets offered

Guchkov a deal. They proposed that the two factions work out an agreed list of bills. The Kadets prepared their list and Guchkov accepted much of it,[1] but neither the main Octobrist faction nor their Moderate Right allies were ready to accept the arrangement and Guchkov retreated. "While there is no formal alliance between us and the Moderate Right," Guchkov explained in an interview, "it is no secret that we have close and friendly relations. The Moderate Right's actions are in accord with ours. We share many basic convictions."[2] On November 1, the Octobrist faction decided: "Since there is a possibility that the Left factions may try to introduce a series of bills designed only for propaganda purposes, the faction intends to oppose these initiatives."[3]

The mood of the Octobrists changed perceptibly after Christmas vacation to one of more opposition. The winter session of 1909 opened with the acceptance of an interpellation concerning the suppression of the press, which, in spite of the October Manifesto, had been continuously censored and its publishers fined and imprisoned. The interpellation concerned the restrictions on the press imposed by the governor general of Moscow. On December 15, 1908, Guchkov supported the acceptance of the interpellation as urgent. He complained that "the citizens of Moscow are subject to the arbitrary rule of the local administration."[4] When the interpellation was brought before the plenum, M. V. Rodzianko, usually considered to be a right-wing Octobrist, explained that "our faction has to admit that the present laws on the press contradict the principles of the October Manifesto."[5] However, he opposed the proposal of the Social Democrats that demanded complete freedom of the press. The Union's resolution recognized "the necessity of the fastest review of the laws concerning the press following the principles proclaimed in the Manifesto of October 17, 1905."[6] The formula was adopted by a vote of 168 to 112, with the Union joined on this issue by the Kadets, the Progressists, and the Polish Koło. The two extreme wings provided the opposition.

The condemnation of the behavior of the local administration in the Caucasus on February 5, 1909, was an exception to the pattern followed by the Duma until then, for most of the interpellations concerning repression in the provinces were defeated by the antirevolutionary coalition. This time the Octobrists voted for a formula that demanded an investigation of the behavior of the local authorities and the "subjection of the administration of the Caucasus to the Council of Ministers."[7] This was a clear reminder that the "visible government" had no effective control of the provincial authorities.

Baron Alexander Meyendorff, opening the general debate on the budget, accused the Finance Department of systematically subverting the Fundamental Laws, particularly in the floating of foreign loans.[8] Many laws were implemented as edicts of the tsar, without passing the prescribed legislative process. To applause from the Left and strong protests from the Right, Meyendorff stated that the "new Fundamental Laws have not yet penetrated the consciousness of those who have to be most careful in their execution."[9]

The Ministry of the Interior came under fire for the continued use of emergency regulations. Octobrist I. V. Godnev maintained that if the Russian Empire was indeed a state governed by law "then at the present there are no laws permitting administrative exile nor the use of emergency and extraordinary regulations."[10] The government had been using decrees that became void with the convocation of the legislative chambers, he contended, and therefore all the extraordinary regulations must be rescinded. The statement was greeted with applause from the center and the Left.[11]

S. I. Shidlovskii repeated his theory that the police had come to characterize the Ministry of the Interior.[12] In the provinces, Shidlovskii maintained, things have changed only for the worse, principally because of the

> extraordinary regulations. . . . There has to be a simple, equally applicable and well-defined law that will replace the role of arbitrariness . . . there is no ground for the continued existence of the extraordinary regulations on the scope in which they are presently applied.[13]

This criticism did not come from a man who strived for unlimited freedom—but rather one who pled for more security; he wanted the authorities to give the citizen the opportunity to know what to expect. Shidlovskii asked to live in a state of law, if necessary even a bad and restrictive one, one to which all conformed.

P. G. Kurlov, representing the Ministry of the Interior, replied curtly that in his opinion "the country has yet to be pacified. Therefore, there is the need to maintain the extraordinary regulations." [14] Although regrettable, he maintained, the use of the extraordinary regulations was the only way to fight the sedition still prevalent in the country.

The Octobrists attached a three-point resolution to the approval of the budget, stating that there was no need for the continued use of emergency regulations over the larger part of the empire, that to renovate the empire and implement the principles of the manifesto it was absolutely necessary to return to normal conditions. The resolution included a demand to impose stricter supervision over the activities of the political police. The third point required the authorities to prepare a reform program that would change radically the organization and functions of the police. [15] The Moderate Right offered its own formula with the result that neither of the formulas received the necessary majority, and the budget was passed without any Duma "wishes" attached.

Beginning in February 1909, the Right started a systematic campaign intended to disrupt the Duma. It was clear that this was a deliberate policy that had President Khomiakov as its main target. He was too liberal for Purishkevich and Markov, the leaders of the Right. Assaulting the Duma president was the best way to disrupt the Duma. The attack took the form of direct personal disobedience of the rulings of the president, unwarranted and repeated protests, and crude behavior on the podium and on the floor. The rightists' behavior typified the general attack of the reactionary forces against Stolypin and the Duma. *Novoe vremia*'s Duma correspondent reported: "the rightists are trying to prove that the Octobrists encroach on the tsar's prerogatives and now try to invade the field of foreign policy, and they [the Right] safeguard them." [16] The Union repeatedly condemned the outrageous behavior of the Right, but without result. [17]

The "Gololobov Affair" was the first open manifestation of the crisis in the Union caused by the assault of the reactionary element. In February 1909 the Octobrists decided to support an interpellation of the Social Democrats that accused the government of persecuting labor unions all over the country. The faction decided in this case to impose party discipline but hadn't reckoned with the Interpellation Committee, which decided, unexpectedly, to reject the interpellation. Ia. G. Gololobov, an Octobrist, cast the deciding vote. In spite of strong party pressure, Gololobov, appearing as the speaker for the committee in February 1909, defended the decision. The Octobrists, in cooperation with the Left, succeeded in passing the interpellation. Several days later Gololobov openly attacked his faction's resolution.[18] The faction's meeting on March 11 was extremely stormy, with a sizable group opposed to decisive action against Gololobov. The left wing demanded the adoption of a clear and well-defined political program and exclusion from the faction of those who would refuse to follow it. It also demanded the application of sanctions against Gololobov, a move endorsed by Guchkov. He demanded the creation of a genuinely united faction, and the prevention of actions that would compromise the Union.[19] On March 15 the faction adopted unanimously Guchkov's proposal to censure Gololobov for his speech and the Union's Central Committee decided to expel Gololobov from the party.[20] Following the opening of the third session, Gololobov became the leader of a small splinter group called the Right Octobrists.

Confrontation with the Right on Religious Freedom

The major confrontation between the Octobrists and the factions to the right took place during the debates on religious freedom. It was an expression of the continued attack by the Right on the alliance between Stolypin and the Union. The Union got its most consistent support from the Kadets and, surprisingly, the Left. Internal discord in the Union reached new peaks during that period.

The bills dealt with: (1) abolition of civil and political limitations on persons who decided to leave the ranks of the clergy; (2) abolition of legal and civil disabilities of the Old Believer communities; (3) abolition of the restrictions imposed on people who changed their religious affiliation. The three were enacted by the government by the use of Article 87 in 1906. For the Third Duma these were the first bills that actually tried to implement the civil liberties promised by the manifesto.

The Orthodox church was considered by the autocracy as one of the main pillars of the established order. Changes and reforms in its status though deemed necessary by many, could have had grave repercussions for the future of tsarism. The presence of a large contingent of Orthodox clergy among the parties of the Right gave the issues of religious freedom an explosive character. The issues were important to many Octobrists, who considered religious freedom among the basics of a "state ruled by law"; it was also for them a test of whether they would fight for their proclaimed principles.

The Octobrist leadership led the liberal and left wings in the conflict, straining to the utmost the internal relations of the Union and the coalition. Guchkov, who insisted on passing the bills in the second session, had a special interest in the bill granting equality to the Old Believer communities. He, as did many other Octobrists, came from an Old Believer family.[21]

It was made clear by the Octobrists, as well as by their liberal allies, that their aim was not to harm the Orthodox church. At most they wanted to reform it and to make it more relevant to the people's life so it would not be just a department of the government. During the debate on the budget of the Holy Synod, the Union's spokesman expressed the Octobrist hope that more attention and money would be allocated by the church for the parish and its clergy and that greater emphasis be put on the local needs of the believers.[22]

The law abolishing the civil disabilities of clergymen who left or were forced to leave their vocation did not raise much opposition and was passed on May 5, 1909. The head of the Holy Synod opposed some of the amendments made by the Duma's committee, contending that the Duma had no right to interfere in matters concerning the church.[23] P. B. Kamenskii, speaking for the Union, retorted: "The Duma should not pay any attention to this attempt to curtail its rights." He was greeted with applause from the center and the Left and was booed by the Right.[24] The attempt of the Right to return the bill to committee was defeated.

The major struggle developed around the bills on the Old Believer communities and the bill on conversion from one faith to another. The first gave religious freedom to the various sects that came under the Old Believers' name, permitting them to conduct their services openly and to form religious associations for worship and for educational and philanthropic purposes. Those voluntary associations were granted wide rights of self-government.[25] The Duma committee introduced only slight changes in the government's bill, granting the Old Believers not only the right of worship (*ispovedenie*) but also the right to propagate their faith (*propovedovanie*). The committee lowered the minimum number of members required to form an independent association from fifty to twelve. Other amendments were of minor importance.

In spite of their innocuous nature, the committee's amendments were violently opposed by the Right, Moderate Right, and important members of the Union itself. Most of them thought that even the original government bill was too liberal and considered the bill an attempt to ruin the Orthodox church.

V. N. L'vov, a prominent Octobrist, presented views differing sharply from those of the majority of his party. He welcomed the bill on the Old Believers but objected to the proposed amendments.[26] The amendment granting the Old Believers the right to preach meant, according to L'vov, the privilege to conduct missionary work, a right that should be reserved for the Orthodox church only.

S. E. Kryzhanovskii, secretary of the Ministry of the Interior, represented the government in the debate.[27] He maintained that the Duma amendments represented an assault on the Orthodox church, that granting the Old Believers the right to preach and to call their officers clergymen instead of "spiritual-men" (*dukhovnie litsa*) could not be accepted by the government, because of the special relationship between the Russian state and the Orthodox church. Threatening openly, Kryzhanovskii stated that "neither the government nor the Holy Synod will ever under any circumstances accept these two amendments."[28]

Kamenskii, again speaking for the Union, stated categorically that "the faction, in response to the suffering prayers and hopes of the Old Believers, will support entirely and by every possible means all the amendments and clarifications of the committee for the Old Believers."[29]

On May 15, 1909, Guchkov made a most touching speech to the Duma,[30] in which he said that millions of Old Believers all over Russia were praying that the Duma would adopt the bill with the committee's amendments. His personal stake in its adoption led him to put the prestige of his leadership behind the bill. The Old Believers had been subjected to harassment and persecution for 250 years, Guchkov said, and the amended bill would finally liberate them from the administration's harassments, that those who objected to the law had little faith in the people and the church if they required artificial protection for its survival—the "promised freedoms" that had been denied under the pretext of a state of emergency and revolution should be implemented in the area of freedom of conscience. The bill passed with all the committee's amendments.

The bill regulating the conversion from one faith to another was of an even more controversial nature, for it freed converts from the requirement of obtaining a conversion permit from the authorities. The majority of the Duma recommended complete freedom of conversion. Kamenskii explained that the principle that guided the committee was that every normal person, after reaching a certain age, should be allowed to believe and practice according to his own conscience.[31] The committee recommended permission for the conversion of children under fourteen with their parents, even to a non-Christian faith,[32] a recommendation that became a major issue.

Stolypin personally represented the government in the debate,[33] his first appearance in the Duma after the government crisis, which naturally added interest to his presentation. To dispel any misunderstandings as to the policy of his government and to refute the accusations of the Right that the bill represented an attempt to placate the Octobrists, Stolypin stated:

> I was told that the bills on religion have been presented at this particular time out of political considerations. They ask whether the government has moved to the right or to the left. But those gentlemen should not forget that our government cannot deviate to the right nor to the left. . . . since our government could follow only one road, that indicated by the sovereign.[34]

Stolypin explained his policy on matters concerning the Orthodox church. He rejected the idea put forth by many, from the Right and even by the liberals, that the church must have complete autonomy. Only in the field of religious dogma and canon law was the church to be autonomous; in matters of the relation between church and state, the latter had full authority, even though the government had to make every effort to reconcile religious freedom with the interests of state and the ruling church. Therefore he opposed the amendment that permitted formally the conversion from a Christian to a non-Christian faith.

The national spirit and tradition deserved special concessions, he argued, revealing a new nationalistic stress in his policy. "You should remember that the religious laws will be implemented in the Russian state, and it will be ratified by the Russian tsar, who for

more than a hundred million people was, is, and will be the Orthodox tsar."[35]

D. A. Leonov replied for the Union[36] that in order for the Union
to defend orthodoxy, the church had to reform its structure, to give
greater freedom to the parish, to bring together church and people—
that the existing restrictions only helped to spread indifference.
Leonov's speech was frequently interrupted by crude remarks and
outbursts from the Right.

The right wing of the Duma, supported by a sizable group of
Octobrists, voiced their objections vehemently, accusing the spon-
sors of the religious freedom bills of being promoters of sedition,
preachers of revolution, and tools of the Social Democrats. A genuine fear that the Orthodox church, by losing some of its coercive
powers, might lose its battle with other religions, particularly in
the western provinces, was implicit in their speeches. Bishop
Evlogii, on May 13, came very close to admitting that even the
slightest reforms might have grave revolutionary repercussions in
the country.[37] Others stressed the role the Orthodox church had in
Russian nationalism and as a means of Russification. The Right,
afraid of change, considered the bills the beginning of the collapse
of a mainstay of the established order, a fear that partially explained
the violence and crudeness of their behavior during the debate.
When Meyendorff very politely asked Bishop Evlogii to stop his
remarks on the national minorities and the Kadets, Markov responded
from the floor with "away with the German!"[38] In the chaos that
followed, the meeting had to be adjourned. The Moderate Right
joined the Right in a protest against Meyendorff, while the opposition denounced the hooliganism of the Right.[39]

All three bills were passed, with most of the amendments introduced by the Duma committees. The effective majority was composed of Octobrists, Kadets, Progressists, and Socialists. But this
was a Pyrrhic victory. The government took back two bills—on the
Old Believers and on freedom of conversion—on the eve of the
third session. None of the bills was ratified by the State Council
or the tsar.[40]

The Union was seriously weakened by this conflict with the
Right; it almost reached an open split. Realizing the forthcoming
internal crisis, the Duma faction of the Union decided to let its

members vote according to their conscience,[41] a "solution" that had been used frequently when important issues were at stake. Guchkov tried to get the support of the entire faction, particularly for the Old Believers bill, but failed. Many opposed the official party line and were ready to leave the faction. Nine Octobrists, among them the cochairman of the faction, Rodzianko, voted with the Right. [42] Rumors circulated in the press that an attempt had been made by the right wing of the faction to oust Guchkov from its leadership and replace him with Rodzianko.[43] According to A. Stolypin, the premier's brother, N. G. Cherkasov proposed to the prime minister that he (Cherkasov) split the Union and together with the Moderate Right create a new center.[44]

On May 15, as head of the faction's bureau, Guchkov offered his resignation, explaining that it was the result of disagreements in the Union on basic issues. In his letter of resignation he said that there were Octobrist deputies who opposed even the October Manifesto. Rodzianko and the rest of the faction's secretariat followed Guchkov after preparing a five-point resolution to be discussed by a general meeting of the faction, a resolution recommending the imposition of stronger party discipline and the expulsion of members who would not accept the party line.[45] The general meeting held to discuss the resolution culminated in unanimously re-electing Guchkov as its leader and a request to Rodzianko to withdraw his resignation as cochairman. On May 19, the faction decided to expel Cherkasov from the party. This was a bold attempt on Guchkov's part to assert his leadership as well as to bring more cohesion and discipline into the party, but the new unity was transitory.

Interpellation on the Union of the Russian People

The second session ended with the adoption of an interpellation on the activities of the Union of the Russian People and its relations with the police, which was signed by seventy-four members, including Socialists and Octobrists. On May 27, 1909, A. D. Protopopov, an Octobrist, defended the committee's recommendation to accept the interpellation. He contended that the Duma, which had condemned revolutionary terrorism, must demand a thorough investigation of the charges brought against the Union of the Russian People and its connections with the police.[46] This was a far cry from the mood that prevailed when the first session debated the law on compensating the victims of terrorism. Since many of the leaders of the Right in the Third Duma belonged to the Union of the Russian People, the interpellation was obviously directed against them.

The second session ended with the Octobrists losing twenty-three deputies of their number, mainly right wingers, leaving the "trustworthy" majority that served as the basis of Stolypin's Duma support in complete disarray. The conflicts over the credits for establishment of the Naval General Staff and the religious bills had created rifts within the Union and unpredictable combinations during the voting. On many occasions the Octobrists found themselves in one camp with the Kadets, fighting against their closest allies, the moderates. Stolypin and the Octobrists were assessing their mutual relations, as well as possible new political combinations.

Following the second session, the possibility of closer cooperation between the Octobrists and the Kadets was raised again. Union leaders such as N. P. Shubinskii, A. V. Eropkin, and Guchkov did not exclude future cooperation with Kadets on political and constitutional issues. Guchkov even expressed his delight concerning the "patriotic" behavior of the opposition on matters of national security, while maintaining his conviction that except on problems concerning religion and national minorities the former alliance with the Moderate Right would continue.[47]

The tone of the third party convention in October 1909 was more liberal and oppositional than the preceding two. Many delegates from the provinces demanded from the Union's faction that they be more consistent in adhering to the principles of the manifesto.[48] The convention adopted a series of guidelines for the future legislative activities of the Union, including reforms in the educational system, positive legislation to implement civil freedoms, reforms of local self-government, and the establishment of self-governing rural district (*volost*) institutions, and social insurance for workers. In spite of lively debate, the resolutions were adopted unanimously.[49] The Union expressed in this convention the oppositional mood that was resurgent in the country.

Nationalism, the New Credo

While the Union was voicing its differences with its allies,

Stolypin was looking cautiously for less compromising associates in the Duma. Since the conflict over the appropriations for the Naval General Staff there had been a definite estrangement between the prime minister and the Union. The publication of the "August regulations," which curtailed the budgetary rights of the Duma on military matters, was met with obvious disapproval by the Union. Several days before the opening of the third session the government refused to transfer to the State Council two of the bills on religious freedom. Guchkov announced that the Duma would pass the bills again.[50]

At the same time Stolypin was encouraging the formation of the Nationalist party. He hoped to include most of the right wing of the Duma, as well as many Octobrists. The result was the eventual merger of the Moderate Right with the nationalist group at the end of 1909 in one Nationalist party. Its political program was one of a chauvinistic Great Russian nationalism, expressed in fanatic anti-minority and anti-Semitic feelings. Their major goal was, in the words of its leader, P. N. Balashov, "to repulse the onslaught of the foreigners (*inorodtsy*)."[51] The party had strong ties with the rightists and considerable influence in the court and on the administration, which made it even more attractive for Stolypin, after his realization that the major opposition to his premiership came from the far Right. For a while Stolypin kept aloof from relations with the various Duma factions.

The third session started with a feeling of uncertainty. Two new groups appeared in October. One, which included peasants from all factions, claimed that it had been formed to represent the special point of view and interests of the Russian peasant.[52] The Right Octobrists comprised the other. Although they had only ten members, the Gololobovtsy (the group of Octobrists who left the faction with Gololobov), as they were often termed, were very vocal, and constituted a permanent threat to the Union through their influence on its right wing. An unexpected by-product of the formation of the Right Octobrist faction was the relative strengthening of the Octobrists' left wing. It soon became evident that the so-called government coalition could not function, and that a new basis for cooperation had to be found.

The third session opened with the adoption of the Social Democrats' interpellation concerning the legality of the "August 24 regulations." Guchkov, speaking for the Union, stressed the need to clarify some points concerning the regulations,[53] although he did not take a position on their content or constitutionality. He proposed to accept the interpellation and redraft it in committee, obviously wishing to use it as a means of expressing his displeasure with the government's policies.

There were recurring clashes between the Octobrists and the Right and a deterioration of their relations with the Nationalists during the third session. On October 30 the Octobrists voted for the Progressist Sokolov as Duma secretary, defeating the rightist Zamyslovskii.[54] It was a clear demonstration against the obstructionist tactics of the Right.

The Octobrists became more outspoken in the criticism of the administration's actions, further eroding relations with the factions to its right. Octobrists A. D. Protopopov[55] and Baron Meyendorff[56] accused the authorities of systematically interfering in the regular activities of the trade unions, thus violating the Fundamental Laws. The contemptuous answer from the administration to the accusation evoked an angry response from Meyendorff, who was in turn hissed down by the Right. The Octobrists, voting with the opposition, passed a resolution demanding that the authorities observe the legal rights of the citizens.[57]

The Volost *Courts Bill*

The fate of the bill replacing the *volost* courts with elected justices of peace proved to Stolypin that he could not rely on the Nationalist coalition. He realized that he had to look for a new platform that would bind together the various groups of the coalition and ensure its support of government policies.

Before the bill was introduced, Stolypin met several times with the Octobrist leadership, making it clear that there were several conditions *sine qua non* for the government: that the candidates for the office of justices of peace have a property requirement; that they be subordinated to the Ministry of Justice; and that the president of the assembly of justices be designated by the administration and not elected.[58] The Octobrist leadership promised to support the government's line, but the membership of the Union acted independently, rejecting the pledge made by the leadership.

The reform was based, the right-wing deputy Shubinskii maintained, not on class principles (*soslovnost*) but on educational qualifications. The left wing and the peasants opposed, in the strongest terms, the proposed reform. M. D. Chelyshov[59] complained that although the good of the peasantry was the main objective of the reform, the peasants had never been consulted as to their wishes and the reform would only impose new burdens on the impoverished villages, creating new jobs for "officials" (*chinovniki*). M. Ia. Kapustin[60] and A. E. Favorskii[61] from the left wing of the Union demanded the reform of the *volost* courts, instead of adding new officials to the Ministry of Justice, which, they held, would only confuse and undermine peasant self-government.

The bill passed on November 13, 1909, but ran into unexpected trouble during the second reading. The Right had consistently opposed the proposed abolition of the *volost* court. When the vote on the property qualifications was taken, they cynically announced that they would join the opposition's proposal to abolish this requirement, and thus make the bill unacceptable to the State Council and the government. Many left-wing Octobrists voted for the abolition of the property requirement, thus defeating their leadership's promise to Stolypin.[62] Shubinskii stated the obvious when he told reporters that "there is no stable majority in the Duma. Many votes have an episodical and accidental character."[63] The bill was finally passed with several amendments that were sternly opposed by the government. Many Octobrists voted against their own leadership.

The Octobrist leadership considered the abolition of the *volost* court and its replacement by elected justices of peace an important reform, but even the most consistent supporters of Stolypin among the Octobrists became increasingly restless with the lack of any movement toward the implementation of the "promised freedoms."

The bill on "personal immunity" was introduced in the Duma on November 13, 1909. Although it was prepared by a committee headed by Gololobov and G. G. Zamyslovskii, both outright reactionaries, instead of reconciling the Union and the government, the bill became another source of embitterment and tension.

The Octobrists decided to recommend the return of the bill to a new committee. N. I. Antonov[64] explained that the bill, instead of securing the rights of the individual, rather broadened the scope of police arbitrariness. V. K. Fon-Anrep justified the return of the bill to committee on the grounds that the speakers of the Right had convinced him that the bill actually was not intended to defend the citizen, and thus could not accomplish its stated goals.[65] The Octobrists and the opposition succeeded in excluding Gololobov and other reactionaries from the new committee, whose speaker was Meyendorff.[66]

On January 20, 1910, the Duma adopted one of the few bills initiated by its own members in the field of civil rights. The Duma's Justice Committee approved a proposal by thirty-nine deputies to abolish administrative exile in the northern provinces and altered it to include the entire empire. E. P. Bennigsen and Antonov, both Octobrists, rejected the government's objections and maintained that administrative exile had not achieved the purpose it was designed for, the rehabilitation of those suspected of revolutionary activities.[67] Like many other Duma initiatives, this bill never became a functioning law and remained buried in the Duma archives.

Opposition characterized the Octobrist speeches on the budget of almost every ministry for 1910, yet in spite of the criticism, sometimes radical in tone and argument, the Octobrists voted for the budget. The Union became oppositional only in words: in its actions it remained "loyal" and "trustworthy."

During the debate on the budget of the Ministry of Education, Fon-Anrep complained that all the wishes and criticisms expressed by the Duma in preceding years remained unanswered by the government and expressed his indignation at the tone of condescension and contempt clearly apparent in the speech of Education Minister Shvarts. The ministry could function and improve the educational system only through close cooperation with the "representatives of the people, who also express the needs of the people," the Octobrist declared.[68]

But the peak of tensions between the Union and the government came during debate on the budget of the Ministry of the Interior, by now an almost traditional occasion to review the entire internal policy. After three years the Union's speakers could hardly be distinguished from the Kadets, but unlike the Kadets, they voted for the budget.

Prince Golitsyn spoke for the Budget Committee, and repeated more emphatically the accusations of former years:[69] in spite of repeated requests from the Duma, the police had not been reformed and the future of freedom in the country depended upon a radical reform of the police, particularly its political department. "I have

to remind you that the present conditions cannot be tolerated any
further. The activities of the secret police are not only illegal but
simply unbearable."[70] The freedoms promised in the October Manifesto remained a myth, Golitsyn said, as he drew a sordid picture of
arbitrariness, coercion, violence. He described the systematic erosion of the feeling of security among the regular citizens from the
continuous use of extraordinary regulations. The political police
"ruin the peaceful flow of the life of the ordinary citizen (*obyvatel'*).
This takes place when the last patches of the dreadful clouds have
disappeared, when the political barometer unmistakably records
clear weather."[71]

The Octobrists sounded impatient, restless, disappointed, but
there was no change in their attitude toward the form of government
or in their basic political orientation. More than five years had
passed since the October Manifesto, and the Duma was in its third
session. Revolutionary activities were at a lull, but government
repression had decreased only slightly, and in the provinces appeared even more arbitrary and reckless. With the disappearance of
revolutionary anarchy, the simple, orderly citizen became the main
victim of repression. The Union did not change, but with the passage
of time the achievement of its goal had not come any closer. The
Octobrists' hope for a secure existence in a state governed by law,
where the future could be anticipated with confidence, receded further and further. Five years had passed without a perceptible effort
on the part of the authorities to "renovate" Russia. This "wasted"
time brought a change in the Union's tactics and became a dynamic
factor in shaping the attitudes of many Octobrists. Guchkov expressed eloquently the feelings of frustration he shared with his
friends when he concluded his speech on the internal policy with
the exclamation: "We are waiting."[72]

Octobrism as an ideology and as a movement whose purpose was
to renovate the country, to strengthen it internally, and to restore its
prestige abroad had reached a blind alley. The Octobrists had made
a genuine effort to cooperate with tsarism and achieve peaceful
change in a country whose foundations were shattered by defeat and
revolution, but after three years in the Duma they found themselves
defeated in an important by-election and estranged from the government. The Union's supporters were baffled by its inaction and in-

ability to work out a clear political program. "Time is passing and the clock continues its movement, but the public still does not know what an Octobrist is," remarked an editorial on February 29, 1910, in *Novoe vremia*. "We feel that on certain problems we are isolated here and in the country," Guchkov said, speaking for the Union on the budget.[73] He repeated in stronger terms the criticism voiced by other members of his party. The Union thought that the country had regained permanent peace, and therefore, said the leader of the Union, "I and my friends do not recognize any more those obstacles that justified the slowing down of the implementation of civil liberties. . . . We cannot see any obstacle to a faster introduction of a stable rule of law on all levels of our national and social life."[74] Guchkov accused the central authorities of doing nothing to improve and adapt the administration to the constitutional regime. "We are waiting," was again the refrain of Guchkov's speech. The Octobrists had been waiting for a long time in vain. Now their waiting became more impatient.

In their dissatisfaction, the Octobrists proposed to remove a token sum of 174,360 rubles from the 52,067,000 rubles budget of the Police Department,[75] a move taken, explained Godnev, to force the abolition of administrative exile. In spite of strong protests from the Right and the Nationalists, the proposal was accepted. Purishkevich remarked from the floor "there still exists the State Council," openly threatening the Duma with the power of the reactionary council.[76]

Guchkov's "We are waiting" received no official reply. The government did not even bother to send one of its major representatives to appease the Union. The relations between the Octobrists and the government were reaching a turning point; so were their relations with the Nationalists and the Right.

It became known on March 4, 1910, that Khomiakov had resigned from his post as the president of the Third Duma. On March 8 Guchkov was elected as his successor. The resignation signified the peak of a process of internal disintegration and chaos in the Third Duma; the election of Guchkov meant a renewed effort to establish a "workable and cooperative" majority.

Observers who followed the daily proceedings in the Third Duma were not surprised at Khomiakov's resignation. It was the result of the convergence of the intensified campaign against him by the Right, the lack of respect for the Duma by the government, and the differences of opinion within the Union.

The unfinished and undefined nature of the post-October regime had given the Duma's president a role that was much more significant than that of an ordinary speaker in Parliament. The October Manifesto and the Fundamental Laws did not establish a functioning constitutional monarchy and the forces that tried to turn back the clock were numerous and well entrenched. In such a time of transition, the president of the Duma was not only a man responsible for the observance of the rules but actually "the mediator between the representatives of the people and the Highest Authority," [77] P. B. Struve observed. Khomiakov had been weak and too gentle to fulfill such a task and to restrain the conflicting tendencies that threatened to wreck the Duma.

By its deliberate campaign against the president, the Right tried to subvert the work of the Duma and prove its uselessness. Khomiakov had already resigned once in December 1908, after a series of severe attacks from the Right and its press [78] and had resumed office only after an expression of strong support from his own party. From the beginning of the third session, the Right sharply escalated its attacks on Khomiakov and provoked the left wing with a chauvinistic and anti-Semitic campaign. Anti-Semitism became one of the major weapons of the Right in its attempt to obstruct the regular legislative work—Purishkevich, Markov, and Zamyslovskii introduced anti-Jewish amendments to each bill discussed in the Duma, meanwhile accusing their opponents of being the pawns of the Jewish revolutionary movement. On numerous occasions the Right, supported frequently by the Nationalists, attacked Khomiakov as a tool of the revolutionaries. The situation became particularly acute toward the end of 1909 and the first months of 1910. On December 2, 1909, Purishkevich had been suspended from participation in five meetings after directing an obscene attack on the Kadets and threats against the Octobrists, [79] and Markov was suspended for fifteen meetings on January 25, 1910, following an attack on the president. [80]

During the debates on the budgets of the Holy Synod, Ministry of the Interior, and the Police Department, the tensions between the Octobrists and the Right reached their peak. When Godnev criticized the Ministry of Justice, the Right succeeded in disrupting the meeting in spite of Guchkov's warning that the Octobrists would prevent attempts at disruption. "We won't let you destroy the Duma," exclaimed the leader of the Union.[81]

Another major reason for Khomiakov's resignation was the deterioration of relations between the Duma and the government. In a letter to the Princess Chertvenskaia in 1908 that was intercepted by the political police, Khomiakov remarked that while everybody was tired of disorders and wanted peace "the government is unable to use the general mood to its own benefit. It continues by its lawlessness and arbitrariness to alienate and destroy this good will."[82] Khomiakov had had to apologize for his mild rebuke to Kokovtsov for denigrating the Duma in 1908, and the forced apology had left the Duma president humiliated and indignant.

Condescension and even open insult toward the Duma was apparent in the administration from the opening of the second session: minor officials appeared during major debates; many inquiries and criticisms by the Duma remained unanswered, particularly when directed against the Interior, Education, and Justice departments. Even *Novoe vremia*, a consistent supporter of Stolypin's government, complained in an editorial on March 6, 1910, that certain departments showed contempt toward the Duma as the supreme legislative body. From 1908 on, A. N. Shvarts, the minister of education, treated with sarcasm the complaints voiced year after year by the Duma. The Duma committees found it increasingly difficult to obtain data and documents that were readily available to the State Council. Many important bills remained lodged in the State Council with no chance to pass. Khomiakov, because of his position as president and his personal sensitivity, reached utter despair. Shvarts's sarcastic speech on March 4 and a provocation directed at the Kadets that was initiated by the Right finally precipitated Khomiakov's decision to resign.[83]

In an interview with the *London Times* correspondent, Khomiakov said the Right had deliberately disrupted the Duma. The Left, however, by responding to the provocations of "Purishkevich and company" had unwittingly helped the designs of the Right and thus was also responsible.[84] The ex-president remarked, "I would like to emphasize that members of the cabinet, too, were responsible for the constant excitement in the Duma," and singled out I. G.

Shcheglovitov, the minister of justice, and Shvarts, the minister of education, for their contemptuous behavior. Khomiakov noted that Stolypin's attitude towards the Duma "was always proper and benevolent," yet even he had contributed to its deterioration by not appearing in the Duma in the previous eight months. The "legislative strike" of the State Council undermined the trust in the Duma as a purposeful instrument of reform, Khomiakov said. He went on to explain that his resignation was designed to draw attention to the Duma's disintegration as a legislative instrument, so that government and society alike would try to stop the fatal process.

The increasing alienation between Khomiakov and the Union that rose from a new attempt to reestablish a "workable" government majority was another factor in his resignation. Khomiakov, a Slavophile liberal of the Shipov type, had never been an enthusiastic party member but had an inherent suspicion of political parties and of professional politicians struggling for power. Although he did not leave the Union when Shipov did, Khomiakov had stayed aloof from the internal strife and from close identification with the Union, probably one of the reasons that he had become the Duma's president. But when he needed the unwavering support of his party in his daily battle with Left and Right, it did not come in the forthright way that he had expected. Khomiakov, as president of the Duma, did not hesitate to criticize the Union when he thought it deserved censure. In an interview with the *London Times* correspondent, Khomiakov castigated the Octobrists for their failure to live up to their role—"they do nothing and remain in the same place."[85] He blamed them as accomplices, by default, to the continuous use of the extraordinary regulations.

The estrangement between the Duma president and his party was no secret. When asked immediately after his resignation whether he was still an Octobrist, Khomiakov answered that he was opposed to the idea of parties in general and to party discipline and tactics in particular. As to his being an Octobrist he said: "I do not know how many of the Octobrists are Octobrists. I have no idea how far they are from their original platform. I sympathize with Octobrism's original platform, but at present it is rather an anachronism."[86]

In the months preceding Khomiakov's resignation the Union had systematically refused to stand behind the assailed president.[87] Attacked from Left and Right, indignant over the government's attitude toward the Duma, and isolated from his own party, Khomiakov decided to resign. On March 8, 1909, the Duma elected Guchkov as its next president, signifying a new phase in the history of the Duma and the Union of October 17.

6

Guchkov's Presidency—
The Nationalist Coalition:
Phase One

Guchkov's election to the presidency of the Third Duma signified a new effort by Stolypin and the Octobrists to reestablish a workable majority. From the governmental crisis in the spring of 1909, it had become increasingly apparent that the majority that had supported Stolypin since 1907 was disintegrating. By 1910 he realized that none of the internal, religious, nor juridical reforms he proposed would get the Duma's support without being amended to unacceptability by the court clique and the State Council. He refused to accept the advice to dissolve the Duma again. Since the Nationalists had not supplanted the Octobrists as the working majority, Stolypin decided to raise the banner of militant Great Russian nationalism as the standard of a revived Nationalist-Octobrist coalition. Khomiakov was not a suitable Duma president for such a new course, and Stolypin supported Guchkov to succeed him.

Nationalism as a political slogan and ideology had been used by the Russian autocracy even before the Polish rebellion of 1863, and it suited both Stolypin and the Octobrists. Stolypin's background and experience as governor in the western provinces made him susceptible to the ideas of Great Russian nationalism as an alternative to the failure of the policy of internal reform. It was one of the major political tenets of the Octobrists for they saw in it the possibility of unity for the empire and its internal and international strength. They conceived it, not in its chauvinistic and suppressive aspects, but as a hope for "unity and indivisibility," a counterforce to the separatism and autonomy that had threatened the empire in the revolutionary years.

If Guchkov thought that militant nationalism would unite the disparate forces within the Union, however, he soon learned his mistake. Its left wing wanted a unified empire where the national minorities could develop their culture and way of life; the right wing tended toward Russification and suppression of national minorities. If he thought that close cooperation with the government to implement its nationalistic program might heal the wounds of recent conflicts, he soon learned that it could also bring out as never before the inherent contradiction between an unreformed tsarism and a still fledgling house of representatives.

Why did Guchkov accept the presidency of the Third Duma? He did it out of personal ambition as well as more general considerations. After the defeat in the Moscow elections before the third session, it became evident to Guchkov that those who elected him disapproved of the line followed by the Union in the Duma. His influence at court was on the decline since his attacks on the grand dukes and his continued "meddling" in military affairs. By becoming the Duma president Guchkov hoped to gain greater influence at court on military affairs through his personal contacts with the tsar [1] and to strengthen and unify the Duma vis-à-vis the State Council and the executive authorities, giving it a stronger voice in shaping the destinies of the country. He still nourished some illusions about the true nature of tsarism; he still thought that things failed to change for the better because the tsar did not know the facts, because the truth and the wishes of his people did not reach the sovereign. In 1917, Guchkov recalled:

> When I accepted the presidency I considered it my goal to bring to the attention of the sovereign everything that others had not dared to talk about. I said to His Majesty, "Your Highness, you must forgive me, but I decided to specialize in telling you the unpleasant truth. I know that you are surrounded by people who inform you only of what is pleasant; please reserve for me the right to tell you about the unpleasant." [2]

Whether Guchkov actually spoke so to the tsar cannot be ascertained, but by the time Guchkov became Duma president he was among the least popular figures at court and Nicholas was not the type to, let the "unpleasant" truth change his basic attitudes and relations. Guchkov quickly learned that "behind the sovereign stood other wills, other influences, that the tsar was not his own master. . . . It did not suffice to convince him, one had to overcome other obstacles that stood behind him." [3] If Guchkov had hoped to convince the tsar to follow his advice, he had been gravely mistaken. Nicholas treated the newly elected president with obvious coolness and reserve during the first audience. [4] A. A. Polivanov, one of Guchkov's friends and deputy war minister, recorded in his diary on November 27, 1910, that Guchkov's frankness with the tsar and his meddling with "unsuitable" military subjects left a rather negative impression on Nicholas. [5] Guchkov's desire to be more influential in his new post in shaping the future of Russia was doomed from the beginning.

Guchkov's candidacy raised strong opposition inside the Duma faction because many thought that he was needed as the leader of the party more than as president of the Duma, that his absence from the faction's leadership would create too much internal friction. Only a slight majority of the 110 Union deputies supported his candidacy, but the entire faction voted for him in the Duma. [6]

Most of the other Duma factions reacted favorably to Guchkov's candidacy, as did the public at large. There was a feeling that the country needed a man of his talents and position to lead the house of representatives.

Guchkov delivered his first speech as Duma president on March 12, 1910. [7] He outlined some of his beliefs, some of his hopes, and spoke of the external and internal forces that were obstructing the Duma's fruitful work. About the external difficulties, he warned: "We should not close our eyes to them. We will have to take them into consideration, and maybe we will even have to fight them." [8] This warning was directed at the State Council and its "legislative strike." By this time, the third year of the Duma, Guchkov was left with few illusions. At the opening of the Third Duma, during the debate on the address, he had maintained that the manifesto had established in Russia a constitutional monarchy; three years later he merely declared,

I am a convinced follower of the constitutional-monar-
chical regime, and have been one for a long time. I cannot
conceive of a peaceful development of present-day Russia except as a constitutional monarchy . . . where the
people's representatives are invested with broad legislative rights and supervision over the executive, but
with a strong government responsible only to the monarch, not to the political parties.[9]

Reactions to Guchkov's acceptance speech were favorable.
That he came out as a "convinced constitutionalist" brought
praises from the Kadets and their press. A. A. Kizevetter recalled
that the speech impressed the country at large as honest and a defense of the Duma and the constitutional regime.[10]

Guchkov's presidency was not a "sell-out" of the Union's constitutional principles. It represented rather a somber and realistic
attempt to defend the constitutional achievements and the Duma
and to try to influence the course of Russia's political development.
It followed the basic pattern of attitudes of Octobrism toward autocracy and revolution. In 1910, as before, the Union was not an opposition party, and did not try to use its power, particularly the budget,
as a means to fight for its principles. Octobrists of all shades of
opinion were rather afraid that such a course might endanger the
existence of the Duma and trigger a new revolutionary outburst.
Nevertheless, they were not blind supporters of the government nor
did they give automatic approval to its actions. The same pattern
was followed during Guchkov's presidency. Criticism became less
frequent and more subdued since a conscious attempt was made to
avoid problematic issues and concentrate on what the Union and
government had in common, yet differences of opinion did not disappear and found their expression in committee and plenum in amendments to government bills and allocations of credits. Guchkov's
presidency was an attempt by both sides to work together.

Although Guchkov's election was meant to be a beginning of
reconciliation, the Union pushed through, on March 23, 1910, a
resolution refusing for the third time to allocate credits for the
dreadnoughts. Even more amazing was the unanimous adoption by
the Duma of a resolution calling for the tsar to appoint a senatorial
investigation board to look into the management of the Naval

Ministry.[11] Preceding the vote were two speeches by the Octobrists A. I. Zvegintsev and N. Savich, who criticized in as strong terms as in the previous year the lack of substantial reforms in the navy.[12]

But the leitmotif of the beginning of Guchkov's presidency was cooperation, the removal of problematic questions and avoidance of embarrassing interpellations. On March 19, 1910, the committee that dealt with the interpellation on persecution of trade unions decided that there were no grounds for complaint, a retreat from the position taken by the Union when the interpellation was first introduced. The committee decided not to bring it up for discussion before the Duma plenum.[13]

The Interpellations Committee refused to support the Social Democrats' interpellation on the August regulations that curtailed further the Duma's budgetary rights over military expenses, another evidence of the new cooperation between Stolypin and the Union. N. P. Shubinskii defended the committee's decision on March 26, 1910,[14] explaining that the committee refused to deal with the question of whether the regulations contradicted the Fundamental Laws or whether the tsar acquired by them certain rights that he was denied by the Fundamental Laws. The committee thought that the interpellants had raised the problem for negative reasons: as an edict of the tsar, the regulations did not represent an infringement upon the Fundamental Laws and were instructions for the administrators rather than new legislation.[15] "Only actions by ministers or their subordinates are subject to interpellations," and since no interpellation has been presented concerning actions taken according to the regulations, there was no basis for their discussion. Shubinskii's explanation was a clear attempt to avoid a discussion of the constitutional implications of the August regulations on technical and formalistic grounds. At issue were not just certain legalistic aspects but the anticonstitutional and anti-Duma spirit behind the publication of the regulations, and the forces that brought them about. The Octobrists understood the issue but they refused to confront it.

Stolypin was more candid in his response to the interpellation.[16] He directed himself to the accusation that the regulations were meant as an affront to the Duma, an indication of a reactionary policy. The prime minister assured his audience, in his first speech in the Duma in eight months, that the government intended to realize the reforms promised by the tsar as well as to fight abuse of power by the various executive agencies. Stolypin maintained that there was a genuine desire on the part of the authorities to return to normalcy and that "this would be achieved by the proper cooperation between the government and the representative institutions." [17] But he made it clear that military matters and decisions concerning the administration of the armed forces were off limits to the Duma. The regulations would prevent any misunderstandings by either the Duma or the government as to the exact limits of the competence of each. In military affairs the Duma's main function was to allocate or refuse the required appropriations, and this was made definitive in the August 24 regulations. In actuality, Stolypin was reminding the Duma that Russia was still an autocracy and the tsar had complete monopoly of the armed forces. The Duma could criticize, advise, or protest, but did not have rights equal to those of the administration. Stolypin knew that this was political reality in Russia and acted accordingly.

N. V. Savich defended the regulations on the grounds that they actually represented the defeat of a concerted effort by the reactionary forces to destroy the constitutional achievements of the manifesto, restore the old bureaucratic order, and overthrow Stolypin. [18] The State Council was the center of that conspiracy—a small clique was frightened by the fruitful cooperation between government and Duma and had tried to ruin the mutual confidence between the tsar and his government, between the tsar and his people, but had failed. Savich's speech expressed the renewed understanding and closer cooperation between the Union and Stolypin.

The debate dragged on until May 5, 1910, and became gradually more acrimonious. Concluding it, Shubinskii sounded very much like his rightist competitors, [19] accusing the Kadets, and particularly V. A. Maklakov, of fostering sedition. The revolution had not yet disappeared, Shubinskii argued, and "in such a period of disintegration men of strong will and energy were needed—men ready to fight relentlessly." [20] Shubinskii sounded very different from his friend Golitsyn, who had denounced the internal policy of Stolypin only three months previously. It was a far cry from Guchkov's "We are waiting." Now, nine weeks later, Shubinskii declared that: "We came here not just to complain but to cooperate with the authorities in the legislative work. . . . We are assured by the government's promise that there was not and will not be any encroachment on the Duma's rights."[21] He was enthusiastically applauded by the center and Right when he denounced the Kadets and promised to support the government.

Only Barons Meyendorff and Shilling, Octobrists of non-Russian descent, raised their voices against this party line. Meyendorff held that the regulations defining the relative spheres of Duma and tsar could not pass as mere instructions from the tsar and were therefore a clear breach of the legislative process prescribed by the Fundamental Laws.[22] Baron Shilling announced, after the vote was taken, that "[I] could not agree that the Fundamental Laws be interpreted by way of instructions from the throne and therefore I could not vote for the rejection of the interpellation."[23] It took courage, in the atmosphere of militant nationalism that reigned in the Duma, for the two non-Russians to vote the way they did.

It is interesting to note that the regulations *were* used by the War Ministry to circumvent the Duma. V. A. Sukhomlinov, the war minister, recalled that he used "the tsar's command" to get the necessary resources for his department, in order to cut short "the delaying character (*volokitnogo kharaktera*) of the allocation procedures." He thought that "it could not be interpreted as something reactionary nor a breach of the Duma's rights."[24]

With the removal of the embarrassing interpellations the road was clear for the "positive" activities of the nationalistic course. Its basis was established with the election of Guchkov as Duma president and Stolypin hoped to use it to avert criticism from reactionary circles and to revitalize the government majority. He could confidently expect a favorable response from the Third Duma, for its majority was "Russian by spirit." From the Octobrists to the extreme Right, slogans such as "Russian nationalism," "Russian historical principles," and the "unity and indivisibility of the Russian Empire" were extremely popular. The nationalities problem presented itself as one way of averting the disintegration of the empire and only the Progressists and the Kadets would have given more autonomy and freedom to the national minorities, maintaining that more repression and denial of cultural freedom would strengthen separatist movements.[25] The extreme Left and the national minority groups strongly objected to the Great Russian chauvinism, although no minority group took a positive stand when other nationalities were concerned. But the opposition was powerless to affect the new course: Great Russian nationalism was the order of the day, expressing itself in the most virulent attack on foreigners and on the opposition parties, which were frequently accused of being unpatriotic and tools of a "Jewish-foreigner" conspiracy to subvert Russia. Although supported by the majority, the course had certainly not achieved the needed calm for a "workable" Duma.

Two bills epitomized the nationalistic course: the bill establishing zemstvo institutions in six of the nine western provinces and the general bill regulating the relations between the empire and Finland in matters relating to the empire as a whole. Both discriminated against the non-Russian elements as well as encouraged the Great Russians' interests. The debates that took place showed how widespread and how intense Great Russian chauvinism was in many Duma factions. Frequently one could hardly distinguish an Octobrist from a rightist.

Zemstvo Institutions in the Western Provinces

The initiative to establish zemstvo institutions in the western provinces indirectly originated in the State Council. A group of thirty-three State Council members, mainly from the southwest, led by D. I. Pikhno, the editor of the *Kievlianin*, one of the most important nationalistic papers published in Kiev, proposed to change the suffrage in the nine western provinces (Kovno, Vilno, Grodno, Vitebsk, Mogilev, Minsk, Volhynia, Kiev, and Podolia, which comprised Lithuania, Belorussia, and the Right-Bank Ukraine) in a way that would secure the election of six Russians and three Poles to the State Council instead of the present nine Poles.[26] Stolypin had supported the proposal and defended the bill before the Duma earlier, on May 20, 1909,[27] maintaining that the present situation was unjust, since the Poles who comprised only four percent of the population had all the representatives. The landholding role of the Poles, relic of Polish rule over these areas until the eighteenth century, gave them economic dominance over the Lithuanian, Belorussian, and Ukrainian peasants, and zemstvo institutions had not been established before because of the dominance of the essentially hostile Poles. As new elections were coming up, the government would not have time to prepare and pass a zemstvo bill that would ensure a more equitable representation of the Russian elements. Stolypin held that the proposal was an attempt to rectify an historical injustice towards the Russian Orthodox majority, since he considered Orthodox Belorussians and Ukrainians as simply "Russians," and therefore responsive to the Great Russian nationalist idea.[28] The government proposed to delay the upcoming elections for a year to be able to prepare an election law on the lines proposed by Pikhno.

The proposal was opposed by the Union. N. I. Antonov argued that the representatives from the western provinces should be elected through the same institutions, the zemstva, as in other parts of the empire.[29] But since the government agreed and promised to introduce a bill for the establishment of zemstvo institutions in the following year, the Union would support a proposition that the elections during that summer (1909) would be for one year only. The elections of 1910 would take place using the zemstvo institutions established by then. The Union's proposal thus changed the original government bill by stressing that the same results, a more equitable Russian representation in the State Council, would be achieved by the introduction of the zemstvo and instead of delaying the elections, representatives were to serve for a year only, according to the existing suffrage. Stolypin accepted, and agreed to pass in a year a bill establishing zemstvo institutions in the western provinces.[30]

An amended zemstvo bill was introduced in the Duma on May 6, 1910. It contained several important departures from the existing laws governing the elections and composition of zemstvo institutions in Russia proper.

The law of June 12, 1890, that regulated the elections to the zemstva had been based on the principles of class origin and the amount of real property owned, bringing about a preponderance of gentry landowners over peasants. Had the same principles been transferred to the western provinces, the Poles would have had a majority, for the Polish landowners were more numerous and prosperous than their Russian competitors. The non-Polish peasantry was weak economically and culturally, but nourished strong anti-Polish feelings. To overcome these disadvantages, the government bill would give a "Russian" majority by changing some basic principles that applied to the Russian provinces. The bill applied only to six provinces, the problems in the other three (Vilno, Grodno, Kovno) required other measures, because there were few Russian landholders in two, and administrative unity required inclusion of the third in the Lithuanian group. The zemstva were to be classless and the electors were segregated into two national curiae: Polish and non-Polish. These curiae became the principal tool for carrying out the nationalistic policy. In order to insure Russian domination, the percentage of representatives allocated to each national group was fixed artificially: the percentage of land in the province held by each group was added to the percentage of the population each group comprised, and divided by two. The property requirement for voting in the landowners' class was lowered, thus enabling more small holders to be better represented, to the detriment of the richer Russian and Polish landowners. The peasantry was given a third of the electoral votes on the district (*uezd*) level but not on the provincial level. The government's bill proposed a fixed number of Orthodox clergy to be among those elected to the zemstvo, stipulating also that the president and at least half of the boards and employees had to be non-Polish. The Jewish minority, which was larger in numbers than the Polish, was denied suffrage.[31]

The Duma's committee on local self-government, where the Octobrists predominated, introduced several amendments designed to liberalize slightly and to modify the bill's nationalistic bias. The committee recommended, instead of the two voting standards of population and property for the determination of the number of voters in each national curia, the establishment of the standard of property only. It meant a slight increase of the Polish representation. It also recommended the reduction of the property requirement by one-half for participation in zemstvo elections. Recommended as well was the introduction of the principle of *fakul'tativnost'*, that on the district level the two national curiae could assemble in a single electoral chamber when this was desired by a majority of two-thirds of each curia. The committee recommended lowering the number of Orthodox clergy in the provincial chambers and rejecting the requirement of a Russian majority in the executive boards of the zemstva and among zemstvo employees, which would be assured anyway by the composition of the assemblies.[32] In the committee itself the Nationalists and right-wing Octobrists objected to some of the amendments, principally those concerning clergy representation, the *fakul'tativnost'* principle, and the Russian majority on the boards.[33] This bill, which was designed to restore harmony in the Duma, became eventually a source of discord between the Union and the Nationalists and intensified the internal struggle in the Union's Duma faction.

The zemstvo bill became the cornerstone of Stolypin's nationalistic course, as well as the basis of the newly established cooperation between the Octobrists and the Nationalists. Stolypin regarded it as joining a nationalistic approach with the liberal principle of local self-government. The prime minister himself took the podium in the first meeting that opened the debate on the bill [34] and outlined his nationalistic philosophy and attitude toward the proposed amendments. The aim of the proposed bill, he explained, was to introduce local self-government in the six western provinces and at the same time to safeguard the rights of the "Russian" majority, in accordance with the government's "national goals" in those provinces.[35] The economically and culturally weak Russian majority could not be left to the arbitrary treatment of the Polish minority, and the zemstvo idea in the western provinces must therefore be subordinated to the national idea. Past efforts to placate the Polish minority had failed, maintained Stolypin. During the revolutionary upheaval of 1905 the Poles revealed strong anti-Russian feelings and the history of past antagonism and exploitation of the Russians by the Poles in those provinces required a special effort to create separate national chambers. He opposed most of the committee's amendments, expressing anxiety over Polish assertiveness and the lack of local Russian initiative. The bill's goal was not the oppression of the Polish minority, explained the prime minister, but to protect Russia's historical principles and to affirm "openly and without hypocrisy that the western region is and will forever remain Russian."[36]

The Right and the Nationalists consistently supported the original government bill. The only amendment acceptable to the Nationalists was the lowering of the property requirement by half, their spokesman, S. M. Bogdanov, announced.[37] Purishkevich, from the Right, went even further and warned the Octobrists that the government would take the bill back if the committee's amendments were passed. Rightist Markov[38] spelled out the true aim of the bill—the creation of a Russian majority in the western zemstvo institution. Bishop Evlogii declared that the problem was "who will be the master of the western provinces—the Russians or the Poles." The bill had to destroy once and for all the Polish aim to make the western provinces part of Poland.[39]

The Kadets, Progressists, and the Socialists opposed the bill in the strongest terms. The Kadets argued that the government's policy of Great Russian chauvinism would encourage separatist movements among the national minorities, and thus contribute to the revolutionary tendencies in the empire. Kadet F. A. Golovin accused the government of trying to divert popular attention from real grievances and of artificially fostering national hatreds.[40]

The debate over the introduction of zemstvo institutions to the western provinces revealed the increasing disintegration of the Union into two wings after Guchkov's election to the presidency. The militant Great Russian nationalism and the closer cooperation of Guchkov with Stolypin aggravated internal discord rather than helped to heal it. The absence of Guchkov's direct and daily involvement in the faction contributed to the same effect. The Union's Duma faction could not reach an agreement as to Guchkov's successor as head of the faction. Facing the danger of a formal split, the faction decided that M. V. Rodzianko and V. K. Fon-Anrep would be coleaders.[41] But the different wings in the Union openly took opposing positions on many issues. The left-wing Octobrists in the Judicial Committee supported the demand to abolish capital punishment; they voted with the Kadets against most of the Octobrists.[42] Rodzianko's relations with the faction became so strained that he ceased to participate in its bureau meetings.

Even before the dissent over the zemstvo bill, *Golos Moskvy*, the Union's main publication, printed an admission that "recent events force us to concede that Guchkov's absence had fatal consequences on the Octobrist faction. It is impossible to hide it anymore, it is even harmful to do so."[43] Neither Guchkov nor Stolypin had anticipated the growing estrangement between the two wings in the Union as a result of the militant nationalistic course.

In spite of strong pressure from Stolypin and Guchkov there still remained a sizable group of Octobrists who refused to support the bill as a whole. After three years of relative tranquillity they objected to implementation of a policy that would heighten national animosities and divert the Duma from a constructive course. Twenty-two Octobrists voted with the opposition against the bill, even in the form presented by the committee.[44] When it came to the amendments, internal discord within the faction was even more pronounced, for the differences concerned whether to adopt the amendments or the original government bill.

The Octobrists who defended the bill maintained that the Russian majority in the provinces was weak, exploited, and needed the help and protection of the central government, that the Polish minority, and particularly the Catholic clergy, abused their economic power and deprived the Russian Orthodox peasantry of its national and religious rights. It is worth noting that only Union back-benchers took part in the general debate. A. P. Sapunov, V. A. Potulov, and G. V. Skoropadskii, Octobrists from the western provinces, repeated Stolypin's arguments, but did it less eloquently. They reviewed again and again the long history of hatred, wars, and repression since the Middle Ages.[45] I. S. Klimenko from Chernigov reminded his party of its erstwhile principles, to their great embarrassment, quoting the proclamation where, together with the pledge to defend the unity of the empire, the authors promised to encourage local self-government and equality of all the inhabitants of the empire, regardless of nationality, race, or religion. The present bill was a blatant travesty of those principles, Klimenko accused.[46] The Octobrist announced that he would vote against the bill since it negated the principles of the Union: "The Third Duma has been in existence for three years and for three years we, the orthodox Octobrists, had to endure, to submit, and to retreat from our principles. I think that it is enough and in the future I intend to follow only the program of the Union."[47] This was an unwelcome reminder for the Union's leadership.

The Union's faction was in complete disarray when the amendments came to the vote. The major issue that separated the two wings was whether to support a single property standard, as recommended by the committee, or a double standard of property and population, as presented by the government. A rump meeting of the faction decided on May 11, 1910, by a vote of 25 to 19, to vote for a single standard.[48] Two days later, the Union resorted to its old technique of granting its members the right to vote according to their own choosing.[49] On the Duma floor the most virulent insinuations had been exchanged among the Octobrists themselves. Prince V. V. Tenishev[50] opposed the idea of national curiae and called the two-standard principle "political opportunism" that was entirely contrary to his political beliefs. M. Ia. Kapustin defended the two-standard proposal,[51] unable to see any contradiction between the Union's principles and the bill. He reminded Klimenko that equality for other nationalities was promised in the proclamation "within the limits of state interests and the protection for those nationalities who need it." "The state interests are Russian and the nationality that needs protection in western Russia is Russian," explained Kapustin.[52] G. N. Glebov was the main spokesman for the Octobrists who stood for the one-standard principle. In the name of those who proposed the amendment, he announced that they too "want to protect the interests of the Russian state no less than you [referring to the critics], but while we agree to protect the Russian interests we refuse to introduce the principle of extraordinary regulations to the zemstvo."[53] Savich opposed the committee's amendments and announced that "out of state considerations I and many members of our faction, regrettably not a majority, will vote for the bill as presented by the government."[54] Rodzianko too promised to vote for the original government bill.[55]

To prevent misunderstandings about where the faction stood M. A. Iskritskii announced that the majority of the Union had decided to vote for the committee's amendment. The interests of the Russian majority had been secured by adopting the principle of the national curiae. The two-standard principle, contended Iskritskii, "will not serve to protect the interests of the Russian population in the region. It would be an unjustified encroachment upon the rights of the Poles. . . . We consider such limitations as contradicting the Russian national interests." The Left greeted this announcement enthusiastically.[56]

The committee's amendment was defeated by a vote of 182 to 165.[57] Among those who voted against the government's proposal were outstanding and principled Octobrists such as Prince Golitsyn, I. V. Godnev, A. V. Eropkin, P. B. Kamenskii, I. I. Kapnist, and Baron Meyendorff. The same happened to the *fakul'tativnost'* principle, which was defeated by a combination of the Right, the Nationalists, and many of the Octobrists.[58] On the other minor amendment the entire Union faction supported the committee. As on other occasions, the Right used the zemstvo bill to express its anti-Semitic feelings, their crude and insulting behavior proving that the stress on nationalism by the majority of the Union did not suffice to placate the extremists. During the debate Purishkevich and Zamyslovskii became so obnoxious that they were expelled for several meetings. When the Duma voted on the bill as a whole some of the rightist deputies voted with the opposition to display their displeasure with the minor amendment adopted by the Duma. [59] Instead of providing it with an atmosphere suited for cooperation, the nationalistic issues intensified the Duma's conflicts.

The Union came out bruised and divided from the struggle over the western zemstvo bill, the result of a long process of estrangement between the two wings in the Union. The absence of Guchkov's leadership certainly had its effect in bringing those contradictions into the open. But although many predicted a formal split, again they were wrong.

Regulation on Finland's Autonomy

The bill regulating the legislation of laws concerning Finland and relating to the entire empire followed. A milestone in the nationalistic course adopted by Stolypin and his Duma allies, the bill gave a new opportunity to demonstrate the "patriotic" character of the nationalistic coalition. Although it had the support of a large majority of the Union, the debate and the form in which it was conducted indicated the disintegration of the Union as a political entity.

Finland had kept its own laws and institutions when it was united with Russia in 1809; only through the Russian monarch, who became the Grand Duke of Finland, was it part of the empire. Under the guise of regulating the methods of legislation concerning matters of common interest to Finland and the rest of the empire, an attempt had been made to curtail its constitutional rights and autonomy. Stolypin continued the policy of encroachment initiated by A. I. Bobrikov and V. K. Plehve in 1899, but he also had a special score to settle concerning Finland's role during the revolutionary years 1904–7, when it became a refuge for many revolutionaries and had itself a strong revolutionary movement.

The Finnish problem had already been raised in the first session by interpellation both from the Right and from the Octobrists when they asked the government to clarify Finland's position in the empire after the publication of the October Manifesto, which, in its change of the legislative system, by implication changed Finland's obligations to the tsar. Left Octobrists, such as Shidlovskii, Kamenskii, Meyendorff, and V. M. Petrovo-Solovovo, objected to the interpellation, and there were rumors that it was introduced because of government pressure.[60]

Stolypin responded immediately to the interpellation and outlined his basic ideas concerning Finland.[61] It was clear from his speech that the restoration of Finland's constitutional rights in 1905, its shelteringof Russian revolutionaries, and the sheer presence of a more advanced and freer Finland presented a threat to tsarism. Stolypin's main premise was that "Finland is an integral part of the Russian Empire, and the empire is governed by a unified government that is responsible to the sovereign for everything taking place in the state."[62] Matters affecting Finland and the rest of the empire had to be decided "through institutions representing the entire empire," he maintained. He was clearly appealing to the Duma for popular support for the curtailment of Finland's freedoms. To enthusiastic applause from the center and the Right, the prime minister declared that by following a policy of combating separatism in Finland the Duma would secure "Russia's lands in the Finnish gulf . . . and the historical rights of the Russian Empire."[63] The prime minister's explanation satisfied the Union and their allies and the interpellation was withdrawn.

When the Finnish problem came up again, the Duma was at the peak of the nationalistic course and Finland became one of its major expressions.

On March 16, 1910, the tsar published a manifesto on Finland, regulating the legislative procedures on matters common both to Finland and to the rest of the empire. It was composed by a Russo-Finnish commission, functioning since 1909, which had had to decide what subjects would be transferred from the jurisdiction of the Finnish to the imperial legislature. The manifesto seriously encroached on the constitutional rights of Finland: such matters as taxes, military service, the status of Russian citizens, language, state security, education, associations, tariffs, commerce, railways, and so on, were excluded from the competence of the Finnish Diet and came under the jurisdiction of the imperial institutions.[64] In effect, the proposed bill abolished Finland's autonomy.

Contrary to the usual routine of delay, the Duma committee was quick in dealing with the bill. It was greeted with enthusiasm by the Octobrists and it took only one day for the committee to conclude the general discussion of the proposal. The head of the committee, P. N. Krupenskii, prevented any attempt by the opposition to continue the discussion. The majority responded by complete silence to all the arguments presented by the opposition and the latter left the committee.[65] The bill was first discussed in committee on April 27 and was completed after going through its details on April 29.[66] By May 7 it was introduced in the Duma with only slight changes.

The debate in the Duma plenum started on May 21, 1910. *Golos Moskvy* characterized the bill and the debate as representing a high point in Russian constitutional development,[67] an editorial commenting that the tsar responded to the genuine wishes of his people. Finland did enjoy special rights compared to the Russian people, the editorial continued, and after the establishment of the representative regime this injustice had to disappear. The editorial concluded that by the proposed bill "the old order is being condemned and the national Russian forces start their great task."

A connection crucial to the nationalistic policy was made in this article by associating strong nationalistic feelings with the idea of constitutionalism. Russia's true national aspirations could be expressed, the article said, only after the establishment of the new regime in the empire. The implications of this connection could be explosive, and could endanger the future cooperation between Russian nationalists and tsarism.

The debate and the acceptance of the bill demonstrated the harshness of the nationalistic course. It was recognized as of special urgency, and contrary to the accepted procedures on such matters,[68] the debate took place in a highly tense atmosphere with all the ministers present. For the Nationalists and the Right it became a test of the "true patriotism" of the Union and Stolypin. Both lived up to expectations, to the great disgust of the opposition and many Octobrists. E. P. Bennigsen, an Octobrist expert on Finnish affairs, gave the necessary technical explanations: the bill's purpose was to clarify and define the relation of Finland to the Russian Empire, a relationship that had never been fully resolved;[69] the basic assumption was that Finland was an integral part of the empire that had a special autonomy only in its internal affairs; Finnish laws would in the future apply only to matters that would be specifically decided upon by the Russian legislature; Finland would be represented in the imperial Duma by five members; the Finnish Diet would have only advisory functions on matters relating to the empire as a whole.[70]

Stolypin represented the government in the debate. While he did not say anything substantially new, his speech contained a virulent attack on Finnish nationalism and its supporters in the Duma.[71] The prime minister noted the increasing deterioration in the ties between Finland and Russia—the Finns had encouraged and participated in the revolutionary movement, there were no legal safeguards to secure Russian interests in Finland. The government thought that while "Finland enjoys broad local autonomy . . . matters pertaining to Russian interests should be beyond the competence of the Finnish Diet."[72]

The debate over the bill gave the Octobrists an excellent opportunity to prove their patriotism. Kapustin's speech was particularly scathing of the opposition, especially of the Kadets,[73] reminiscent of the strident castigations of the Kadets in the first session, when they were accused of being proponents of revolution. The proposed bill would only secure the Russian interests and make Finland a truly integral part of the empire, maintained Kapustin. The true national spirit of Russia was expressed after the establishment of the representative regime. Kapustin's speech stressed the connection between nationalism and the constitutional regime, a connection from which the autocracy could not benefit whether the Octobrists realized it or not.

The usually restrained Fon-Anrep delivered a chauvinistic speech that embarrassed even his friends.[74] "When dealing with a problem of such major national importance one should keep uppermost in his mind the nation's and the state's needs, rather than elaborate juridical rights," he explained at the beginning of his speech. The interests of the empire ought to supersede any and every particularist rights or privileges:

> A true national policy [in the borderlands] . . . has to steer clear from any attempt to gain the love of the minorities. One has to announce explicitly and openly, not being intimidated by liberals nor constrained by notions of universal rights, justice, equality, that the highest

form of justice is to protect the national interest. . . .
We want the respect, we do not need the love of the nationalities.[75]

Even the members of Fon-Anrep's own party remained silent
when he accused the opposition of lack of patriotism, of cosmo-
politanism, of a deficiency "in genuine love for Russia."

It was no wonder that the arch-chauvinist Purishkevich enthusiastically accepted Fon-Anrep into the fold of "true" nationalism:
"It is not a matter of names, one could be an Anrep and a Russian,
and one could be a Miliukov and a *Zhid* [Jew]. . . . I would like to
hail this outburst of nationalism by the Union of October 17, so
eloquently expressed by Fon-Anrep."[76]

A sizable group of left-wing Octobrists, with Meyendorff as
spokesman, joined the Kadets in opposing the bill.[77] He warned
against the incitement and mudslinging that accompanied the debate. No one had the right to present himself as the incarnation of
patriotism, nor should the people who object to the bill be branded
as traitors, said Meyendorff. The problem of Russo-Finnish relations were too complicated to be decided by a bill passed under
pressure. He objected to the encroachment upon Finland's constitutional rights. Stolypin's strong-arm policy towards the minorities,
he contended, would only encourage separatism and hatred. Turning
to the supporters of the bill in the Duma and his own party, he lev-
eled the accusation that by encroaching upon Finland's constitution
"you think that you are performing a great national deed. I do not
have any desire to have any part in this 'national' achievement."[78]

The bill passed the three required hearings in four days, with the
majority limiting the speakers to twenty minutes. The opposition,
particularly the Kadets, tried to point out the unconstitutionality of
the bill and its infringement on Finland's historical rights, but to
no avail. On May 26, 1910, the opposition left the hall in protest,[79]
accompanied by a group of twenty-three left Octobrists.

The Union emerged from the debates over two nationalistic bills
so divided that again many predicted a formal separation between
the two wings. However, N. P. Shubinskii, in an interview with Duma
reporters, rejected the idea that the Union would cease to exist as
one party. "The differences in our ranks concern only secondary,
not principal matters. We have our different opinions and even

votes. We have never strived to impose an iron discipline on our members," he explained, as one of the principal nationalistic leaders of the faction, that "each member in the Union has the right to express his views and vote accordingly."

The very loose internal ties of the organization helped the Union to retain its formal unity, and apathy and inertia contributed their share in achieving the same results. But if Guchkov hoped to strengthen and unify the party by following the nationalistic course, he was gravely mistaken. Nor was it enough to sustain friendly relations within the coalition or with the government.

7

Guchkov's Presidency—
The Nationalist Coalition:
Phase Two

The fourth session of the Third Duma, until the zemstvo crisis in March, 1911, was characterized by a gradual disintegration of the nationalistic coalition. The seeds of this disintegration were in the alliance itself. A militant nationalism could bring together Octobrists and rightists as long as its main expression was directed outward, but it created tensions when proposed internal reforms excited the rightists' sterile chauvinism. The Duma reflected the uneasiness that was beginning to reappear in the country: the elections to the Fourth Duma were already on the minds of many deputies, and there was a gradual movement of the Union to a more oppositional stand, yet the nationalistic coalition did not disappear; like the preceding government majority, it went through a period of conflict, but the characteristic pattern remained. The nationalistic course only revealed once again some of the contradictions inherent in Stolypin's policies.

The fourth session opened in the fall of 1910 under the shadow of unrest at the universities and of demonstrations occasioned by the death of S. A. Muromtsev, the president of the First Duma. Laws had been passed to suppress national minorities in the borderlands, but no movement of reform stirred in Russia itself. The politically conscious public was not satisfied, and still there was no obvious response from the Duma to the changing mood of the populace.

The first conflicts of the session occurred when Prince Volkonskii, the acting president (Guchkov resigned for a short period, following his involvement in a duel), refused to honor Muromtsev after being threatened by the Nationalists and the Right with disruption of the Duma.[1] Guchkov denounced Volkonskii for succumbing to threats made by the Right,[2] and, with the opposition and a large group of Octobrists, left the hall, followed by shouts of derision from the Nationalists and the Right.

The gap between the Octobrists and the Right was again emphasized when the Right opposed the adjournment of the Duma meeting on November 8, 1910, in tribute to Leo Tolstoi following his death. A delegation headed by M. V. Rodzianko asked Stolypin to rescind the prohibition on conducting memorial services for Tolstoi but was rejected.[3] The bigotry and crudeness that the Right had shown about Tolstoi troubled and alienated the Octobrists, who found themselves cooperating inadvertently with the Kadets, reflecting their growing tensions with both the Right and the government.

Guchkov was re-elected Duma president with a smaller majority than before, 201 to 137. The Right opposed him; he was not nationalistic enough, and his cooperation with Stolypin only made him less acceptable to the "true Russians" of the Right.[4]

Despite these events, at the beginning of the fourth session the Union looked more unified than it had. On November 23, 1910, it elected as its head Rodzianko, who defeated V. K. Fon-Anrep by a vote of 79 to 16.[5] The holding of an election indicated a greater unity—it had been avoided for nine months from fear of a formal split, and the outcome showed the growing strength of the right wing, a trend that had been detectable in the second half of the third session.

But this shift to the right among the Octobrists was not enough to satisfy the Nationalists and the Right. When the Duma started its deliberations on major reforms in the elementary educational system, the chauvinism of the Right brought almost complete disintegration to the nationalistic coalition.

Among the most important of the Octobrist goals were basic educational reforms, in the struggle for which their closest allies had been the opposition, particularly the Kadets. Their achievement in this area during the Third Duma was most impressive—from the first session the Union had followed a consistent policy of furthering the spread of education and improving the system, with major efforts concentrated on the elementary level. They had exerted much time, planning, and pressure to provide Russia with an adequate educational system, which they thought of as prerequisite to the progress and strengthening of the country. The defeat in the Russo-Japanese War was attributed by many to the low educational standard of the Russian soldier; the development of sophisticated weapon systems required more learning from its users; and education was necessary to improve the lot of the peasantry. A certain minimum education was a prerequisite for a genuine constitutional regime, for a state ruled by law (*pravovoe gosudarstvo*), the cherished aim of the Union. Stolypin, too, recognized the importance of education in his scheme to move Russia forward, and gave his support to the initiatives and plans of the Union. But not all the members in his cabinet realized the need for a quick modernization of the educational system, not all the ministers gave it the same priority, nor were they even ready to accept new ideas. Financial considerations motivated V. N. Kokovtsov, the finance minister, when he tried, unsuccessfully, to limit the increases in the education budget. Fears of the revolutionary potential of popular education, particularly in view of recurrent disturbances in the universities, motivated A. N. Shvarts and his successor L. A. Kasso in the Ministry of Education to oppose basic reforms in the traditional system.

During the first two sessions the Union limited itself to the expression of recommendations, wishes, and pleas, usually attached to the budget of the Ministry of Education. But in the third session their tone became more demanding, even threatening, as a result of an almost open contempt shown by Minister of Education Shvarts toward the Duma. Fon-Anrep, the Union's expert on educational matters, was explicit: the Union's demands were modest, "but we will not retreat from them." [6] If the ministry should follow its plans of limiting the development of the educational system, "then I can assure you," the Octobrist warned, "that there will not be any sense in bringing them to the Duma. I have every reason to believe that my opinions in this respect will be supported by many other groups and factions, not only by the Union." [7] The Union's program included the integration of the different educational levels into one coordinated system, from elementary school to the university, with the purpose of abolishing class distinctions and enabling the talented student to reach the highest level of education. This required suitable changes in the structure of the elementary and high school systems. The reform had to follow decentralization of the educational system through giving the system more independence from the ministry, Fon-Anrep explained. The program also demanded the granting of autonomy to locally elected self-governing institutions in the administration of the elementary education.[8] Fon-Anrep demanded more autonomy for the universities, and to the great delight of the Left, announced that the primary function of the Ministry of Education was not to fight "sedition" but to promote education. This would be achieved "only when the ministry will forget its police functions and engage in public education."[9]

The Union's educational policies were more or less in line with Stolypin's aspirations. The prime minister and his allies succeeded on October 15, 1910, in introducing a bill to the Duma on "the introduction of universal education in Russia." Most of the fall of 1910 was devoted to the debate on that bill, which was slightly changed in committee by the Octobrists and the opposition.

Fon-Anrep presented the bill as prepared by the Duma committee,[10] explaining that it followed two principles:

> (1) The school has to be a state school, it has to be always under the supervision of the state. (2) The development of education and its success can be achieved only with the full cooperation and with the broadest rights being given to local institutions of the zemstvo or city self-government.[11]

The management of the elementary educational system would be given to educational councils, composed of locally elected representatives and officials of the Ministry of Education. The Duma committee objected to the original government proposal that the "district nobility leader" preside over the district educational councils. The councils would have extensive rights in the management of the schools. The committee recommended teaching in the native language for the first two years in those localities where Russian was not the children's native tongue, but Russian had to be taught from the very beginning. The use of the native tongue could be extended by petitioning for a special legislative act.[12] The committee recommended that all the schools, including parochial, that benefited from the financial support of the state had to abide by the rules established by the educational councils.

The bill represented an attempt to balance conflicting attitudes and interests and at the same time to move forward in establishing a more efficient and equitable educational system. It was bound to alienate various interest groups, particularly the Right. As on previous occasions when internal reforms were at stake, the Octobrists found themselves cooperating with the Left.

The status of church schools, the teaching of non-Russian languages, and to a lesser degree the presidency of the district councils were the major issues that divided the Duma.

The Right and the Nationalists, supported by the government, objected to the amendments made by the committee in the original government proposal. Some even found faults in the government's bill itself. They demanded a stronger stress on Russian nationalism and a more decisive voice for the clergy and nobility in the management of the educational system.

N. N. L'vov, a Progressist who was once a Kadet, opposed vehemently the subjection of church schools to the supervision of local boards and the Ministry of Education.[13] He considered the proposal harmful to the church, that it would have a ruinous effect on the religious consciousness of the masses and would facilitate the spread of revolutionary ideas.

N. E. Markov went even further. He accused the Octobrists of fostering sedition by introducing the bill.[14] The Octobrists, in his view, were just second-rate Kadets who, by weakening the church, opened the way to revolution and chaos. "You flirt with revolution, and the revolution will destroy you," Markov warned the Octobrists.[15]

The speakers for the government took a stand almost identical to that of the Right and the Nationalists. Ober-prokuror Lukianin of the Holy Synod objected to the inclusion of the parochial schools into the general system. He argued that the church and its educational system were the main repositories of morality and state order in the empire and had to remain autonomous.[16] The minister of education followed the same line, rejecting most of the minor amendments made by the committee.[17]

In the Union itself not everybody was happy with the amendments. M. Ia. Kapustin, following the militant nationalistic line of the previous session, demanded that provisions be made to secure teachers of Russian descent for the minorities. This he demanded "in spite of the attitude of my own faction."[18] The schools in the Russian Empire must be Russian, the Octobrist declared. He was promoting a policy of Russification when he said that "all the peoples living in Russia have to be acquainted with the Russian language, Russian literature, and attracted to the Russian culture. . . . Our major goal and the most important national interest has to be to strengthen Russian nationalism."[19]

It is interesting that peasant back-benchers came out as the strongest supporters of the supervision of parochial schools. They brought personal evidence of the deficiencies and corruption of the church educational system.[20]

The most detailed defense of the amendments and the most incisive attack against the Right was delivered by Fon-Anrep.[21] Only a few months before, when he defended the Finnish bill, he was the hope of the Great Russian chauvinists; now he became the main target of their attack, which reminded him of his German ancestry. Fon-Anrep retorted that the Right did not have a single creative idea but only sterile criticism. "Your behavior," he said, pointing to the Right, "is an insult to all of us."[22] No attempt was made by the committee to harm the Orthodox church, nor its educational system, the Octobrist explained. He rejected with indignation the rightist and Nationalist insinuations that there was lack of patriotism on his part. The scandalous behavior of the entire right wing of the Duma provoked a sharp attack from Fon-Anrep on the corruption of the church, particularly of its higher dignitaries. He contended that the church had lost its hold and moral influence on the people, that the clergy was subservient, lacked moral courage, and was dependent upon the administration. "Have they preached courageously? Could they open their mouths when . . . the people needed their word? Was it not true that the priests of the church were commanded to preach only what they were told? . . . Have not those who dared to speak . . . paid dearly for their courage?"[23] Fon-Anrep, in the best tradition of anticlerical liberalism, accused the clergymen among the rightists and the Nationalists of opposing reform out of self-interest. Never before had an Octobrist expressed in such strong terms his criticism of the stifling effect of the established church hierarchy.

The most violent clashes between the Octobrists and their allies in the nationalistic alliance occurred during the second reading of the bill. The Octobrists voted with the opposition in most cases. Guchkov, as president, reprimanded V. M. Purishkevich in strong terms for his assaults on the Kadets and the Russian intelligentsia.[24] The repeated attempts by the Right and the government to change the committee's amendments and reject the more liberal amendments introduced during the debate were defeated again and again, amid violent verbal exchanges.

Purishkevich reacted with contempt. It could have been a source of despair, he said, but "one could not take the amended bill seriously. . . . We know . . . that the legislation passed by the Duma is being radically changed and rehabilitated by the State Council."[25] There were no grounds for fear, he proclaimed, that the government bill that had been "distorted" by the Octobrists would not be "rehabilitated" by the State Council. This was not far from the truth. All the bills passed by the Duma that contained anything distasteful to the reactionary State Council either bogged down in committee or were so radically changed by the council that there was no possibility of compromise between the Duma's and the council's versions.[26] The Nationalists voted with the Right against the final form of the elementary education bill. Militant nationalism proved to be a stumbling block rather than an asset for the nationalistic coalition.

A companion bill designed to secure money for the maintenance and gradual development of elementary education followed. The Duma had been consistent in its policy of increasing its annual allocations for education, going above the budgetary requirement of the ministry. Thus it added eight million rubles in 1908 and 1909, and ten million in 1910 to the education budget.[27]

On January 24, 1911, the Duma passed a bill on "the designation of allocations for elementary education." The bill proposed to fix an annual addition of ten million rubles, starting with 1912, for the purpose of developing the elementary educational system, until the year 1922, when universal elementary education would be provided in all parts of the empire. V. I. Kovalevskii, the speaker for the Duma's Education Committee, explained that the government objected to the idea of fixing beforehand the annual increment.[28] The government finally accepted the idea of allocation but only of eight instead of ten million rubles. The committee insisted on its original proposal.

Kokovtsov, the finance minister, explained that the government's opposition to the idea of fixing a definite sum was mainly on formalistic grounds,[29] yet announced that the government retreated from its opposition to allocation but insisted on limiting it to eight million rubles. The Duma nevertheless adopted the committee's proposal by an almost unanimous vote.[30]

An unexpected development took place when the bill came up for the third reading. Fon-Anrep, in the name of a group of Octobrists, had proposed adoption of the original government proposal of eight million. The ensuing debate brought on a general assault on the Octobrists, from all parts of the chamber. V. K. Tychinin, a Nationalist, explained that only a small section of the Octobrists in the Education Committee endorsed the agreement between Fon-Anrep and Kokovtsov.[31] The agreement was also rejected by most of the Octobrists, and I. V. Godnev announced that the Budget Committee objected to any changes. Fon-Anrep tried desperately to defend his proposal,[32] holding that the principle of allocation, and not its exact amount, was the most important part of the bill. Fon-Anrep told the Duma that Kokovtsov made it clear that if the Duma would not accept his proposal, the government would not support the bill in the State Council, and thus it would be doomed. A strong rebuttal to the veiled threat from the government revealed by Fon-Anrep came from his own faction. V. A. Kariakin, a back-bencher, said that he could not believe that the government would oppose the bill if its figures were not accepted. It was long overdue, he complained, to do something for the people, "I am not frightened by the challenge presented to the representatives of the people by the minister of finances, that he might put obstacles in the path of realization of the bill because of two million rubles."[33] Fon-Anrep's proposal was defeated by a majority that included members of all the Duma factions.

The defiance apparent in the speeches of many Octobrists during the debate on the bill on financing the development of education in the country indicated a change within the Union. The pendulum was moving again to an attitude more critical of Stolypin's government.

The causes and manifestations of the changing mood among the Octobrists were different, sometimes contradictory. The more politically conscious elements in society were restless and the

Union's leadership became aware of the frustration of the voters in a series of meetings, where many potential voters expressed their disenchantment with the Union's close cooperation with the government.[34] Strikes were becoming more frequent. From the end of 1910, the universities had a series of student and faculty demonstrations that were dealt with harshly by Minister of Education Kasso. He curtailed the autonomy of the universities and fired many teachers. The Octobrists joined the opposition in a request for the authorities to explain their actions.[35]

But, as on previous occasions, the developments that pushed the Union toward a more oppositional attitude came from the Right and the various reactionary cliques in the State Council and court. In spite of the nationalistic line of the Union in the preceding year, the court and the extreme Right did not change their opposition to Stolypin and his cooperation with the Union in the Duma. When the premier's brother, A. A. Stolypin, praised the Octobrists' role and achievements in an article in *Novoe vremia* on January 8, 1911, the tsar sent a note to the premier expressing his reservations about the Octobrists, hinting to his prime minister not to be too closely identified with them.[36]

The second half of the fourth session witnessed a gradual but growing estrangement between the Union and the authorities. Its first expression was the defeat of a minor bill giving the administration the right to intervene in the management of the municipal services of St. Petersburg, to carry out certain municipal public works where and when the elected authorities refused or were incapable of executing them.[37] Stolypin himself tried to convince the Octobrists that the bill did not imply a curtailment of local self-government, but to no avail. The Octobrists voted against the bill and it was defeated.[38]

On January 26, 1911, the Duma passed a resolution, sponsored by the Union and presented by N. V. Savich, condemning the Naval Ministry for negligence that led to the sinking of the destroyer *Slava*. The resolution declared that "this was not an isolated case. It was the outcome of negligence during duty by those in command as well as the result of the entire system of service and management of the Naval Ministry."[39] On February 24, 1911, there followed the rejection of the financial agreement between Fon-Anrep and Kokovtsov on the financing of the elementary education system.

The peak of criticism, and growing oppositional mood, was reached on February 27 during the debate on the budget of the Ministry of the Interior. Criticism and even incisive denunciations of the government's internal policy had become by now almost traditional when the ministry's budget was discussed in the Duma, but in the fourth session there were new elements in the presentations and arguments of the Octobrists. They could hardly be distinguished from those of the Kadets. For the first time, the speeches contained not only criticism but also outrage and despair, not only disillusionment and disappointment but also a feeling of helplessness and signs of militancy.

The official speaker for the Budget Committee, Prince Golitsyn, admitted that his report would not include an analysis of the internal policy. It had been done in previous years, but "the Interior Ministry has done very little concerning the desire expressed by the Budget Committee." [40] The main recommendation made by the committee was a request that the government introduce a bill for the reform of the Police Department. In response to this demand, N. P. Zuev, the director of the Police Department under Assistant Minister of the Interior P. G. Kurlov, gave assurance that Makarov's committee appointed to investigate and propose reforms of the Police Department had already prepared the required bill and it would soon be presented in the Duma. In the fourth session this sounded like a hollow assurance. It was being repeated for the fourth time, but had not yet led to any result.

The most devastating attack on Stolypin's internal policy came from S. I. Shidlovskii. [41] His speech reflected disillusionment and the dawning of the realization that the major goal of the Union—the establishment of *pravovoe gosudarstvo*—was not being accomplished and actually was becoming less and less attainable. In many ways Shidlovskii's speech was an admission of failure by the Octobrists to bring about the "renovation of Russia" by peaceful means.

The trend, he declared, was more toward administrative lawlessness than toward the implementation of the promised freedoms. He explained: In 1911 Russia was undergoing a new phase in its internal development; the first phase had been a gradual absorption of the Ministry of the Interior by the Police Department; at the present stage the cabinet was being systematically transformed by the

Ministry of the Interior and Russia was actually becoming a police state. He went on: Departments that by definition had nothing to do with the police revealed an increasing tendency to use police methods; the primary cause for this development was the use of all kinds of extraordinary regulations that freed the different ministries from the need to follow normal legal procedures, which in fact enabled the administration to disregard any law. For the fourth time in the Third Duma, one could hear the same arguments, the same complaints—a rather sad spectacle—but this time, Shidlovskii said, speaking for the Octobrists,

> . . . the troubles [which the government used to justify the continued use of extraordinary regulations] were to a great extent the result of the tendency of the Ministry of the Interior to find sedition where there was none, and the troubles could in no way justify the use of extraordinary regulations.[42]

Shidlovskii's words were unequivocal; he held that the use of the extraordinary regulations destroyed the faith and confidence of the people in law and government, that the ordinary citizen stood bewildered and helpless, not knowing what the law was nor why it was abused by the authorities, that he was disappointed that the Octobrists had failed to accomplish their major goal (the establishment of a regime of law and order, where citizens would be safe from both revolutionary anarchy and administrative abuse), and that although revolutionary anarchy had been curbed, the life of the Russian citizen remained insecure, unpredictable, and without the protection of consistent law.

Shidlovskii's speech was of special interest because it was well documented, represented the mood of many Octobrists and their provincial constituencies, and provided ample evidence of the disintegration of the state mechanism, recorded already by the same speaker and others in 1908. By 1911 the conclusions had become even more ominous: the promises of the manifesto were not realized, but what was even more disturbing was that "normal life became utterly impossible for the orderly citizen."[43] Frequently the question was put: "Who is the first revolutionary in Russia?" and the answer given was "the administration!"[44]

Shidlovskii's speech continued, describing in emotional terms the agonizing dilemmas faced by Octobrism. Six years after the promulgation of the October Manifesto and in the fourth year of the existence of the Third Duma, the Union of October 17 had made little progress toward achieving its major goals. Yet there was no change in the basic tactic. An Octobrist would criticize the policy of the government, admonish the administration, but would remain on the side of the established authorities, the official government. Shidlovskii defended the Union's cooperation with the authorities; as far as he was concerned, there was not yet an alternative course.

> I could criticize, reject, or oppose the government's policy, using any legal means at my disposal. I could argue and vote against it. But there is no reason to condemn me for my willingness to cooperate with the present government. . . . We do not give our moral support to the repression practiced by the authorities, yet we consider it our duty to work together with the government. Had we refused to do so we would have been lacking in the fulfillment of our obligations to the country.[45]

Shidlovskii's speech was one of the clearest statements of policy made by the Octobrists in the Third Duma because it prescribed the boundaries of political maneuvering that the Union set for itself. The Octobrists were not the government's party; in many instances they were a source of embarrassment rather than an asset for Stolypin, yet there was no doubt as to their position between the authorities and the forces who tried to change radically the political structure of the country. In the Russia of 1911, the Octobrists were in a powerless and thankless position, with only a slight chance to succeed, and many of them knew it.

A mood of frustration and powerlessness settled upon the Duma, particularly on the Octobrists. It came at a time when the reactionary forces were preparing a new assault on Stolypin and the representative regime, and it soon became apparent that a real battle had to be waged to guard the modest constitutional achievements. Further progress was almost a lost cause. The rightists in the Duma conducted a vicious campaign of slander against the Union, assuming the dual role of the Union's accusers and defenders of the national-historical interests of Russia. In the context of heightened nationalistic tensions in the Duma, nationalistic sensitivities in

court, and the international situation, it was extremely difficult to
combat their obstructionist tactics. Added to this was the "legislative strike" of the State Council, which systematically distorted or
simply avoided all the bills passed by the Duma that meant any
meaningful change or reform. When Purishkevich threatened the
Duma that the State Council would change the education bill that
was not palatable to the extreme Right, he merely recorded the
obvious—the State Council and the extreme Right in the Duma
presented a threat not only to fruitful legislative work, but also to
the entire representative regime.

The anticonstitutional elements, whose centers of power were
the State Council and the court cliques, directed their attack against
Stolypin's system, his cooperation with the Duma, and particularly
his cooperation with the Octobrists. Guchkov, upon accepting office
as Duma president on December 20, 1910, had warned the State Council, predicting a decisive clash between it and the Duma, because
the State Council fought the Duma and government alike.[46] There
was a natural identity of interests between Stolypin and the Union,
and between Stolypin and the cause of Russian constitutionalism
on this issue. But when the conflict occurred, the shifting of emphasis revealed Stolypin in opposition to the Octobrists, who found
themselves, together with the State Council, defending constitutional principles.

8

The Crisis Over the
Western Zemstvo Bill and
Its Aftermath

On March 4, 1911, the State Council rejected by a vote of 92 to 68 the clause on separate national curiae in the western zemstvo bill. The vote represented a direct assault on Stolypin and his Duma allies, the Octobrists. The western zemstvo bill was the symbol of Stolypin's cooperation with the Union's leadership and its rejection precipitated the so-called zemstvo crisis, whose causes can be found in the political alignments and intrigues in the council and the court. The crisis had grave implications for the viability and reality of the constitutional regime in Russia. It had far-reaching repercussions on the relations between Stolypin and the Duma, the government, and the Union. Furthermore, the crisis resulted in the collapse of the nationalistic coalition initiated by Stolypin and Guchkov and in many ways was the dialectical outcome of the nationalistic course.

Although the formal reason for the crisis was the rejection of what Stolypin considered a major policy line, there were deeper causes. An attempt was made by the reactionary cliques to get rid of Stolypin and his policy of cooperation with the Duma and the Union. Dissatisfaction and bitterness were in the ascent in the Union, because of lack of substantial changes and reforms, yet the real threat to the modest constitutional achievements developed within the circles of the devout supporters of the old regime.

Since the governmental crisis in the spring of 1909, Stolypin's

137

influence in the court was on the decline. Stolypin had been very close to losing his office then, but succeeded in avoiding dismissal by loosening his ties with the Octobrists and by adopting a nationalistic course that would appeal to the court and strengthen a government majority in the Duma. Stolypin's continued support of the Duma raised the fear of the reactionary cliques that he might try to implement the second half of his political formula—reforms. The reactionary forces had regained their self-confidence and some were even thinking of returning to the pre-October regime.

By 1911 it became evident that Stolypin was not moving to implement the constitutional promises of the October Manifesto, but at the same time there were no doubts that he was against a return to the old order. Thus, even before the crisis, Stolypin was isolated from the constitutionalists and reactionaries alike. The zemstvo crisis was the result of Stolypin's decreasing influence in the court, and it became the cause of his eventual defeat.

The strength and influence of the "irresponsible forces" became a major aspect of Russia's political life at the time.[1] Guchkov identified three centers of reaction: the court clique, a group of veteran bureaucrats in the State Council, and the organization of the United Nobility, which had the vocal support of various monarchistic organizations.[2] The power of these backstairs influences grew as the fear of revolution receded. Stolypin retreated before their pressure and by doing so actually weakened his position. The reactionary forces considered Stolypin a greater threat than they thought the revolutionary parties were. They believed in their ability to crush any radical outburst, but feared Stolypin's reform plans.

The right wing of the State Council became the spearhead of reaction and opposition to Stolypin and his policies. Some of the reasons for this attitude have been explained in connection with the first government crisis in 1909. Half of the members of the council, mostly its right wing, were appointed by the tsar; they consistently blocked any bill that had some liberal implications, even when the government stood behind it. The council, packed with seasoned bureaucrats, maintained close connections with the court and the tsar's immediate entourage. The right wing in the council, under the leadership of V. F. Trepov, P. N. Durnovo, and S. Iu. Witte, pretended to be the custodians of the "true Russian principles," which meant pragmatically a negative attitude toward change and reform. Such "patriotism" and personal connections in the court gave the group special leverage with the tsar. Stolypin's genuine attempt to cooperate with the Third Duma was considered by them to be a dangerous game, for, in spite of the "trustworthy" composition of the Third Duma, many in the State Council still regarded it as a hotbed of sedition. The strained relations between the two chambers prevented any meaningful reforms. Even direct government pressure brought little result—particularly true for any bill that tried to implement the October Manifesto. All three bills on religious freedom had been deliberately kept in the State Council's committee, which had tried on several occasions to curtail the rights of the legislative chambers. During the first session it opposed the allocation of money for famine-stricken provinces, holding that such actions were the prerogative of the executive, not the legislature. They also refused to act on the credits for the Naval General Staff, and in the area of international loans.[3] The council made the appropriations whenever the Duma refused or cut the sums requested by the administration. Such was the case with the funds for building a high-seas fleet—the Duma refused for four consecutive years to allocate the credits, but the council agreed to give the funds.

According to the Fundamental Laws, when such disagreements existed between the chambers the government was free to use the funds allocated by either house until an agreement was reached.[4] The government, however, made a special effort to satisfy the council and tailored the bills it promoted to fit the council's taste. Thus it agreed to change the bill on the reform of local courts and re-establish the *volost*, or township, court. The reform of the *volost* that established self-governing rural bodies was stuck in committee, in spite of strong protests by peasant deputies in the Duma. The educational reform bills passed by the Duma had been changed by the council to such an extent that they lost their original purpose.[5] That the council was conducting a "legislative strike" was the impression of many political observers, and some means had to be found to break the impasse.

The Octobrists became increasingly restive when the council blocked or distorted even those few liberal bills that the Duma succeeded in passing. Guchkov included a veiled threat of a coming showdown with the council in his presidential acceptance speech.

In interviews and speeches the Octobrists warned against the dangerous course followed by the council. "Even the October Manifesto would not have been compatible with the spirit of Russian law as Durnovo and company understood them," remarked N. P. Shubinskii in an interview.[6] The Union considered as one of its major objectives the stopping of the obstructive methods used by the council and there were rumors that Guchkov asked the tsar to pack the State Council with Octobrists. "In the Duma the slogan is to assault the council and present it as an obstacle to the liberal initiatives of the Duma," recorded V. A. Bobrinskii in his diary on December 11, 1910.[7] Stolypin was the Union's natural ally against the reactionary policies of the council, but neither he nor his Duma allies wanted a confrontation. During the entire period of the Third Duma, the political initiative was with the reactionary forces.

The seasoned bureaucrats in the State Council sensed that Stolypin's authority was decreasing, particularly in the imperial court, and they seized the western zemstvo bill as a pretext for an attack on Stolypin and the Duma. While it was true that some of their reservations concerning the bill were genuine, it soon became apparent that they had ulterior goals in defeating it. Deliberations over the bill dragged on for months, but Stolypin was confident that eventually it would pass.[8]

The council showed the strongest opposition to the clause lowering the property requirement for the electors and to the establishment of national curiae. The right wing argued that national curiae contradicted the idea of the "unity and indivisibility of the Russian State," that national curiae would encourage separatism among the national minorities, and that lowering the property requirements would lead to democratization of the electoral laws in other areas.[9]

But the important part in the debate was not the one that dealt with the technical aspects of the western zemstvo bill but was the all-out attack on Stolypin's policies. The prime minister was accused of trying to limit the sovereign rights of the tsar and increase the power of a small clique of politicians—the same argument used by the reactionaries in 1909.

Stolypin took the floor three times during the debates in the council. He agreed to lighten the property requirement for small holders and made other minor concessions, but he stressed that the national curiae clause was central to the bill, and the government would insist on its acceptance. M. G. Akimov, State Council president, informed the opposition that the tsar had let him know that he wanted the bill passed. But during a personal interview with V. F. Trepov, the tsar granted the council members the right to vote "according to their conscience."[10] Stolypin was not aware of these developments. Therefore, when the clause on the chambers was rejected on March 4, Stolypin and the entire government were utterly surprised.[11] The following day Stolypin submitted his resignation. For several days it was generally assumed that Nicholas would accept it, but on March 10 it became known that the tsar had agreed to certain conditions made by Stolypin to remain in office. The tsar was convinced by several members of his family to retain the prime minister and to agree to the suspension of Durnovo and Trepov from the State Council. Stolypin had stipulated another condition—to adjourn the chambers for three days—and while the chambers were not in session to use Article 87, the emergency clause, to pass the western zemstvo bill. Probably the major reason the tsar agreed to Stolypin's ultimatum was his reluctance to accept a resignation of his prime minister forced through rejection of his bill by one of the chambers. A. Ia. Avrekh believes that this could have been a dangerous constitutional precedent for tsarism.[12]

Stolypin acted in the belief that his confrontation with the State Council would have the support of the Duma, particularly of the Octobrists. "I assume that the Duma will be satisfied that the law, which it worked out with such care, was saved by Your Majesty," Stolypin remarked to the tsar on winning his conditions.[13] The prime minister thought that the Duma would consider the punishment of the upper chamber a blow to the council's reactionary policies, but he was badly mistaken. The Union, rather than approve the ends, saw the means as completely destructive of all they had sought, and to Stolypin's surprise, opposed his action. It was a personal tragedy for Stolypin and the Octobrists as well as a fatal blow for Russian constitutionalism.

For a long time the Octobrist leadership had been preparing itself for a confrontation with the State Council, whose actions were considered an affront to the constitutional regime as well as a threat to Stolypin, in his close orientation to Octobrism. But when the actual event took place the Octobrists found themselves defending the council against Stolypin.

The nationalistic course, whose aim was to cement the alliance between the Union and the government, had inadvertently revealed the gap that existed between the interpretations of Stolypin and those of the Union about the post-October regime. It also revealed the extent of Stolypin's blindness to some of the basic forces that motivated the Octobrists. The results were far-reaching, although not immediately evident.

The Union's reactions to the crisis underwent several stages: disappointment at Stolypin's resignation, disbelief in his actions, strong criticism and opposition, confusion, retreat, and finally sullen submission. But quite a few of the Octobrists had finally despaired, not just of Stolypin but of any hope of changing the regime and the forces that shaped it.

When it first became known that Stolypin submitted his resignation, despondency pervaded the Duma. The resignation was considered a mortal blow to the constitutional regime, a loss for the cause of reforming Russia by peaceful means, for Stolypin was considered a staunch advocate of the Duma against its enemies in the court.[14] It took only two hours to get more than two hundred signatories to submit the bill again to the Duma, when it became known that Stolypin would retain his post.[15] His conditions for remaining in office had not yet been revealed. Their disclosure shocked the Union, and the Union's reaction came as a complete surprise to the prime minister.

On March 12 the Duma faction sent a delegation to Stolypin to ascertain whether the premier indeed intended to use Article 87 to implement the western zemstvo bill. Stolypin refused to retreat and insisted that his actions were meant to teach a lesson to the State Council and to curb those reactionary currents that wanted to destroy the Duma. There was no intention to harm the Duma, Stolypin explained: the bill would be promulgated in the form in which they passed it.[16] Stolypin was so confident that the Union would support his actions that he had not even informed the Union's leadership of his plans.

Whether out of principle, insult, or of being tired of the role of a docile tool in the hands of the prime minister, the Octobrists reacted sharply. On the same day, the faction's bureau announced that it would vote against the bill if Article 87 were to be used. The faction's meeting on the same day revealed an unprecedented unanimity in denouncing Stolypin's intentions. The bill could be passed through the regular legislative channels, while the use of Article 87 could create a precedent that might be used in the future against the Duma, the Octobrists argued. By a unanimous vote the Union's Duma faction decided to bring to Stolypin's attention its view that the use of Article 87 in the case of the western zemstvo bill and the adjournment of the Duma were illegal acts. The faction warned that it would vote against the bill when it came up again before the Duma and would also introduce an urgent interpellation if Stolypin went ahead with his plans. The Octobrists decided to ask those of their deputies who expressed their intention to resign from the Duma to wait until the next faction meeting. The most important decision was to announce the resignation of Guchkov from the Duma's presidency on the day the bill was promulgated and not to have a Union candidate for that position.[17]

The Duma was adjourned on March 12; on March 14, when the bill was promulgated, Guchkov resigned, despite Stolypin's pleas not to do so. What prompted the leader of the Union to take this action? It is clear from Guchkov's actions and statements, during the crisis and after, that Stolypin's behavior was not the only reason. Even before the crisis Guchkov felt that his goals when accepting the Duma presidency were unattainable. In his personal audiences, Guchkov only alienated the tsar; his renewed alliance with Stolypin had not brought the Union closer to achieving its goals; his party was in complete disarray. The crisis convinced Guchkov that the forces opposing change were stronger than he imagined, and that as Duma president he was least effective in moving the country toward "peaceful renovation." Guchkov was also personally insulted that Stolypin had not considered it necessary to inform him of his intended moves. Mutual trust was a prerequisite to fulfilling his role as an "intermediator" between the Duma and the government, and Stolypin destroyed such trust by his actions. Explaining many years later the reasons for his resignation, Guchkov said that Stolypin had violated the constitution, undermining

the state order that he tried to defend against its enemies.[18] By
his actions during the zemstvo crisis Stolypin alienated all the
political forces in the land.

> Regardless of my good relations with Stolypin, I had
> to move away from him by some act of protest against
> his antiparliamentary action. This was particularly nec-
> essary to prevent the impression that I and the Octobrist
> party . . . who fully supported Stolypin's bill on the west-
> ern zemstva, were in sympathy with his clearly uncon-
> stitutional action.[19]

Stolypin was surprised when he heard from Guchkov that he intended to resign. The prime minister thought that since the bill
would be passed in the form approved by the Duma, there were no
grounds for grievance. Guchkov pointed out that the prime minister's
actions had discredited the State Council and dealt a mortal blow
to the fledgling constitutional regime, but more important was the
political suicide that the prime minister had committed.[20] One may
question the details of Guchkov's version of his conversation with
Stolypin, but its basic arguments fit their natures well. Stolypin
was a man of action, ready to circumvent constitutional formalities
when they presented an obstacle to achieving what he considered
was right. While he accepted the legislative chambers as a permanent part of Russia's regime, he considered the tsar and his administration the supreme authority in the land. This was the reality of
Russia in 1911. Guchkov considered it his role to ensure that the
tender beginnings of Russian constitutionalism would not be brutally shattered. The tragedy of the situation was that Stolypin and
Guchkov cherished compatible goals, yet found themselves opposing each other. "The Octobrists have pleaded in vain with Stolypin
not to act in such an unlawful manner. This is the end of Stolypin:
He had such a convenient party on his side and how foolishly has
he lost it," Bobrinskii recorded in his diary on March 14, 1911.[21]

After the first outraged reaction, a gradual retreat was begun
by the Union. Guchkov stopped in Moscow on his way to the Far
East, where he had decided to investigate "the measures taken by
the local authorities to fight the plague." The Moscow Central Committee decided to support the faction's decision not to vote for the
bill and to introduce an interpellation, but objected to Union mem-

bers resigning from the Duma.[22] A. I. Zvegintsev explained that
Stolypin's actions were "rather unsuitable" but not illegal. Actually, explained the Octobrist, promulgation of the bill in the form
passed by the Duma "proves the primacy of the Duma over the council whenever the Duma and the government are in agreement against
the council."[23]

The faction decided on March 14 to oppose the resignation of
its members from the Duma, and eight members favored supporting
the zemstvo bill, in spite of Stolypin's actions. At the same time
the Moscow Central Committee went a step further—it decided that
Guchkov's resignation was unjustified.[24]

When the Duma reconvened on March 15 it had on its agenda
four urgent interpellations. The Union's interpellation was the most
moderate: It questioned Stolypin's right to use Article 87, since no
emergency was created by the State Council's vote; it pointed out
that Article 87 could be used only when the chambers were not in
session, and since no bill could become a law without passing the
chambers, the use of Article 87 to enact the western zemstvo bill
was illegal. The Union asked the prime minister to explain his reasons and justify his actions.[25] The Octobrist interpellation was
very mild compared to the first outburst of outrage and indignation
expressed by the Union's speakers when Stolypin's actions first
became known and had created complete confusion among the Octobrists. While the left wing demanded drastic and dramatic actions,
such as resignations and the rejection of the budget, the majority
was far from being prepared to follow a consistent oppositional
course. Moscow's Central Committee further dampened the oppositional ardor of the Union's Duma faction and the result was a moderate interpellation. Yet the Octobrist speakers in the Duma were
more militant—another case of discrepancy between the Union's
words and deeds. G. G. Lerkhe declared,

> We have frequently heard in this hall how our laws
> were being violated by the agents of the government, but
> now we are faced with a problem of a different order; we
> deal with a violation of our Fundamental Laws by the
> same prime minister who has on many occasions stated
> that he strived to uproot such violations and to estab-
> lish in Russia a state of law.[26]

S. I. Shidlovskii followed the same line and warned against the anticonstitutional precedent established by Stolypin's actions.[27] In an ironic situation rising out of the peculiarities of Russia's political structure, Shidlovskii defended the legality of the council's vote and held that the government's high-handed treatment of the higher chamber was a threat to the entire representative system. An Octobrist, he yet had to defend the chamber that consistently blocked any innovation by the Duma, and had to remind the Duma that "once you decided to defend your rights, you could not separate yourself from the upper chamber: the violation of its rights is also a violation of yours." [28] There should not have been any doubts about the Union's position as to the use of anticonstitutional means by the prime minister in his struggle with the council, said Shidlovskii, "It is regrettable, awful, and tragic to think . . . that such means, that such a brutal violation of the law, could be expected to receive our endorsement." [29]

Only the Nationalists and parts of the Right objected to the interpellations, maintaining that the tsar, who was unlimited in the exercise of his authority, could do anything and still be within the confines of legality. He was the sovereign—and as such there were no limitations that could prevent him from adjourning the Duma and passing the bill by using Article 87. On March 19 the Interpellations Committee drafted a single interpellation instead of the four adopted by the Duma. It included two questions directed to the prime minister: (1) Did the prime minister know that by his actions concerning the western zemstvo bill, he abused Article 87? (2) What did the prime minister intend to do in order to correct the law? This formula was adopted in the committee by a majority of the Left—Progressists, Kadets, and Octobrists.[30]

When Guchkov resigned as Duma president, the faction decided that no Octobrist would run for the office again, a resolution adopted under the shock and excitement following Stolypin's actions. It took only a few days before the trend changed. Pressure was put on the Duma faction by the Moscow Central Committee and different provincial branches against the resolution, and the Union chapters in the western provinces opposed the Union's decision to vote against the western zemstvo bill when it was again brought before the Duma. Almost unnoticed, the decision not to run any Octobrists for the presidency was shelved. As early as March 17, *Novoe vremia* noted that the problem being discussed in the Union was whether the right-wing Octobrist M. V. Rodzianko should run for office.

Rodzianko's candidacy was opposed vehemently by the left Octo-brists, who still maintained that no Union member should be a can-didate. On March 18, a large majority decided to have a Union can-didate run for office.[31]

The decision meant that the Union was returning to its tradi-tional Duma role. But it was doing it amid continuous internal fric-tion, threats of splits, and mistrust among its component groups, not a new phenomenon in its short history. By now the internal disunity in the Union had become one of the regular features of Russian political life that the aftermath of the zemstvo crisis only accentuated, reminding those who expected a new unity to emerge on the grounds of a consistent and effective opposition to the anti-constitutionality of Stolypin's actions that the majority of the Oc-tobrists were not ready to follow such a line. Because of social background, personal experience, and basic political orientation, the majority of the Union tended to side with the authorities, in spite of having reservations regarding the wisdom, desirability, or legality of their actions.

The left wing in the Union, accepting finally the advantages of having an Octobrist candidate, went to great lengths to prevent the election of Rodzianko and proposed M. M. Alekseenko, head of the Duma Budget Committee. He was chosen by a majority of fifty-eight; only thirty-six voted for Rodzianko. Alekseenko refused to accept the nomination after some pressure had been put on him by the right wing and the Nationalists, who objected strongly to his moderate views on the Jewish problem.[32] Rodzianko was finally nominated by a vote of fifty-eight to twenty-three.[33] A devout mon-archist who served for many years in the army, Rodzianko was sure to continue the former policies of the Union. His election as Duma president signified the defeat of those Octobrists who advocated following a consistent oppositional policy towards Stolypin's gov-ernment. A sizable group of left-wing Octobrists voted against Rodzianko even in the Duma; Guchkov, who had been elected again as the faction's leader, was pointedly absent during the vote.[34]

The Union went through a period of internal turmoil and confu-sion following Stolypin's actions. There were those who called for moderation and caution, while others demanded the following of a consistent oppositional policy. One wing wanted the faction to limit itself to an interpellation, the other insisted on voting against the zemstvo bill. The two wings clashed over the candidacy of

Rodzianko. When he was nominated, four members of the faction's bureau, Fon-Anrep, Shidlovskii, Lerkhe, and Golitsyn, resigned and retracted their resignations only after Guchkov's personal intervention.[35]

Guchkov's behavior during and after the zemstvo crisis was puzzling as well as suggestive of a complication of purposes. At the height of the crisis, when the country was still in turmoil, he had taken off for a prolonged "inspection tour" to the Far East. The Duma, the party, and the entire country underwent a traumatic period but the leader of the major party took a "vacation," remarked P. B. Struve.[36] Guchkov probably left in order to let Rodzianko mend the Union's relations with Stolypin, but this can be only a partial explanation. He had a strong personal sympathy for Stolypin, sharing many of his views and policies, and even after his resignation, Guchkov still thought that Stolypin's government was the best the current regime could produce. He was therefore reluctant to end their friendly relationship and perhaps for that reason disappeared from the center of public attention to facilitate the reconciliation. But at the same time, one gets the impression from Guchkov's actions, during the crisis and in the years to come, that he had lost faith in the future of Stolypin's government, in Stolypin's ability to survive. In his actions there is also the suggestion that the zemstvo crisis reinforced a conviction that the regime was doomed because of those forces that defeated Stolypin. Yet the prime minister remained in office, and the leader of the Union still had some hope left.

On April 27, 1911, Stolypin took the floor to answer the interpellation.[37] He rejected from the beginning the right of the chambers to question the government's legislative initiatives. The chambers had the right to reject or accept government bills but not to supervise its legislative initiatives. Therefore, Stolypin concluded, the bill could be rejected but there was no question of its legitimacy. There were no legal limitations on the use of Article 87, and while the rejection of the western zemstvo bill by the council was considered by the Duma a legitimate act that did not create an emergency situation, the government had an opposite view and therefore was justified in using Article 87. The behavior of the State Council created an intolerable situation, Stolypin contended: they froze all bills passed by the Duma; they defeated major reforms; by rejecting the western zemstvo bill, they forced the gov-

ernment to use Article 87—the misery of the Russian population
living in the western provinces justified the use of emergency legislation. Stolypin, obviously appealing to the nationalistic feelings
of his audience, went on: the Duma was by itself powerless to cope
with the problem; the government selected by the tsar to execute
his will had to take decisive actions, not to evade its responsibility to the nation. The Duma remained unmoved by the speech and
only scattered applause was heard from the benches of the Nationalists.[38]

The Octobrists rejected Stolypin's explanations. P. B. Kamenskii, speaking for the Union, maintained that there was a basic
discrepancy between the government's actions and the Fundamental
Laws.[39] Article 87 gave the government the right to pass emergency
legislation when the chambers were not in session, but what ran-
kled the public was the government's attempt to justify its actions
on formalistic grounds while in essence they were contrary to the
law. An attempt had been made by the government to pursue a sham
legalism, "which signifies a return to our not so old and good memory of the past," Kamenskii charged.[40] Those methods, he continued, violated the basic ideas of law and raised the fear of return to
the old regime; Stolypin's actions demonstrated the fragility of the
legal guaranties. The Octobrist expressed a fear of a return to the
past, but at the same time wondered if the past had ever really disappeared. He warned that actions of the kind taken by Stolypin
might ruin the accord between the chambers and the executive.

Baron Meyendorff followed the same line of argument:[41] The
Duma expected a bona-fide use of Article 87, a use that was certainly absent in this instance—such disregard might ruin completely the remnants of respect for law and legality that still existed
in the country.

The Union's resolution[42] stated that the use of Article 87 to
introduce zemstvo institutions to the six western provinces constituted a violation of the Fundamental Laws, which might become a
harmful precedent for the various branches of the administration
and which put new obstacles in the way of a more fruitful cooperation between the Duma and the government. Therefore the Union
proposed to decide that the prime minister's actions constituted a
violation of Article 87 and his explanations were unsatisfactory.
The only faction that defended Stolypin's actions were the Russian
Nationalists, a party that had been organized by Stolypin and heavily

subsidized by his government. The Union's formula, which was prepared with the Progressists, Kadets, and the Left, was adopted by
a vote of 203 to 82.[43]

The zemstvo crisis was officially over with the adoption of the
Octobrist formula denouncing the prime minister's actions. The
Union did not dare and actually was not willing to go further than
this mild rebuke. The crisis, with some dramatic flavor, brought into
the open the basic weaknesses of Russian constitutionalism. Stolypin, feeling that Russia was not yet ready, socially or education-
ally, had never really accepted a full-fledged representative regime.
He was aware of the real distribution of political power in the country, but would cooperate with the Duma when he thought it would
not be harmful to the government. The Duma had accepted most of
Stolypin's initiatives, although sometimes reluctantly. Much of the
importance of the zemstvo crisis was the focus of public attention
on some of the attitudes, relationships, and forces operating in Russia. It also epitomized Stolypin's attitude towards the representative regime.

The crisis revealed that Russia was going through a period of
change, although the forces of the past were still strong and still
monopolized the political sphere. The crisis involved new as well
as old political forces and behind-the-scene intrigues of veteran
bureaucrats and favorites as well as the clash with newly established institutions. It revealed that the court and the bureaucracy
had changed very little and showed to what extent those who wielded
political power were divorced from Russian public opinion, its mood
and aspirations. The zemstvo crisis laid bare the extent of the continued existence of the autocratic principle, even in the legislative sphere.

One of the basic defects of the "old regime" had been the lack
of any separation between the legislative and executive branches
of government, when an edict or even simple administrative instructions could change established laws. The October Manifesto and
the Fundamental Laws that defined the legislative competence of
the chambers constituted a departure from these practices, and for
the first time a clear distinction was drawn between the legislative
and executive branches. But this distinction had never become a
functioning reality and the zemstvo crisis only proved it once again.

The government had usurped legislative functions, despite the
introduction of the new legislative bodies, for a number of reasons.

The same people who were in the administration before October 1905 remained in those positions after. Many of them had never accepted the new regime as final and considered it only a temporary retreat; others simply could not change long-established practices and traditions. The various constitutional changes that had been introduced while the country was living through a revolution facilitated the infringement on the legislative rights of the chambers because in that period the authorities had been forced to adopt some of the legislative functions, thus establishing a precedent for further encroachments. The use of Article 87 was the most important manifestation of the administration's intervention in the prescribed legislative procedures.

Provisions similar to those of Article 87 that enable a government to take action when the legislatures were not in session exist in every parliamentary system, but in Russia it was used by the government to adopt legislative functions denied it by the Fundamental Laws, making Article 87 a weapon for coercing the chambers (an utter distortion of its purpose). Its use during the zemstvo crisis only continued a tradition that started with the dissolution of the First Duma. Most of the laws passed between the First and Second Duma could not be considered emergency legislation—yet they were passed using Article 87. This was certainly true with the laws concerning Stolypin's land reform. It was obvious that the government used Article 87 as a legislative means to circumvent the regular legislative process.

The Third Duma did nothing to counteract this practice. It passed all the bills that were previously enacted by the government and did nothing to stop legislative initiatives by the executive that distorted the meaning of the Fundamental Laws. During the zemstvo crisis Stolypin developed the theory that the government was not only responsible for the execution of legislation, but in certain cases, for the content of the legislation itself. Since no emergency conditions that could have justified the usage of Article 87 existed at the time, Stolypin contended that the government was the one to decide when and what emergency conditions were, that it had the duty, not just the right, to correct the shortcomings of the legislatures. According to Stolypin, Article 87 was a means of control to be used by the government when it deemed necessary. The Octobrists as well as a majority in both houses understood the dangerous implications for the representative regime in Stolypin's interpretation but did nothing, apart from the mild censure included in the Duma's resolution, to combat this development. In reality, Stolypin's interpretation brought him a new victory; never passed by the Third Duma, the zemstvo bill yet became a functioning law in the western provinces.

The use of Article 87 was the most conspicuous but not the only infringement on the rights of the legislature by the administration. There was a continuous encroachment upon the legislature by "administrative instructions," which actually were the interpretation of the existing law.[44] The confusion between the tsar's ukase and law continued to exist and the Duma took no decisive action to stop it. There were the various extraordinary regulations that had been extended year after year by the tsar's instruction. From 1881, when they were first introduced, until 1905, these regulations were prolonged by a simple decree of the tsar every three years. In 1905 they had been renewed for another year in order to prepare a fundamental reform concerning them, for it was becoming clear that the regulations could not be used indefinitely without passing the newly established legislative process, that is, being ratified by the chambers. Article 83 of the Fundamental Laws stipulated explicitly that any action that implied a limitation of the civil freedoms that had been enacted during an emergency situation had to pass the chambers, but the emergency regulations had been extended by the tsar's decree year after year. The Fundamental Laws gave the tsar control of the armed forces, but the emergency regulations curtailed the chambers' rights even on legislative procedures concerning them. On matters relating to the civil rights of the Orthodox church there was a continuous erosion of the chambers' legislative rights—the Holy Synod, which was in actuality a government department, succeeded in avoiding any meaningful supervision of its management. The Duma, although aware of the illegality of the situation, took no decisive stand against it. Among the major obstacles it faced in opposing this systematic infringement of its rights were the broad budgetary rights given the executive by the Fundamental Laws, and the Third Duma did very little to change that situation.

Following the zemstvo crisis the Duma made a half-hearted attempt to broaden some of its budgetary rights. It could have been pure accident, yet it looked like a challenge to the administration when on May 11, 1911, the Duma adopted a resolution that recognized the urgency of the bill dealing with the broadening of the legislature's budgetary rights. It was a rather insignificant attempt to strengthen its "power of the purse," a traditional weapon of all representative institutions.

The Fundamental Laws were vague and general on the budgetary rights of the Duma. The house of representatives shared, according to the Fundamental Laws, equal rights with the upper house. In addition, a wide range of incomes and expenses was excluded from the jurisdiction of the Duma's Budget Committee. The income from railways, many of them government owned, was managed by a special committee of the Ministry of Finances. The price of liquor, a state monopoly and one of the major sources of its income, was fixed or changed by the Finance Ministry itself. Tariffs and customs duties concerning commercial agreements with foreign countries were also excluded.[45]

The "March regulations" issued on March 8, 1906, defined the Duma's budgetary rights. These regulations placed considerable limitations on the representative assembly in the matter of voting appropriations and determining the sources of revenue,[46] and were designed for a consultative, not a legislative, Duma. It set January 1 as the latest date for the Duma to pass the budget, an empty provision since the government needed no authorization to spend money. One of the most important aspects of the regulations was the exclusion from the competence of the Duma of a whole series of expenditures called the "ironclad" parts of the budget. They included the entire budget of the court, the payment of interest on government loans, and a special ten-million ruble fund. Appropriations based upon existing statutes or upon imperial administrative decrees could not be changed without repealing these statutes by the usual method of legislation. Every department in the government had a certain part of its expenditures shielded this way from the Duma's intervention, expenditures that were protected by "legal titles."[47] Thus only 1 percent of the Holy Synod's budget could be discussed and changed by the Duma; 13 percent of the War Ministry's budget; 19 percent of the Ministry for Foreign Affairs. Almost 47 percent of the 1908 budget was "protected" from the supervision of the Duma.[48]

The government had other means as well to circumvent the Duma's financial purview. Articles 87 and 17 of the Fundamental Laws gave the government the right, in emergency situations, to request financial appropriations without specifying amount, time, or specific reasons. The law required that within a period of two

months after such an appropriation had been made, the government
had to detail the expenditures, yet even this requirement could be
avoided when the government decided that there was a need to keep
such details secret. This was an open door to money without endorsement by the Duma. In addition to all these circumventions, all
matters concerning appropriations or preparations for war had been
explicitly excluded from the jurisdiction of the Duma.

As a result of the vagueness of the regulation on certain matters
as well as of the weakness of the chambers, the Duma's rights had
been encroached upon even further. The way Article 96 was interpreted by the "August regulations" decreased the Duma's rights in
financing the military. State guarantees to private railways had
been granted without passing the Duma. The chamber had also very
limited influence on the conditions of issuing state loans. Of crucial importance were Articles 13 and 14 of the March regulations.
They stipulated that when the chambers disagreed on certain allocations and a committee representing the two houses could not
reach an agreement, the government could use the sum closest
to that included in the budget of the preceding year or any of
the sums allocated by one of the chambers.[49] This provision mark-
edly weakened the bargaining position of the representative chamber, as in the case of the appropriations for the construction of the
dreadnoughts.

Yet even the endorsement of a budget by the Duma did not mean
that the government would implement the Duma's decisions. Article
31 of the Fundamental Laws gave the Duma the right to supervise
the implementation of the budget by receiving an annual report from
the state comptroller, but the article never became a functioning
reality. The comptroller, who had the rank of a government minister,
had been denied the independence needed to fulfill his duties prop-
erly and many areas, such as the court and Holy Synod, were outside
his control. His reports were not made public, thus making his position even less effective.[50]

The Third Duma made no real effort to achieve the "power of the
purse," nor even to use effectively those limited budgetary rights
it had. Unlike the first two dumas, the third annually passed the
budget, and only on rare occasions refused appropriations. Despite
the Octobrists' inclusion of a demand to broaden the Duma's budgetary rights in their program, they did very little to implement it.[51]
When it was brought to the attention of the Duma (usually by the

Kadets), that the government was encroaching even upon its limited budgetary rights, the Octobrists usually tried to avoid the issue. The August regulations and the allocation of funds for the building of the dreadnoughts demonstrated the basic subordination of the legislative branch of the government to the executive.

A bill intended to achieve a broadening of the Duma's budgetary rights had been introduced by the Kadets on November 10, 1907, and was strongly opposed by the government. When the "desirability" of such a bill had been first discussed at the Duma plenum on January 12, 1908, V. N. Kokovtsov, the finance minister, rejected the idea in the strongest terms.[52] Lerkhe proposed in the name of the Union to acknowledge that the March regulations needed certain "corrections." He proposed to transfer the Kadet proposal to the Duma Budget Committee and added that there was no need to rush, nor did the matter deserve highest priority.[53]

When the Duma Budget Committee discussed the Kadets' proposal, the government's representative rejected any proposed changes in the existing laws. He even lodged a protest against the subject having been brought up at all.[54]

Only in the wake of the zemstvo crisis, more than three years after the Kadets' initiative, did the Budget Committee propose some amendments to the March regulations. R. Ia. Ergardt, representing the committee,[55] justified the proposed changes in the light of the experience gained in the previous four years; the bill was intended to clarify as well as to amend some of the shortcomings in the preparation of the budget and in the competence of the Duma. The committee proposed to bring the special ten-million ruble fund under the Duma's budgetary supervision. The committee refused to change Article 9 of the March regulations, which stipulated that the Duma could neither change nor exclude from the budget revenues or expenditures based upon existing laws, edicts, and regulations, but proposed to limit the protected items to those issued before April 23, 1906 (the day the new Fundamental Laws had been published).[56] It also proposed to rescind Article 17, which gave the administration the right to use credits before they passed the Duma, in cases of special urgency. This provision, explained Ergardt, was used by the administration to circumvent the Duma on the crucial issue of the use of credits in cases of disagreement between the Duma and the council. The committee came out with a rather evasive solution. If no agreement could be reached between the chambers, the Duma committee proposed to use the low figure.[57] No attempt had been made by the committee to face the issue occurring when one of the chambers rejected and the other accepted a certain item on the budget. The proposed bill included a whole series of propositions intended to smooth and clarify the Duma deliberations on the budget.

Ergardt made it clear that the committee had no intention of replacing the March regulations by a new budgetary bill. The goals of the committee were limited from the very beginning: to use the experience accumulated in the Duma in order to correct some of the regulation's defects and shortcomings.[58]

Alekseenko, the Octobrist chairman of the Budget Committee, emphasized the limited objectives of the proposed bill,[59] saying that the state comptroller had admitted that the goal of the March regulations had been to "protect the government from the legislative institutions and provide the administration with independent sources."[60] Yet although the Octobrist expert on budgetary problems recognized the true nature and motives behind the existing budgetary laws, he rejected the idea of trying to change them. The proposed bill tried only to "accommodate the regulations to the Fundamental Laws," Alekseenko stressed.[61] The apologetic tone as well as the rather timid amendment to the bill itself reflected helplessness and resignation. The bill could not be considered, by any criteria, a real attempt to strengthen the Duma against executive power, but only demonstrated the subordinate nature of Russia's legislative institutions, as Stolypin's behavior had demonstrated during the zemstvo crisis.

Yet even such an innocuous bill was considered intolerable. Kokovtsov was ready to accept only its minor procedural parts. The government made it clear, he explained, that "it does not exclude the possibility of reviewing the budgetary rates within the limits necessary to improve, change, or refine them, but without touching their essentials and the limits of the rights given the Higher Authority."[62] The finance minister acknowledged that the bill was very moderate compared to the original proposal made by the Kadets, yet it still contained some elements that would be utterly unacceptable to the government.[63]

The bill passed the Duma the way it was prepared by its committee. Kokovtsov took part in the debate during the second and third readings. His tone, condescending to the point of insult, evoked several sharp exchanges, particularly with A. I. Shingarev, a Kadet. The entire bill went through the required three readings in two days (May 11–12, 1911), after a majority vote approved it as urgent. This, more than its spirit or content, testified to the mood of the Duma after the zemstvo crisis. The bill never passed the State Council, strangled by the very body whose rights had been defended by the Duma.[64]

This mild censure and the undertones of defiance that accompanied the passage of the bill amending the budgetary rights of the Duma were the most tangible manifestations of displeasure with Stolypin's actions during the zemstvo crisis, yet the crisis had more lasting effects on many Octobrists. It had brutally shattered many illusions about the real changes in the country after the introduction of the representative institutions. The Octobrists realized how fragile were the constitutional elements and how strongly entrenched were the powers of the past. Many were losing faith in the regime in spite of the mood of "normalcy" that soon asserted itself in the government-Union relations.

In spite of the shock and frustration, the majority of the Octobrists still considered Stolypin the best hope that Russia had. Rodzianko was elected Duma president with the Nationalists' and Stolypin's support, and after some wavering the nationalistic coalition agreed on a new series of "nationalistic bills."[65] To complete the reconciliation, the Union's leadership agreed to an earlier adjournment of the Duma to prevent the danger of a clash over the western zemstvo bill, which was introduced on the last day of the fourth session. The authorities intended to implement the bill during the vacation and thus face the fifth session with an accomplished fact. The Octobrists made no attempt to oppose those obvious tactics.

But the Octobrists who still clung to Stolypin as the best man, one who might still follow the road of peaceful renovation, cherished "senseless dreams." The zemstvo crisis, in spite of his apparent victory, actually signified the end of Stolypin's political career. By his actions during the crisis he had isolated himself from the major political forces in the country: the tsar, the two chambers, and public opinion. Stolypin's dismissal by the tsar was only a matter of time—Nicholas never forgot nor forgave his prime minister's ultimatum, and looked for an opportunity to get rid of him. The reactionary forces that triggered the crisis were only too willing to nourish Nicholas' displeasure with Stolypin. His assassination on September 1, 1911, killed him physically; politically he had been dead since the zemstvo crisis. Stolypin's assassination and the circumstances surrounding it signified for the Union an end of an era, of great hopes and faith in the man that was trying to renovate Russia. For many Octobrists Stolypin's death was a confirmation of the defeat of their hopes.

9

The Union in the Fifth Session:
Between Great Russian Nationalism
and Opposition

The Union of October 17 entered a new phase after the assassination of Stolypin. During the last session of the Third Duma there were two concomitant developments among the Octobrists. This was a period of the strongest expression of militant Great Russian nationalism in the Union, occasionally with anti-Semitic undertones, and at the same time, the strongest manifestation of opposition. Neither of these phenomena was new, nor were they contradictory, but in a way they supplemented each other and were inspired by the same sources. A growing sense of disillusionment with the existing regime, hurt national pride, and a feeling of helplessness in the struggle to work within the system as it was constituted and manned were among the causes that brought the Union toward more outspoken opposition. For the first time Octobrists attacked the regime and its most prominent functionaries, stopping short of a direct attack on tsarism itself. It was an expression of indignant nationalism. Belonging to the Russian Empire was felt by many Octobrists to be a humiliation, whether at home or abroad.

These feelings and attitudes were not shared by the entire faction. Because the Union had never been a true political party, but had in its ranks contradictory and conflicting personalities and trends, it had always been more a coalition of people with diverse political orientations that were united by a common goal of preventing a violent revolution and preserving the established socioeconomic order. It was a coalition that tried to ensure the Russian citizen a measure of freedom and security denied him by the pre-October regime, but apart from these general goals, the Union was divided on almost every major issue. As in the past, the main spokesmen of the oppositional trend in the last session of the Third Duma came from the left wing of the Union, as well as from Guchkov, who again had become the official leader of the faction and its major speaker. But opposition was not confined to Guchkov and the left wing—loss of faith in the regime was spreading among the faction's rank and file.

This growing loss of faith may be traced to tsarism itself and the influences behind the throne that shaped the destiny of the country. It was a gradual disillusionment that had been accelerated by the zemstvo crisis and heightened by the assassination of Stolypin, one that extended far beyond the Union's left wing. The combination of militant Great Russian nationalism and increasing criticism of the regime was found in other circles of Russian society, not only among the Octobrists. It was present even in the so-called patriotic press in the provinces and the capitals.[1]

Apart from tsarism itself, two other factors account for this development of nationalism and criticism. Growing international tensions and frequent crises that threatened to become major wars led to an accelerated arms and naval race. From the time of the annexation of Bosnia-Herzegovina in 1908 the possibility of war with Austria and Germany had been present, and the tensions in the Balkan peninsula, which was of special concern to Russian nationalists, were a constant reminder that Russia had to be ready for war. The disintegration of China and its possible partition among the major powers was a second issue that had interest for Russian nationalists, but it was an issue beclouded by the rankling memory of the humiliating defeat by Japan. The Russian nationalist had the feeling that his country was doing very little in the way of preparing itself for a major crisis, and an even more frightening suspicion was dawning: that it was sliding backwards. There was a growing awareness that the "visible" government was not in control, that the fate of the country was being shaped and decided by "irresponsible forces." The tsar, the incarnation of authority and the source of political power in the empire, was not his own master. The idea that a regime that provided the backing for activities destructive to Russia as a nation had to be radically changed had not yet occurred to many Russian nationalists. In 1911 they confined their main efforts to the elimination of forces behind the scenes that were considered detrimental to Russia and the tsar.

Disillusionment and loss of faith found their strongest expression in Guchkov. His prestige in the Union had suffered some damage, but he was still Octobrism's major spokesman, and although his conclusions had the special mark of his personality, they also largely represented the mood of the Union. Stolypin's death had a profound influence on Guchkov's attitude toward the government and the regime, but it took him some time to express this change publicly. "With the disappearance of Stolypin one could sense a sigh of relief among the dignitaries in court circles," recalled Guchkov in 1917. "With him disappeared the man whose presence reminded them of given promises and of future-threatening miseries."[2] With Stolypin's death the influence of "irresponsible forces" became more evident and more provoking for the Russian nationalist.

> But even before the physical death of Stolypin, I had lost faith in the possibility of a peaceful evolution of Russia. As Stolypin was gradually dying politically it became increasingly clear to me that Russia would be forced . . . to follow a different road—the road of a violent change that would sever the ties with the past, that Russia would drift along the shoreless seas of political and social searching, without compass or rudder.[3]

In 1912, despite the feeling of impending disaster, the leader and founder of Octobrism had not yet made up his mind to fight the regime. Guchkov still hoped to prevent the disaster. He decided to try, during the fifth session, to neutralize those forces that pushed the monarchy toward its demise. "When there became clear to me the fatal role of the irresponsible forces, centered mainly in the court, I decided that the Duma and Russian society would have to . . . assault them directly."[4] The new government, under the premiership of V. N. Kokovtsov, the former finance minister, had lost control of the situation, Guchkov claimed, and only followed the whims of others. Guchkov's views were shared by many Octobrists, although they did not all express them with the same vehemence and consistency.

The feelings of despair, disillusionment, and opposition prevalent during the fifth session of the Third Duma had their basis in the atmosphere and behavior of the highest center of political power in the empire—the court. While Stolypin had tried to carry out a comprehensive plan of reform and adapt himself or at least cooper-

ate with the newly established constitutional institutions in the
country, his successor was, above all, an old-style bureaucrat who
had spent most of his life in the service of the autocratic regime.
Stolypin's personality gave the semblance of a cabinet and a coordinated policy to his government. Kokovtsov could not fulfill that
function. Each minister reported directly to the tsar, without previously consulting with the titular prime minister. It meant a return
to the premanifesto situation, when policies had been decided between the tsar and each of his ministers, without following a sus-
tained policy.

When Kokovtsov was appointed to his post it was made clear to
him that his line had to be different from that of his predecessor.
On October 2, 1911, the tsarina remarked to the new prime minister:
"for those who are not with us today, it is because they had fulfilled
their role. . . . He had nothing more to accomplish. . . . I am convinced that Stolypin died to make room for you, and that it is for the
good of Russia."[5] The tsar and the people who influenced him
wanted a prime minister who would be purely a bureaucrat, who
would disengage from those troublesome parties that occasionally
upset the "Autocrat of all Russia." Alexandra, whose influence on
her weak-willed husband was by then no longer secret, was explicit:

> We hope that you would never follow those awful polit-
> ical parties, whose only dream is to gain power and sub-
> jugate the government to their will. . . . *Do not seek the*
> *support of the political parties: They are so unimpor-*
> *tant. Rely only on the faith of the Sovereign*[6] [italics
> added].

It is apparent that the prevailing attitudes and actions in the
court after Stolypin's death presaged those of 1916–17. The disintegration of the governmental structure, already evident at the time
of Stolypin, became more obvious. It had started in the provinces
and now was attacking the center of power—the capital and the
court. Dubious characters became more firmly entrenched; there
was a growing alienation between the tsar and the people; reaction
dominated the entire governmental structure. "Its goal was to curtail
and diminish the importance of the people's representatives," Duma
President M. V. Rodzianko contended,[7] and Kokovtsov agreed: "Inside the closest circle surrounding the sovereign there was a di-
minishing meaning given to the government and more frequently and

conspicuously there appeared the personal role of the sovereign." [8] The idea that the tsar was and remained the absolute ruler of the country and who had the unreserved devotion of his people predominated in the court, remarked the premier.

Kokovtsov was primarily a bureaucrat, and never developed a close relationship with the Duma. Stolypin had established friendly personal relationships with the Duma leaders and commanded the respect of many of its members and factions, but Kokovtsov was never popular. His speeches were dry, condescending, and sometimes even insulting. Many still remembered his remark in 1908: "Thank God, we do not have a parliament." Never having been in close contact with the Duma leadership or any of its factions, he was able to assure the tsarina, when he received the nomination, of this fact although he could say that he had tried to work with it. [9]

His lack of rapport with the Duma was soon to become one of his major problems. "Kokovtsov's character had a determining influence on his relations with the Duma. As a new institution it tended to overestimate its own value, a fact which Kokovtsov could not bear," noted S. D. Sazonov, the minister for foreign affairs. [10] But Kokovtsov's past behavior and character presented a relatively minor problem; what affected him now was that he was caught between two opposing trends—the tsar and the court cliques were reverting more and more toward old-style absolutism—the Duma was becoming more restless and oppositional. The approaching elections to the Fourth Duma did not make things easier.

The immediate problems faced by Kokovtsov with the Duma were the circumstances and suspicions raised by Stolypin's assassination, and the upsurge of a militant nationalism and anti-Semitism among the traditional supporters of the government. The deputies knew that the new prime minister had different views of the national minorities than his predecessor, and there were uncertainties and fears among them until his policies were revealed. Kokovtsov anticipated with uneasy feelings the coming of the Duma's fifth session.

Stolypin's assassination had been considered by many Octobrists a serious setback, by some even as the loss of a last chance to move Russia in the desired direction. After the event, Guchkov recalled, "I had for the first time unfriendly feelings toward the sovereign." [11] The circumstances surrounding the death as well as

the tsar not deigning to participate in Stolypin's funeral added to
this feeling.

The immediate reaction of the Union to the assassination was
one of outrage, apprehension, and confusion—all overriden by a
mood of militant nationalism. The opposition, which was associated
in the minds of many Octobrists with antipatriotism and support of
separatist tendencies among the national minorities, came under
fire because Stolypin had symbolized, in spite of many aberrations,
the hope for national recovery and renewal. His murder was first interpreted as an attempt by the opposition and national minorities to
put obstacles on the road to fulfillment of the nation's goals and
resulted in an intensification of nationalistic manifestations, beginning with the swift passage of the bills on Finland. For a while
it appeared that the coalition of the first session had regained its
vigor, for the debates were characterized by virulent attacks on the
Kadets and the Left, and by frequent anti-Semitic outbursts. The
fact that Stolypin's assassin was a Socialist Revolutionary and a
Jew was used by the Right and the Octobrists to the utmost.

In an official statement by the Union's Central Committee following Stolypin's death the opposition was accused of fomenting
hatred and provoking murder.

> The time has arrived for every citizen to stop his
> apathy . . . and to engage in an open struggle with the
> opposition. . . . Only the coordinated effort of all the
> people who stand for order and freedom can rescue Rus-
> sia from the fate prepared for her by the leftist parties.[12]

The surge of nationalism following Stolypin's death and the uncertainties surrounding the "patriotism" of his successor strengthened the ties between the Union and the Nationalists.[13] The Octobrists emphasized their loyalty to the principles of Russian
nationalism, while the Nationalists assured the Union that they
supported the principles of the representative regime. On the sixth
anniversary of the October Manifesto the Nationalists were the Union's guests of honor. Both sides, in flamboyant speeches, emphasized their past cooperation and common aspirations for the future,[14]
but it was more an expression of common fears than of newly found
love.

The opposition and the Jews provided only one target for the
allies. The way Stolypin was assassinated, the connection of his

murderer with the secret police, and his quick trial and execution raised many questions among the Octobrists that were voiced by Guchkov in a closed meeting of the Union's Central Committee. The Union and the Nationalists demanded that I. G. Shcheglovitov, the minister of justice, thoroughly investigate the rumors, and hinted that they were suspicious that attempts were being made to hush up the entire affair. The Duma threatened to intervene if the government did not reveal the entire truth to the public.[15]

The urgent interpellation introduced by the Octobrists and Nationalists implied that there was, at the least, criminal negligence on the part of the secret services,[16] and that it was of utmost importance to reveal the truth behind the murder and to punish those who were responsible, regardless of their position. The minister of the interior was asked: (1) whether he knew of any illegal actions by "persons in responsible positions" that led to the assassination; (2) if the minister indeed had such information, what he intended to do in order to bring those people to court; (3) what measures by way of reorganization of the secret services would be taken by the minister to prevent such future occurrences.

Guchkov was the only speaker for the Union.[17] He asserted that Stolypin's murder demonstrated once again the deep malaise that plagued Russia. His denunciation of terrorism was not new, nor was it the major message of his speech—his main demand was that the government prove its courage by exposing the truth about the assassination, even if the task were dangerous.

A. A. Makarov, the new minister of the interior, expressed his sympathy for the motives that prompted the Octobrist interpellation.[18] He justified the use of double agents, following the line taken by Stolypin during the Azef affair in 1909—that any means used to defend the security of the state was justified. Like his predecessor, he avoided the moral issue of such tactics, as well as the actual dangers involved as far as the safety of the state and the relationships of the authorities with the political parties were concerned. Makarov promised, in vague terms, to take the necessary steps to discover and bring to court all those responsible or connected with the assassination. A senatorial investigation, headed by M. I. Trusevich, was appointed to look into the matter. As to the demand to reform the secret services, Makarov was evasive: under the guise of security considerations he refused to deal with the subject at all.

Guchkov's response to Makarov revealed his changing attitude toward those in authority after Stolypin's assassination, and the frequent and stormy applause from the Octobrist benches indicated that he was not speaking only for himself. Guchkov posed two crucial questions for clarification: Who was really responsible for the assassination and what were the system and institutions that enabled him to commit the crime? [19] Becoming even more explicit, Guchkov then asked: Was the assassination merely an accident, a result of negligence of certain people, "or behind it is there something worse, a conscious connivance, a desire to get rid of a man whose presence had become undesirable?" [20] The question carried embarrassing connotations to Kokovtsov, in view of his conversation with the tsarina following Stolypin's murder. Only a court of law could give an unequivocal answer to the "tormenting" questions raised, Guchkov continued, government investigations or declarations would not satisfy the national consciousness. He rejected the argument that a public court would jeopardize the security of the state, remarking that such an excuse was an attempt to refrain from compromising personalities that had great influence. "The people we are talking about are dangerous and very influential. Among them one may even find some who participated in person. These people know too much, it is dangerous to infuriate them, they are capable of doing anything . . . even treason." [21] Although the Octobrist leader mentioned no names, it appeared as if everyone knew that personalities of high standing were implicated in the assassination. Guchkov went beyond the immediate problem of Stolypin's death and directly attacked those who wielded political power in the empire, accusing them of leading Russia to disaster. "If such are these men, then in whose hands do you leave the vital interests of Russia . . . whose guardians you were called to be?" He was greeted with prolonged applause from his own faction. [22]

Although Guchkov criticized in detail the structure and personalities of the secret services, his remarks on the "personalities behind the scenes" were of greater importance because they reflected the general loss of faith in the system that accommodated such personalities.

> If the government does not investigate thoroughly the
> forces behind the assassination, if it takes only half-
> measures, then everything will remain as before and as

before the power will remain in captivity of its servants. . . . If you will follow this road, you are doomed.[23]

On November 11, 1911, the Duma adopted an Octobrist-Nation-
alist formula on the interpellation concerning the assassination of
Stolypin. It contained very little of the strong language and insinuations expressed during the debate. Only an expert could distinguish in its phrasing the vestige of reservation or lingering suspicion. It stated that the Duma,

> after hearing the explanations by the minister of the in-
> terior and expressing its confidence that the government
> would bring to the court of justice those people in re-
> sponsible positions whose guilt would be ascertained
> in connection with the murder of the prime minister, and
> that it would without any further delay start a radical re-
> organization of the political police with the aim of sub-
> ordinating its activities in the provinces to the gover-
> nors, city-heads and procurators, the Duma decides to
> pass to the agenda.[24]

Despite its relative mildness, the formula did not contain an
expression of "satisfaction" with the government's explanations,
phraseology usually included in formulas concerning interpellations
on government actions. It was adopted by a vote of 141 to 101.[25]
The Octobrists were left with the uncomfortable feeling that
behind Stolypin's assassination stood dark forces manipulating the
destinies of the Russian Empire to their private benefit, and furthermore that the few high-ranking police officials who were forced to
resign from service were sacrificed in order to divert public attention
from the real culprits. P. G. Kurlov, chief of the Police Department
and the man directly responsible for the security arrangements in
Kiev where the assassination took place, maintained that no real
attempt had been made to ascertain the assassin's motives. He
expressed doubt that the revolutionary movement was behind the
assassination. The brunt of the investigation was directed against
the people who were responsible for the security arrangements,
and Kurlov implied that no effort was made to find out what stood
behind the assassination or what motivated it.[26] The obscurities
surrounding the murder of Stolypin undermined the faith of many
in the regime.

The nationalistic and anti-Semitic feelings excited by Stolypin's murder extended further than the capital. In the Duma, the Octobrists and the Nationalists declared that their aim was to continue to implement the "national legacy" of the late prime minister. Their doubts about the future of the nationalistic course of the new prime minister lay in his record when Stolypin was alive, and he had then "appeared as the only consistent opponent of the more extreme manifestations of the nationalistic line."[27] And now Kokovtsov opposed the curtailment of the constitutional rights of Finland as well as opposing Stolypin's forceful policies in the borderlands. He thought that the artificial intensification of national tensions within the Russian Empire was counterproductive to the peaceful development of its economy and its position in the international credit market. Yet, in spite of the differences of opinion with his predecessor, Kokovtsov followed the nationalistic course. He had been aware that the Union and the Nationalists intended to "test" him and decided to follow Stolypin's line in the case of Finland.[28] Kokovtsov's only success in stemming the nationalistic wave was his prevention of the outburst of anti-Jewish pogroms following the assassination. The irony of the situation was that one of the few men who opposed Stolypin's militant Great Russian nationalism decided to continue Stolypin's course, and thus defended bills that he personally considered harmful for the empire.

The first bill on Finland was introduced in the Duma on October 29, 1911. It dealt with "payments by the Finnish treasury to the imperial treasury in exchange for personal military service of the Finnish citizens." This was the first bill implementing the general law passed by the Duma that gave the imperial institutions the right to legislate on matters concerning Finland and the rest of the empire. It provided for a proportionate contribution by the Finnish treasury to the defense expenses of the empire, as well as a provision that the Finnish contribution would be lowered if Finns would participate in the armed forces of the empire.[29] The bill "on equalizing the rights of Russian citizens living in Finland with the rights enjoyed by Finns" was the second Finnish bill and was introduced in the Duma on the same day.

The debate over the two Finnish bills became a test of Kokovtsov's policy toward the national minorities in the empire. His comments on the subject had been eagerly anticipated by the nationalistic center and were bound to affect the attitude of the Union to the new prime minister.

His speech, which included the statement "Finland constitutes an integral and inalienable part of the indivisible Russian state," dispelled the fears of the nationalists by the promise it contained to continue his predecessor's course.[30] The time had arrived, he went on, to abolish the special privileges enjoyed by the Finns and end the discrimination against Russians living in Finland; if the Finns nourished any hopes of preserving their privileges as a result of the assassination of the late prime minister, they were manifestly mistaken,[31] for both public opinion in Russia and the empire's supreme authority did not intend to deviate from the line followed by Stolypin. Kokovtsov admitted that he was aware of the fears that prevailed among the nationalists that his ascent to power might presage a change,

> but . . . on matters concerning the vital interests of the state, on matters concerning Finland and being important for our entire state, on matters that determine the integrity and unity of the state, its glory and might, on all matters basic for the satisfaction of the vital needs of the Russian people, *there could be no vacillations nor disagreements between successor and his predecessor*[32] [italics added].

He promised, to the great delight of the apprehensive nationalists of the Union and the Right, that "the successor of the late State Secretary Stolypin, maybe with less power and skill, but with the same devotion, will defend the proposed projects."[33]

Kokovtsov's speech was received with surprised enthusiasm, and was given a long-standing ovation by the Octobrists and their allies to the right. Guchkov called it "A great day. The nationalistic center in the Duma has been restored and will be able to continue its national task as before." It would stop finally the rumors of lack of patriotic ardor in the new prime minister. Other Octobrist leaders reacted in the same way. Kokovtsov had "passed" his test in patriotism.[34]

The Octobrists were delighted. Their expert on Finland, Count E. P. Bennigsen, stated that he and his friends

> listened with a feeling of deep satisfaction to the prime

minister's speech. He has dispelled what has tortured many of us in the last month and a half. He has clarified what many of us wanted to be elucidated. Now there is no ground for our doubts. We know that the government's policy will remain the same. [35]

He added a warning:

> The policy of a Russian government could not be a different one. We can be assured that at present the Russian people will not betray the Russian borderland policy.... . Stolypin is not with us anymore, but his spirit is alive in this hall, the spirit of healthy nationalism.[36]

A militant Great Russian nationalism characterized the discussion of the second Finnish bill, which was to ensure equal rights for Russian citizens living in Finland. The leitmotiv was an unrestricted attack on the opposition, particularly the Kadets, who defended the constitutional rights of the Finns.

The bill was designed only to rectify an injustice that "converted the victors of 1808 into the vanquished of 1911," stated Bennigsen.[37] When the Octobrist tried to explain how and why this process took place, he inadvertently reached some conclusions that could have had ominous implications for the relations of tsarism and popular nationalism:

> There were times when the government's policy had been determined by a few dignitaries, when Russia's vital interests depended upon the whims of one state servant or another. . . . *But these times have passed. At present the national interests became the concern of the entire Russian people*[38] [italics added].

Bennigsen was saying in essence that Russia's national interests could not be determined any longer by a small group of bureaucrats. Russian nationalism was intimately connected with the creation of institutions that gave the Russian Empire the possibility to express its national aspirations and its views on Russia's national interests.

Whether the Octobrist realized it or not, there was danger for the future of autocracy in his use of popular nationalism. As presented by Bennigsen, nationalism was connected with the idea of

constitutionalism and representative institutions. National consciousness rejected the idea that its vital interest could or would
be decided by the whims of a small clique of dignitaries. Its natural
tendency would be to bring about a more decisive participation of
the people in shaping its national destiny, a most hazardous implication for Nicholas II.

To demonstrate the support of the entire faction for the Finnish
bill, the Union chose D. A. Leonov, a left-wing Octobrist, to represent it in the discussion.[39] That Russians were being discriminated
against in Finland "is a humiliation for a great nation such as ours,"
stated Leonov,[40] who then demanded that the bill include special
provisions to punish those Finns who actively or passively opposed
its implementation. N. I. Antonov, another Octobrist, rejected Kadet
Maklakov's argument that the bill was ill-conceived since the Duma's committee devoted only one meeting to its discussion. Antonov
accused the Kadets of being unpatriotic, of encouraging active
Finnish opposition to the implementation of the bill by their behavior and speeches.[41]

The opposition's efforts to delay the passage of the Finnish
bills were defeated by the nationalist majority of the center and the
Right. The debate was a series of acrimonious attacks on the opposition, reminiscent of the first session of the Third Duma. The
Kadets and the Left were accused of being unpatriotic, of fomenting
sedition and treason, and their opposition was attributed to their
intention of preserving Finland as a base and refuge for revolutionary activities. The Kadets were reminded by V. N. Shubinskii that
the Viborg Manifesto was published in Finland,[42] but Guchkov was
even more virulent, accusing the Kadets of responsibility for the
defeat in the war against Japan. The Russian army had to fight on
two fronts in 1905, declared the leader of the Union, "against an
honest opponent—the Japanese—and against those dishonest
men . . . who fomented sedition in the rear, who had corrupted and
brought discord and despair into the army, against those who prevented our victory."[43]

The nationalist trend that had its inception following the Russo-Japanese War of 1905 had, in Stolypin's assassination, an impetus for a dramatic upsurge. Its development may not be attributed
only to manipulation by tsarism and various interest groups, for it
coincided also with the establishment of representative institutions
and with the revolutionary activities in 1905–7 that took place in

the non-Russian borderlands and were connected with local separatist movements. The opposition parties, from the Kadets to the
Left, had espoused a program of granting at least some form of autonomy to the national minorities, which gave a special acuteness to
the political struggles in the Duma. The distinction between those
who favored a nationalistic line and those who favored a more len-
ient and understanding policy toward the minorities' peculiarities
and aspirations on many occasions overshadowed social or ideological differences. Anti-Semitism played an important part in the manifestations of Great Russian chauvinism at the time. It was a major
component of the nationalistic ideology of the Right and the Nationalists, but was found even among the Octobrists. A group of Octobrists organized an Association for the Defense of Russia's Interests with a particular stress on defense against "Jewish violence." [44]
A group of industrialists led by Guchkov demanded that the customs
duties on American cotton be doubled to counteract American pressure to grant its Jewish citizens, while they were in Russia, the
same rights given to other American citizens. [45]
    Anti-Semitism, as one facet of Great Russian nationalism, was
expressed in the Duma on many occasions. The bill on the establishment of municipal self-government in Poland was introduced in
the Duma on November 23, 1911. It provided for national chambers
in the proposed councils but special arrangements were made to cut
the representation of the Jewish population. "Our faction cannot
accept the idea of granting full equality to the Jews," explained
Bennigsen on that occasion. The bill represented the rather ambiguous position of the Union on the "Jewish question."
    There were important exceptions to the anti-Jewish feelings of
many Union members. As a party, the Union tried to avoid the issue
in its program and actions and was under constant pressure from
the Kadets to take a more liberal stand. But on many occasions the
Octobrists followed the violent anti-Semitism of their nationalistic
allies and did not oppose the anti-Jewish incitement of the Right.
Guchkov's rather "practical" attitude towards the "Jewish problem"
was demonstrated during a conversation with the tsar in the summer
of 1907:

> Personally I have no special liking for the Jews. I find
> that it would have been much better had they not been in
> our country. But they were given to us by history and we

have to establish with them some kind of normal relationship, regardless of our attitude towards them. [46]

He proposed to abolish the pale of settlement and some, but not all, of the other restrictions, but the tsar did not accept his advice. The Octobrists, caught in the classic trap of the moderate, took no positive action either for or against.

The extreme Right and the Nationalists commonly used the Jews as a scapegoat to divert popular attention from real issues and as a banner to rally popular support, and when issues relating to the Jewish problem were raised in the Duma, the Octobrists usually evaded a stand. Thus anti-Jewish clauses were added to almost every bill passed by the Duma. The Jews were excluded from certain ranks in the army; a *numerus clausus* was introduced in the professions and schools, and Jews were denied voting rights in the zemstvo. Although the Right and the Nationalists were the instigators of this policy in the Duma, the Octobrists did not oppose it.

A group of 166 Duma members, including several prominent Octobrists, proposed on February 9, 1911, to draft a bill abolishing the pale of settlement. The proposal was transferred to a committee and was never raised again.[47] The Octobrists were put in an embarrassing situation whenever the opposition proposed to abolish certain restrictions on the Jewish population, since they were afraid that support of such propositions would compromise their patriotism in the eyes of allies on the right. But occasionally the Octobrists did reject the Right's crude anti-Semitism: many expressed disgust at an interpellation "on the use of Christian blood for Jewish ritual purposes in connection with the murder of Lushchinskii,"[48] in reference to the Beilis trial in Kiev in 1911–12. Shubinskii refused to recognize the interpellation as urgent and in response to a virulent anti-Semitic speech by Purishkevich, denounced "the attempt to turn this podium into a forum of agitation, even anti-Semitic, as was done here now." [49]

Following Stolypin's assassination, the Union became more inclined to accept anti-Semitic slogans from their "patriotic" allies. The interpellation on Stolypin's death opened with the sentence: "On September the first this year in Kiev an attempt has been made by the *Jew* [italics added] Mark Bogrov on the life of the prime minister." [50] Kadet Niselovich expressed amazement at the stress on the nationality of the assassin, to which Guchkov retorted that Niselovich, as a Jew, should use his rhetorical talents to convince his people not to become agents and terrorists.[51] It was clear that the nationalistic coalition had been using anti-Semitic feelings as a weapon against the opposition and as an expression of "true" Russian patriotism. During the fifth session, anti-Semitism became one of the major expressions of Great Russian nationalism and, concurrently, a source of tensions and disruptions. The Octobrists were mostly on the defensive, embarrassed by the Kadets and dragged along by their nationalistic allies.

Great Russian chauvinism reached its peak during the debate on the Kholm (Chełm) bill, which dealt with the separation of the eastern parts of the provinces of Lublin and Siedlce from the Kingdom of Poland and the creation of a province, Kholm, that would become part of Russia. No other single bill brought out such a rabid display of Great Russian chauvinism as this bill, which during the previous three years had probably been the principal nationalistic issue in "patriotic" circles. It evoked historical studies, statistical research, speeches, petitions, and demonstrations. Bishop Evlogii, the most prominent clergyman in the Third Duma and one of the militant Great Russian nationalists of the period, was the figure behind a special association to "bring back" the lost province to Russia. The association, which included prominent members of the bureaucracy, the State Council, and the Duma, conducted a vicious anti-Polish campaign among the population of the districts planned for separation. It became an international issue when the Poles of Galicia conducted a countercampaign and asked the intervention of the Austro-Hungarian Foreign Ministry.

The issue raised emotional reactions because it had its roots deep in the relations between Russia and Poland, dating back to the Union of Brest in 1596, when the Uniat (Ukrainian Eastern Rite Catholic) church was created. A process of Polonization took place in the region, which, when it was conquered by Russia, endured a reverse process of forced Russification and persecution of the Uniat church. When freedom of religion was proclaimed in 1905, the Uniat church began to flourish again and the proposed bill was designed to reverse that trend.[52]

The official arguments for the Kholm bill were presented by Minister of the Interior Makarov,[53] who maintained that those districts contained a "Russian" population, as far as its ethnic origin was concerned (the Ukrainians were considered by the Russian authorities as "Little Russians," part of the "Russian nation"). Since there were plans to introduce local self-government in the Kingdom of Poland, the Russian government was naturally concerned with the fate of the "Russians" in those provinces, explained Makarov, and the rights of the Russian minority had to be assured before any move to establish zemstvo institutions could be made. In order to facilitate the introduction of local self-government in Poland, the Russian minority had to be separated; past persecution and national oppression had caused tension between the two people; the separation would correct past injustices and enable the free development of the Russian minority.

The proposed bill did not have the wholehearted support of the Union and during the debate there were many instances of open disagreements between the Union and the government and within the Union itself. It had been in committee for almost three years, partly because many Octobrists were doubtful as to its wisdom and the need for it, yet finally the Octobrists succumbed to the pressure of their Nationalist allies and introduced the bill in the Duma. A last-minute attempt by the opposition to delay the discussion of the bill was defeated by a vote of 174 to 94. Many Octobrists intended to introduce amendments to the bill when it came up for its second call and very few participated in the general debate. The main speaker was G. V. Skoropadskii, who repeated the arguments presented by Makarov,[54] relating again and again the past hardships of the Russian minority, stressing the weakness of the Russian peasant and his need to be told that he was not part of Poland anymore. His speech was actually a reiteration of what was said during the debate over the western zemstvo bill.

A group of Octobrists headed by V. K. Fon-Anrep voted against the bill. Fon-Anrep explained that the bill had no positive content whatsoever and only served to inflame national animosities.[55] Despite his objections, Fon-Anrep apologized for the way he voted, reminding the audience of his patriotic initiatives in the past; his apologies were met by laughter and derision from the floor.[56] Fon-Anrep's speech and the way it was received by some was indicative of the atmosphere during the fifth session—although the group of extreme chauvinists was small in numbers, its demagogical tactics succeeded, outside and within the Duma, in intimidating many, particularly among the Octobrists. Even such a nationalist as Fon-Anrep had to apologize.

The bill passed the first reading, but during the second, when a vote was taken on each article separately, there was an unpredictable development. Article 10 of the proposed bill, the one that provided for the separation of the created Province of Kholm from the Kingdom of Poland, was rejected by 155 to 105.[57] Since this was the central clause, its rejection amounted to a temporary rejection of the entire bill. It happened as a result of a disagreement within the Union's faction. Fon-Anrep's proposal to exclude from Article 10 the provision that the Province of Kholm "will be separated from the Kingdom of Poland," was adopted, and excluded also was the phrase that the new province "will come under the jurisdiction of the Ministry of the Interior," by a vote of 139 to 135.[58] A sizable group of Octobrists voted against separation while many others were absent when the vote was taken, a ridiculous action, since the other clauses that were phrased and contingent upon the separation had passed on the same day.[59] All the amendments, some of which were introduced by Octobrists to diminish the negative effects of the bill on the Polish population, were rejected.

The Kholm bill was passed eventually on the third reading in the form it was originally designed, Article 10 included. Octobrist Antonov explained that the crucial Article 10 was rejected previously because it was misunderstood by many of the Union deputies.[60]

The debate and the votes over the Kholm bill indicated the gradual decline of nationalistic zeal among many Octobrists, who refused to limit their nationalistic feelings to negative forms of discrimination against national minorities. They wanted positive legislation that would raise their national pride and improve Russia's image abroad. Nationalism expressed only in negative terms could not suffice to cement a coalition or to overcome internal dissent within the Union.

10

Indignant Nationalism and
the Struggle Against the
"Irresponsible Forces"

Octobrist nationalism, with all its ambiguities and equivocations, was at its peak in the fifth session. Just as the Union of October 17 had never had a streamlined and coherent political and social ideology, neither had it had a coherent nationalism. It was not a clear-cut ideology nor program of action but rather a combination of ideas, tactics, past memories, and aspirations for the renovation of Russia. Yet, withal, nationalism was a central concept and a motivating force of Octobrism, meaning different things and serving many purposes. There were elements of Slavophile nationalism, with its stress on the peculiarities of the Russian nation and its mission among the Slavic peoples and in the world. Crude Great Russian chauvinism and anti-Semitism could be found on the other end of the spectrum of Octobrist nationalism, serving as a political weapon and a rallying slogan for the Union in its competition with the parties to its right and its attempt to gain the good will of the authorities. The term "nationalism" was used at the time, not only by the Octobrists, for many purposes. Its very vagueness made it a convenient political slogan.

Great Russian chauvinism was only one component of Octobrist nationalism and was not the dominant one, although it found vocal and ugly manifestations throughout the Third Duma. For many Octobrists, nationalism meant more than the persecution of national minorities under the guise of preserving the unity of the empire, it also meant the creation of a better Russia, the regaining of national pride. The Octobrists' nationalism meant, on the most general level,

177

the creation of a Russia wherein they would be comfortable, secure, and proud to live, a Russia whose internal strength and international power would increase, so as to overshadow the disgrace of defeat. In the Russia of Nicholas II, nationalism understood in such terms was a force that pushed many Octobrists toward change and reform, criticism and opposition.

The intensification of Great Russian chauvinism after Stolypin's assassination contained other elements that emerged gradually during the fifth session and which were ominous for the tsarist regime as it was constituted under Nicholas. The circumstances surrounding Stolypin's assassination, the rumors and suspicions, all affected the emergence of other aspects of the nationalistic feelings. Autocracy, all along, was using nationalism as a major ideological bastion and stressed the greatness of the Great Russian. At a certain point its representatives were bound to ask themselves whether it was right that their nation's honor and destiny were determined by a clique of "irresponsible persons." It was inevitable to ask whether those who made the crucial decisions for the nation could fulfill their duties; whether they could secure internal peace and international prestige. The Russian nationalists were beginning to wonder whether "the Great Russian nation," an expression used frequently by nationalists and representatives of the regime, did not deserve a larger share in shaping its own destiny. Nationalists with this turn of mind were dangerous allies for tsarism: they could turn into its fatal enemies.

During the first part of the fifth session, militant Great Russian nationalism helped to re-establish the original government coalition. The two bills on Finland, the Kholm bill, and the virulent attacks on the opposition were reminiscent of the first session. The Union was following the pattern established at its beginning: support of the government with freedom to disagree. But as the fifth session progressed, criticism became more frequent, explicit, and oppositional. A perceptive observer would have seen the trend even at the beginning of the session.

With the opening of the fifth session, Kadet Teslenko introduced an interpellation on the legality of the use of the extraordinary regulations. He maintained that since the convocation of the representative chambers, the extension of the regulation by a tsar's edict violated the Fundamental Laws.[1] Teslenko's move had been obviously designed to push the Octobrists toward a more principled

stand on the issue or to discredit them before the upcoming elections to the Fourth Duma. "At this moment the authors of the interpellation wait to hear what the Duma of June 3 will say. Will it say
that it still remembers October 1905?"[2] asked the Kadet. It was
clear to whom he directed his question. The Octobrists tried to
avoid a direct answer. Their spokesman, I. A. Kurakin, declared that
the faction could not see the urgency in the interpellation and proposed to transfer it to a committee.[3] Yet the interpellation was accepted. Many prominent Octobrists, including Fon-Anrep, Alekseenko, Godnev, Kapustin, Lerkhe, and Leonov, voted for it. Savich
and Shubinskii abstained. Guchkov was conspicuously absent.[4]
Kurakin was obviously not representing the entire faction.

At the height of the nationalistic wave, the Duma passed the bill
"on the changes in the procedures concerning criminal actions in
service," part of a long list of planned legislation to protect the
rights and freedom of the Russian citizen. Its purpose was to provide a more efficient machinery to secure the rights of the citizen
when violated by the administration, and was in line with the Octobrist ideal of making Russia a "state of law." It was also in line
with the feeling that a "great nation" should not be left at the mercy,
whims, and caprices of an irresponsible administration.

The Octobrists considered the proposed bill a landmark in safe-
guarding the citizen's rights. "The transformation of the country
into a state based on the principles of law, requires . . . in particular the establishment of criminal liability of officials for criminal
acts in service,"[5] explained N. I. Antonov, who stressed that the
rights of the Russian citizen would be safely protected only when
they would be guarded by a positive law against the administration's
encroachment. One has to keep in mind the lingering suspicions
about "irresponsible" personalities involved in Stolypin's assassination to appreciate the special significance of the bill, in spite of
its moderate character.

According to the existing system, officials were almost entirely
immune from prosecution when they committed an offense against
a citizen. They were protected by administrative guaranties that
actually left the decision to prosecute to the discretion of the administration, usually the superiors of the delinquent officials.[6] The
offended citizen could complain, but there was no way to get real
redress. The proposed bill did not abolish the administrative protection; it only improved the investigative machinery and gave the

state prosecutor more voice in deciding whether an offense should
be brought to court. Other items were of secondary and technical
importance. Antonov admitted that the bill was the result of a compromise with the government, otherwise it had no chance of being
ratified.[7] Although not perfect, the Octobrists thought that it represented a step forward. For the Russia of Nicholas II it certainly
was.

Again, when the budget of the Office of State Comptroller was
discussed on January 8, 1912, the Duma adopted for the first time a
resolution demanding a radical revision of the composition and management of the office, that the office be separated from the government, and that its higher personnel be given an independent status.
A request to broaden the Duma's supervisory functions over the execution of the budget was included in the same resolution. In spite
of strong opposition from the government and the Right, the Duma
passed the resolution.[8]

In a way these were meaningless bills and resolutions—there
was almost no chance that they would become functioning laws.
For a short period following the zemstvo crisis, a feeling of soli-
darity between the two chambers existed, but it did not last long
and the State Council became again a major obstacle to any positive
legislation passed by the Duma. The bill providing for the financial
expansion of the elementary education system was rejected on May
26, 1911, on the grounds that it did not provide sufficiently for parochial schools.[9] The bills on religious freedom were still held in
committee, as were the bills that provided for the replacement of
volost courts by justices of peace and for creating self-governing
volost units. These were only a few of the more important bills the
council blocked.

In the fifth session, the Octobrists renewed their campaign
against the council. For many of them it represented those "irresponsible forces" that first thwarted and then killed, at least politically, the only man who could move Russia to "peaceful renovation."
Towards the end of the fifth session this campaign against the
council reached its most acute form.

Two issues were chosen by the Union for the attack: the reform
of the peasant courts, passed by the Duma in the second session,
and the establishment of the self-governing *volost* unit, passed in
the fourth. They had been designed to equalize the status of the
peasants with the rest of the population, to provide them with a

more efficient legal system, and to broaden their self-government. The bill providing for the establishment of self-governing *volost* units represented the old demand of the zemstvo liberals for "a small zemstvo unit." Stolypin had been a dedicated supporter of the self-governing *volost* unit and the reform of the peasant court, for the two bills supplemented his land reform and created the groundwork for a strong self-governing peasantry—the basis of his entire political program.

In selecting these bills to use in their attack, the Octobrists were relying on the support of the peasant representatives in the Duma as well as the sympathy of liberal public opinion. Petitions were organized by peasant organizations. Peasant deputies, from different factions, demanded that Kokovtsov and Makarov force the council to pass the bills. The deputies threatened to vote against any government bill if the authorities did not use their influence on the council and, following Guchkov's advice, they also petitioned the tsar.[10] Guchkov and other Octobrists accused the council of defending narrow class privileges to the detriment of the entire nation.[11] The council tabled the bill creating the self-governing *volost* and passed the bill of the local courts only after distorting its liberal meaning.[12]

The debate over the budget of the Ministry of the Interior served again as an occasion for a re-evaluation of the country's internal development. It also gave the opportunity to assess the achievements and failures of the Third Duma. There was disillusionment, helplessness, and even despair in the summary of the Octobrist Golitsyn when he announced that the Budget Committee had not even attached any recommendations: the administration had evaded most of the recommendations in the past; there was no sense in repeating them now.[13]

S. I. Shidlovskii's speech sounded more like a personal confession than an analysis of the budget for his mood was one of resignation, helplessness, and foreboding. The Union deserved a more understanding attitude by the authorities, he complained. Its wishes were not those of an opposition party and its treatment as such by the authorities was unjustified.

During the five years of our activity in the Duma, we received nothing but disappointments. . . . When people who are completely loyal express their views and wishes,

when people whose primary concern is to establish the
rule of law speak out, then the authorities ought to
listen.[14]

Shidlovskii pointed out that those in authority had wasted five
years of tranquillity and good will of the public opinion, that the
government had abused nationalistic feelings to divert public attention from the real problems of the country. Under the banner of
nationalism, Shidlovskii found persecution of national minorities,
particularly the Jews, and for him nationalism meant the unity of
the empire and the opportunity for all nations to live within its bor-
ders free and proud of being part of it. The present policy drove the
voters to support the Left, Shidlovskii warned, but he could see no
hope for change. Before leaving the podium, the disillusioned Octobrist added with a tone of despair: "The present policy of those in
authority . . . is following the wrong track. I personally, to my great
sorrow, cannot see any way out."[15]

As if to demonstrate how little had changed, how the years of
tranquillity had been wasted, came the incident in the Lena gold
fields. On April 4, 1912, 147 striking workers were killed and 193
wounded by an army unit during a peaceful demonstration. Government announcements and explanations were incomplete, contradictory, and demonstrated a general loss of control.[16]

The information that reached the government proved flagrant
exploitation by the mine owners and the guilt of the local army commander.[17] The country was in an uproar, with even the loyal press
denouncing the bloodshed.[18] It demanded understanding and moderation in handling the wave of strikes and demonstrations that
followed the incident.

The Octobrists considered the Lena incident another stain on
their national pride. *Golos Moskvy* wrote that "In the West the most
severe labor unrest . . . goes by without such catastrophes. What
shame it is to write now about Russia, which in the seventies was
presented as an example for England, as a place of respect for
human life!"[19] When news of the incident reached the capital the
Central Committee of the Union decided to introduce its urgent interpellation after Easter vacation.[20]

When the Duma was reconvened, the Octobrists asked the government in their interpellation whether it knew that there was no
justification to open fire against the striking workers; whether it

knew that the company treated the workers contrary to government laws; what did the government intend to do in order to bring those responsible for the massacre to court?[21] Guchkov, who spoke for the faction to justify the urgency of the interpellation, emphasized that the information available indicated conditions unworthy of a twentieth-century country and that the Duma and the empire were waiting for a thorough and impartial investigation.[22]

The government was confused and its actions contradictory. It tried to allay outraged public opinion but at the same time put on a show of determination and authority.[23] While Minister of Commerce Timashev promised a thorough investigation of the mine company's conduct,[24] Interior Minister Makarov tried to justify the behavior of the military.[25] Makarov accused the Social Democrats of incitement and an attempt to use the strike for political purposes, contending that the revolutionary agitators and not those who gave the order to open fire were responsible for the massacre. "The crowd lost its self-control under the influence of malicious agitators and moved towards the army. The latter had no choice but to fire. *This is how it was in the past and will be in the future* [italics added]."[26] It was Makarov's version of Stolypin's "do not frighten us" directed against the revolutionaries in the First Duma. But Makarov was no Stolypin, nor was 1912 another 1906. The reaction to Makarov's speech was almost completely negative, in the press as well as in the Duma.[27]

The government's explanations did not satisfy the Duma. The Octobrists demanded a full investigation through A. I. Zvegintsev, who introduced a motion to stop the debate in the Duma until the government could come up with a complete report on the incident and the measures it intended to take to prevent such occurrences in the future.[28] The explanations of the various ministers brought more confusion than clarity, he remarked, adding that the Duma was left with the distinct feeling that the government was not in control of the situation and lacked sufficient information on what was happening in the country. The Union's proposal to express the Duma's dissatisfaction with the government's explanations and to demand a complete report before the end of the session [29] was adopted by a vote of 162 to 91.

No "full and complete" report was ever given the Duma and probably very few deputies really expected to receive one. The Octobrist resolution was in a way an attempt to avoid the issue, but at the same time it actually stated that those in positions of official authority were not really in control—a reflection of the prevailing feeling that the governmental mechanism was disintegrating.

As the Third Duma was nearing the completion of its term, the country was becoming increasingly restless and dissatisfied. A new outbreak of revolutionary violence was expected by some, feared by others—it was obvious that the tranquil years had been wasted. The Russian nationalist, concerned with strengthening the country internally and internationally, realized to his great chagrin that the Russian Empire was instead going to pieces—in the center, in the provinces, and, in different forms, in the military. The Octobrists, and particularly Guchkov, had tried for years to stop this process; toward the end of the Third Duma they brought the struggle into the open.

Disintegration of the governmental structure had not started with the assassination of Stolypin but had underlain the elements responsible for those who thwarted Stolypin and brought him to his political demise before his physical death. Stolypin could not overcome the entrenched reactionary forces in the court, council, and provinces. Even during the tenure of office of Russia's most statesmanlike prime minister, the provinces and local administrations were governed without effective supervision from the center, for Stolypin had never been able to eradicate the reactionary inertia of the entrenched bureaucracy in the capital, let alone in the provinces. He was forced to retreat from a determined drive for reform, and eventually committed political suicide during the zemstvo crisis, when he tried to fight.

While Stolypin had fought a rearguard battle against the "irresponsible forces," his successor had become their victim. Kokovtsov, himself a product of the traditional tsarist bureaucracy, was incapable of providing leadership during the period Russia needed it most. One of the reasons that he had been chosen to replace Stolypin was the belief that in his mediocrity he would not oppose the whims of the court circles, which were disturbed by the actions of his too-strong predecessor.

In the center and in the provinces, in church and army, Kokovtsov's premiership saw an acceleration of disintegration. As mentioned before, among those who surrounded the tsar there prevailed an amazing alienation from public opinion. They were unreserved proponents of an absolutist regime and, directly and indirectly, contributed to the deterioration of the state machinery. The provincial administration did not follow the directives of the center, a phenomenon that existed when Stolypin was still alive and which now became more frequent, prevalent, and open. But more and more the concern of the public became the court and those who influenced the tsar, particularly personalities of dubious character such as Rasputin.

Toward the end of 1911, Kokovtsov wrote in his memoirs: "The problem of Rasputin became the central question of the near future. It has not left the scene for almost the entire duration of my premiership, resulting in my eventual resignation after two years."[30] Memoirs of the period by other cabinet members, such as V. A. Sukhomlinov, A. A. Polivanov, and S. D. Sazonov, as well as various political leaders, attest to the same. While Russia was approaching a general war, its prime minister was wasting most of his energy and time on a problem that befitted ancient Persia.

Rasputin's position at court became a major political issue for the Duma and its top leadership. His role and exact influence on political decision-making are beyond the scope of this work,[31] but whether his influence was great or not, it is relevant that his presence in the court had great political repercussions. Rasputin troubled the official government and became for Russian patriots the incarnation of the "irresponsible forces" leading the nation to disaster. He became the target of the indignant nationalistic feelings of the Octobrist leadership.

Rasputin's association with the tsar's family dated from 1905; his influence grew with time, and must be understood against the background of the personalities of the royal family. He was one among several "mystery men" influential in the higher society of St. Petersburg in the years preceding World War I,[32] but his shadowy background, despicable behavior, and his close association with the tsar's family provided the enemies of the regime with an excellent weapon. Stolypin understood the possible detrimental effects of Rasputin on the prestige of the monarchy, but he also understood that Rasputin's relations with the tsar's family were complicated and therefore had not raised the issue too often.[33] Rasputin's influence itself had been limited while Stolypin was in office.

From the end of 1911 Rasputin preoccupied the government of Kokovtsov. Letters written by the tsarina to Rasputin began to appear in St. Petersburg society. Rumors were circulating in the Duma and in various papers about Rasputin's influence on the tsar. Kokovtsov and Makarov, who had been asked by the tsar to put pressure on the press to prevent publicity about Rasputin,[34] tried behind the scenes to suppress articles on the subject but failed, and Makarov's efforts brought the issue before the Duma.

On January 24, 1912, *Golos Moskvy* published an open letter by M. A. Novoselov, an expert on the sectarians, in which he accused Rasputin of belonging to one of the extreme sects, the Khlysti. He accused the higher church hierarchy of neglecting its role as spiritual leader of the nation, thereby helping Rasputin corrupt the national soul. The Ministry of the Interior confiscated the entire edition of the paper, precipitating an urgent interpellation in the Duma. The initiative came from the Union's leadership, particularly Guchkov, who was the first name on the lists of interpellants.[35]

"When it became clear to me that while we made an effort to preserve the constitutional regime, such a phenomenon as Rasputin's influence takes place, I decided to pay closer attention to that man," [36] explained the leader of the Union. When he failed to diminish Rasputin's influence through Kokovtsov and Makarov, Guchkov decided to act through the Duma. Guchkov received the endorsement of the Union's leadership to introduce an urgent interpellation. President Rodzianko opposed the move, arguing that it might damage the image of the tsar, and proposed to ask the tsar directly to remove Rasputin from the court. But Guchkov's view prevailed.[37]

On January 25, 1912, the Duma accepted as urgent the interpellation concerning the confiscation of the papers *Golos Moskvy* and *Vechernoe vremia*, which published Novoselov's open letter to the Holy Synod. The letter in its entirety was included in the interpellation, and thus received the widest possible publicity, exactly the opposite of what the government tried to accomplish by the confiscation.[38] The interpellants also included references to government pressure on the press to avoid any publication concerning Rasputin. The Duma asked the government to justify and stop these illegal actions.

Asking the Duma to recognize the interpellation as urgent, Guchkov declared that "Russia is living through oppressive and terrible days; its national conscience is deeply disturbed; dark phantoms from medieval times trouble our state."[39] The church and secular authorities had neglected their duties toward the Russian nation, the leader of the Union accused, and therefore, "it is the patriotic duty of the independent press, the duty of our conscience, the obligation of the people's representatives, to raise their voices and give vent to the feelings of indignation that prevail in the land."[40] The general applause that followed Guchkov's speech testified that he spoke for the entire Duma. The request to recognize the urgency of the interpellation was adopted unanimously.

The interpellation was transferred to a Duma committee, while behind the scenes attempts were made to prevent a general debate on its content. The immediate result was a further deterioration in Guchkov's relations with the royal couple—the tsarina demanded the immediate dissolution of the Duma.[41]

Rodzianko, in cooperation with Kokovtsov, Makarov, and V. K. Sabler, head of the Synod, tried to convince the tsar that Rasputin was not a "true" Orthodox, but a charlatan and a scoundrel.[42] Together with the prime minister and his own party leaders, Guchkov and Shubinskii, Rodzianko prepared a detailed paper to prove his point. The tsar himself provided Rodzianko with documents on the subject, explaining that he expected an unbiased investigation that would clear up the issue.[43]

While Rodzianko tried to convince the tsar to remove Rasputin, the Duma took up the subject during the debate on the budget of the Holy Synod. The attacks came from the Left and Right alike, but the major assault came from Guchkov, on March 9, 1912.[44]

> We have to speak out, because others are silent. . . .
> One feels like shouting that the church is in danger, that
> the state is in peril. You all know the terrible drama
> Russia is living through . . . and in the center of that
> drama is a mysterious tragicomic figure.

Whether Guchkov intentionally dramatized and exaggerated or not, he certainly reflected the general mood of both his party and the Duma. It is difficult to know whether Guchkov believed that Rasputin had the power attributed to him. One may doubt if he actually thought that Rasputin was responsible for changes in policy and determined government appointments, as he insinuated in his speech, but many Octobrists and other Russian nationalists were saying the same. There was reason to doubt that Guchkov was truly concerned when he agreed with Social Democrat Gegechkori that "Rasputin was useful" for the revolution. Guchkov certainly was opposed to this eventuality. Guchkov's question: "Where are the authorities—of church and state?" was a sincere one. We know that the authorities were at a loss, that they tried and failed to prevent Rasputin's presence in the court. Guchkov's speech represents a transition to opposition to the regime as it was effected by Nicholas II. There were times, Guchkov held, when to serve the country and tsar means "something entirely different than to be servile."[45] The leader of the Union, who started his political career as a supporter of Nicholas's "new regime," called it a national and moral obligation to oppose those who wielded official power in 1912. The long and tumultuous applause that came from the entire Duma except the extreme Right testified that Guchkov was not alone in his feelings and conclusions.

Yet in spite of the outrage, in spite of strong oppositional language, the Octobrists followed their established pattern—no concrete oppositional action. The budget of the Holy Synod was passed, and Rasputin was not even mentioned in the attached recommendations.[46]

Rodzianko had completed his report on Rasputin, while in the Duma Guchkov was attacking the highest church and state authorities. The tsar refused to grant Rodzianko a personal audience to discuss his conclusions.[47] He wrote to his prime minister:

> Please inform Rodzianko that I refuse to see him. . . . The behavior of the Duma and particularly Guchkov's speech on the budget of the Holy Synod aggravated me very much. . . . I would be very happy if my dissatisfaction would be conveyed to those gentlemen.[48]

Rodzianko considered the tsar's attitude not only a personal insult but more, an insult to the Duma's president. He threatened to resign if the tsar would not grant him an audience or write a personal letter. Kokovtsov tried to convince Rodzianko to change his mind and prevent an open breach between the Duma and the government. The prime minister eventually persuaded the tsar to write a letter to the Duma president, promising to receive him at a later time and to hear his report on Rasputin. Kokovtsov explained to the tsar that an open clash with the Duma might be disastrous for the monarchy and jeopardize the passage of the financial plan for building a high-seas fleet.[49]

Rodzianko received the tsar's letter and sent his report condemning Rasputin. Rodzianko, a devout servant of the monarchy, considered the outcome a victory for the Duma—yet Rasputin continued to trouble Russian politics and contributed to the collapse of tsarism.

The Rasputin affair proved once again how isolated and divorced from the reality of the nation's feelings was the court of Nicholas II. The tsar was surrounded by people who assured him that the masses were his staunch supporters. The Duma and some of its Octobrist leaders were depicted as a few troublemakers, trying to infringe upon the prerogatives of the monarch, particularly in military affairs.

Toward the end of the fifth session once again a battle was shaping up between the administration and the Octobrists on the problem of military reforms. The influence of "irresponsible personalities" and the deficiencies of the army and navy became prime subjects of concern and indignation of the Russian nationalists. The Great Russian nationalists in the Third Duma lived with the memory of the humiliating defeat by Japan and fear of a new débâcle, this time in Europe. Since the annexation of Bosnia-Herzegovina by Austria-Hungary, the Balkan peninsula had become more and more the center of concern of Russia's foreign policy, for the area had a special emotional appeal for the Russian nationalists. The possibility of a general war in Europe loomed larger as the Third Duma was nearing the completion of its term, but among the well-informed nationalists in the Third Duma there was an uneasy feeling that their country was not prepared for a large-scale war.

Following the conflict over the appropriations for the Naval General Staff in 1909, the authorities had tried to diminish the influence of the Duma, and particularly that of Guchkov, on military matters. Yet this was a subject of utmost importance for the Octobrists and they continued their loyal cooperation with the War Ministry and their futile efforts to reform the army and navy. The Octobrist leadership, and particularly Guchkov, succeeded, in spite of the court's efforts, to continue and even strengthen their connections with the higher military command and the officialdom of the War Ministry.[50] Guchkov "used his role in the Duma so as to gain information and to broaden the circle of his friends on the Naval General Staff and among the officials of the Ministry of War,"[51] Sukhomlinov complained. The Octobrist leader established particularly friendly relations with Polivanov, Sukhomlinov's deputy. The memoirs of both Guchkov[52] and Polivanov[53] tend to confirm Sukhomlinov's observations.

In spite of the sincere desire on the part of the nationalist Duma Defense Committee to help strengthen the military might of the country, they found themselves increasingly alienated from War Minister Sukhomlinov. The Defense Committee realized that urgently needed reforms in the higher command, the development of the military industry, and the supply of up-to-date equipment to the army were dangerously delayed,[54] and yet Sukhomlinov only rarely appeared in person before the committee or its plenum. Polivanov, who succeeded in gaining the confidence of the Duma, usually represented the government.

The antagonism between Sukhomlinov and the Duma's Defense Committee brought an open clash on April 18, 1912. Guchkov accused the war minister of establishing a secret unit headed by S. N. Miasoedov, a police officer of dubious character, to control the political loyalty of the higher military command.[55] The "Miasoedov affair" was openly discussed in the press amid rumors of security leaks in the highest ranks of the War Ministry.[56] Miasoedov did not become the commander of the planned political spying unit, but Polivanov, who supplied Guchkov with the secret information, was fired by the tsar on April 27, 1912.[57] Sukhomlinov used the tsar's antagonism toward Guchkov and the Octobrists to get rid of one of the most talented men in his ministry.

The dismissal of Polivanov was received by the Duma as a setback for the cause of reform in the country's military establishment and was strongly resented by the Octobrists and Nationalists.[58] The nationalists in the Duma decided to make a public attack on the shortcomings of the War Ministry. As usual Guchkov led the assault.

On May 7, 1912, during the debate over the budget of the Artillery Department, Guchkov accused the War Ministry of almost criminal negligence.[59] In a well-documented speech, the leader of the Union proved that the Russian army was lagging far behind its possible enemies in its equipment and readiness for war. The speech demonstrated how the tense international situation and the arms race drove the Russian nationalists to demand reforms and, failing to achieve their aim, to criticize in the strongest terms those who were responsible. For five years, explained Guchkov, the

Defense Committee tried to reform and improve the department, but without results. He had decided to make public the defects, said Guchkov, since he thought that without the determined action of the Duma, nothing would change.[60] Speaking for the Budget Committee, he proposed that the Duma formally recognize that the way in which the Russian army was equipped "presents a serious danger for the security of the country" and to call on the government to take immediately the necessary corrective measures. Justifying his public denunciation, Guchkov spoke for the entire nationalistic camp: "We have given to the reconstruction of our military might our complete devotion, power, time, and knowledge."[61] After five years of futile efforts, the fact that there was no other way open but a public assault led Guchkov to apologize: "then you have to believe me that the cup was full; that no other means but a scream of indignation and the voice of protest, that nothing else was left."[62]

Guchkov's speech was received enthusiastically by the entire Duma. His proposed censure was adopted unanimously.[63]

Through subtle use of court influence, Kokovtsov succeeded in the last days of the Third Duma to pass a bill providing for the construction of a high-seas fleet. The Duma had refused for four years to allocate the required appropriations for the construction of several squadrons of dreadnoughts, and for Nicholas II the construction of a strong fleet had become an obsession. He was subject to the prevailing notions that a strong fleet was the major attribute of a big power and the almost hysterical naval competition between Great Britain and Germany in 1912 had influenced the tsar in its turn.[64] Kokovtsov succeeded in gaining the Duma's approval by alienating a large group of Octobrists from their official leader, Guchkov, through having the tsar give a personal audition to Alekseenko and asking his support for the bill. Alekseenko, head of the Budget Committee, was flattered and promised his support, which was crucial during the debate in the Budget Committee.[65]

During the debate in the Budget Committee, Guchkov, with a group of left-wing Octobrists, voted against the appropriation. But most of the Octobrists, among them his friends Savich and Zvegintsev, voted with the Nationalists and the Right for the bill.[66] The Duma's plenum passed the bill on June 6, 1912. Guchkov and a minority of Octobrists voted against it.[67] A high-seas fleet that involved huge expenditures was not a matter of first priority for Russia's military might. Many understood this, but Russia in 1912 was not ruled by a government that made its decisions by following only true national priorities.

The Third Duma completed its term on June 8, 1912, with a symbolic act of defiance. The Octobrists and the opposition left the hall without passing the bill allocating special funds for the parochial schools, one of special significance to the tsar. The first to leave the hall was Guchkov. This was done in reaction to the hostile reception of the Duma by the tsar on the previous day.[68]

M. O. Menshikov, the ideological leader of Great Russian nationalists, praised Guchkov's and the Octobrists' role in the Duma. He added ominously: "It is quite possible that the regrettable picture of the continuous disintegration of Russia is pushing the nationalists imperceptibly to the Left."[69] The Octobrists left the Third Duma dissatisfied and frustrated. Many of them were thinking of different methods to "renovate Russia" and restore its national honor.

Conclusion

The seven years before World War I were a short interval of relative tranquillity between the defeat and revolution that had preceded it, the war and collapse of the entire sociopolitical structure that followed it. One can hardly overestimate the significance of the developments that took place during this period. Russian society, economy, and culture were undergoing rapid change, but at the same time the political structure of the country was not responding to the other changes that were taking place. The court, the center of political power, became increasingly isolated from the major trends in the country, its social base continued to narrow. The constitutional monarchy established in 1907 came under attack from two sides, the court and the revolutionaries. The court and the reactionaries of Russian nobility thought that the regime was too radical. Time restored to the court its self-confidence, the events of 1905–7 appeared to be an episode, their message of wide and popular discontent was being lost and forgotten. On the other hand, from 1910–11 there arose a clear trend of disillusionment among important segments of supporters of the constitutional monarchy, resulting in the "crisis of the heights." For many, the Third Duma proved that Russia was moving too slowly toward reform. For the Union of October 17, the lesson of the Third Duma was rather ambiguous; while they failed to achieve many of their major goals of reforms and progress, they succeeded in keeping alive the representative institution and thus the constitutional monarchy. The Octobrists' experience in the Third Duma was a repetition of the

basic dilemmas and anguishes faced by Russian liberals all along:
how to bring change and progress without revolution and how to
preserve the integrity of state and society without succumbing to
a reign of autocratic arbitrariness and oppression.

The Union of October 17 was what its name implies: a union of
people and organizations whose aim was to work for the implementation of a tsar's proclamation—the Manifesto of October 17, 1905.
In many respects the Union was a coalition of people devoted to
implement a government policy proclamation that was no more than
a promise and a statement of general principles. The Octobrists
had never formulated a cohesive ideology nor political program.
Yet, in spite of being a coalition of people with different orientations and interests, several elements bound the Union together.

Founded after defeat and amid a revolution, the Union represented those elements in Russian society that strived to regain
internal peace and restore to its former glory the tarnished national
honor. They wanted to achieve these goals without severing Russia's ties with its past and without changing radically its form of
government. They wanted to achieve peaceful renovation without
effecting a change in the ultimate seat of political power. The
Octobrists wanted to live in a state ruled by law (*pravovoe gosudarstvo*), free from the threat of revolution and protected from the
arbitrariness (*proizvol*) of an "irresponsible" administration. Humiliated by defeat and afraid of the separatist tendencies in the
borderlands that threatened to disintegrate the Russian Empire,
the Octobrists strived to reform and strengthen the military might
of the country believing, as other Russian nationalists did, that
this would preserve their multinational empire. Restoration of internal peace and international prestige, both conceived in terms of
national pride and personal security, were the goals of the Union
in the Third Duma. They wanted to achieve it by cooperation with
tsarism.

Stolypin represented for the Union a hope that their goals could
be achieved. In many ways his goals and the goals of the Union
coincided—restoration of peace to the country and strengthening
its government by reforms and repression of the revolution. Stolypin's failure to move much beyond repression of the revolution
signified also the failure of the Union to achieve its goals. Both
Stolypin and the Union were thwarted by the same reactionary
forces, and their ultimate failure could be in part attributed to their

joint acceptance of the location of ultimate political power in the country. Tsarism, as constituted under Nicholas II, proved an insurmountable obstacle to the peaceful renovation of Russia. Since the Union accepted without reservation tsarism's monopoly of political power and actually never tried to contest it, Octobrism was doomed to fail in achieving its major goals in the Third Duma. Tsarism, according to Nicholas II, meant arbitrariness at the center and in the provinces, that is, the opposite of the state ruled by law as the Octobrists hoped. Nicholas's tsarism meant the influence of "irresponsible forces," favoritism, and nepotism that thwarted reform, particularly in the military.

The Union accepted for the Duma a subordinate role in shaping the destinies of Russia. According to the Union's programs, the Duma would participate in legislation and supervision over the administration, but the ultimate decision rested with the tsar. The Octobrists called it a constitutional monarchy. Within this framework the Union tried to act in the Third Duma, where it emerged as the largest faction. During the five years of existence of the Third Duma, the Octobrists, in spite of internal tensions and divisions, supported the authorities, whether represented by Stolypin or Kokovtsov. The Union's natural allies in this policy were the various groups to the right, and together they constituted a coalition that accepted tsarism as the ultimate arbiter of the destiny of the country. Fear of revolution and intense Great Russian nationalism bound together the Union and its allies. During the first session of the Third Duma, when the memories of the revolution were alive, the stress was on the antirevolutionary character of the coalition. When the country regained some semblance of tranquillity, the coalition relied on its nationalism. It must be noted, however, that this periodization is in a way misleading, since both elements were present during all of the five years.

By the end of 1910, and certainly with the death of Stolypin eight months later, the constitutional monarchy in Russia was in serious trouble. The court became more and more isolated from the country. The isolation of the tsar from the people, so characteristic of the period preceding the February 1917 revolution, was almost complete by the close of the Third Duma. It is not so much a phenomenon of the country becoming oppositional but rather more a phenomenon of defection, best seen among the Octobrists, people who were by and large staunch believers in tsarism. Now they had

lost faith. The social basis of the regime continued to shrink. At
the time when Stolypin was trying to enlarge the social basis by
his agrarian reforms, tsarism was causing the gradual defection of
some of its most devout supporters, the Octobrists.

Octobrism's hope to make the constitutional monarchy a living
reality failed but not without leaving a potential for positive results
in the future. The Third Duma was a rather poor example of a representative institution—its powers were limited and even within
those limits the Octobrists had not dared to exercise the Duma's
full rights. The feelings of failure and disillusionment among many
Octobrists toward the end of the Third Duma period were well
founded, yet, going beyond these subjective feelings, the constitutional monarchy as a viable alternative to Russia's political development was served by the Third Duma and its leading faction—the
Octobrists. It is of utmost importance to remember that the mere
survival of the representative institution for five years was no
small feat and it was accomplished by the Octobrists' leadership,
who kept the Duma alive and made it a part of the political process
and structure of the empire. By doing so they kept alive the possibility of constitutional monarchy for Russia—the mere fact of the
Duma's existence, in spite of all its limitations and shortcomings,
represented a major departure in Russia's political history.[1] For
five years the budget (although not all of it) came under public
scrutiny. Government officials, including prime ministers, had to
answer interpellations, and defend their actions and policies. In
plenum and committee, precedents of public criticism and supervision were established and representatives learned the art of government and compromise. The Octobrists had no small part in this
achievement. Stolypin saw the importance for the country of the
willingness of the Octobrists to work within the established framework and sought their cooperation. Meyendorff, one of the more oppositional Octobrists, expressed it thus:

> When I listened to the answer of the minister of justice,
> I was filled all the time with the happy feeling that we
> have in Russia an institution where accusations leveled
> against any government representative get an immediate
> refutation—an institution where there exists freedom
> of thought and expression, and feelings of discontent
> against this or that order find their legal outlet [May 5,
> 1912].[2]

While the Union was moving toward more oppositional attitudes, the experience of a functioning representative institution established an alternative political focus that could have developed, in due time and under favorable circumstances, into a true constitutional regime. While tsarism, Nicholas II style, was losing support by the "defection" of many Octobrists, the ideal of a constitutional monarchy did not suffer accordingly.

The Third Duma period exposed the Union to some basic dilemmas that liberalism faces when it must choose between authority and anarchy. When threatened in 1905 by the revolution, with chaos and the disintegration of the established order, the Octobrists recoiled from a decisive attack on autocracy and chose to support what they believed to be reformed tsarism, or a constitutional monarchy. They closed their eyes to the contradictions between a reactionary, even stagnant, autocracy and the development of national power or the maintenance of Russia's status as a major power. The result in 1905 was a split in the liberal movement between Kadets and Octobrists. The latter tried during the Third Duma period to cooperate with tsarism, offering the court the opportunity to extend its public support. The Union practiced in the Third Duma what one may call "small deeds" in line with the tradition of nineteenth-century zemstvo liberalism, which usually tried to cooperate with tsarism, and their fate was similar: they failed to close the gap between society and autocracy. The Union eventually discovered, as did its predecessors, that small deeds were not sufficient to face big problems. But when the memories of the revolution became distant, many Octobrists were reluctant to accept the slow rate of change and reform. Tsarism appeared more and more an obstacle to the reconstruction of a better and stronger Russia. The result was not necessarily active political opposition but rather a withholding of support, a phenomenon not limited to Octobrists. The Union still maintained an antirevolutionary attitude yet they were suspicious and uncomfortable with the established authority. One important development for the future was the slow but perceptible increase of cooperation between the Union and the Kadets toward the end of the Third Duma. These two wings of Russian liberalism, split in 1905, were closing their ranks, a process that culminated in the Progressive bloc of 1915.

That the Union was the largest party in the Third Duma was not fully reflected in the shaping of policies and initiatives in the house. There were both internal and external reasons for the rather disproportionate role of the Union. It accepted a subordinate role for the representative institution, consequently leaving most of the legislative initiative to the government. There were only a few bills passed by the Duma that did not originate with the authorities. Most of the major legislative initiatives were enacted by the administration through the use of Article 87 of the Fundamental Laws; the Union only modified them slightly when the bills were introduced in the Duma. The composition of the Third Duma, with its "trustworthy" majority, tended to strengthen the dependence of the Octobrists on the administration. The need to form a coalition in order to pass any bill forced the Octobrists to accommodate themselves to the whims of other groups, particularly those to the right. This frequently meant abstention from constructive initiatives by the Octobrists. (Inexperience and lack of self-confidence played an important role in hindering Duma legislative initiative in general.)

The composition and organization of the Union's Duma faction tended further to diminish the strength of the Octobrists in the chamber. The lack of internal cohesion weakened it as an effective political force even within the limited sphere allotted by tsarism to the Duma. The Octobrists did not act as one party in most issues raised in the Third Duma; party discipline was a meaningless term for the Union. Except for Guchkov and a few others, the faction's leadership was mediocre and unable to inspire the rank and file of the faction, let alone the entire Duma.

The coalition functioned mainly as a tool of the government in passing the budget and bills initiated by the administration. Except for agrarian reform, all other reform programs, whether initiated by the government or by the Duma, raised internal conflicts within the coalition, and on many occasions in the Union itself. Here, the opposition frequently cooperated with the Union with the bills on religious freedom and on education, but substantial reforms were doomed because of the nature of the regime. Even those few bills of basic reform were either rejected or distorted by the State Council, which could do it with impunity because it had the backing, active or passive, of the court. The Union's campaigns against the council were actually misdirected: the council only reflected the nature of tsarism.

The conflicts and tensions, splits and crises, within the Duma and in its relations with the authorities "were not serious," as P. B. Struve remarked at the height of the zemstvo crisis.[3] In many ways he was right. The centers of power were outside the Duma and the major developments that shaped the fate of the country took place outside it. The zemstvo crisis proved these facts dramatically to the Union. Stolypin, the Union's ally, knew it all along and behaved accordingly. In spite of continuous disappointments, the Union continued to support those in authority, but with reservations, criticism, and sometimes by symbolic acts of defiance. There was a tangible discrepancy between its mood and its political expression, sometimes even in the same person, and the result was either resignation or defection from active support of the regime.

The achievement of internal security and the rule of law were among the major goals of the Union, as was the restoration of Russia's military might. No wonder that the most acute criticism and the most serious clashes between the Union and the authorities occurred in the areas of the implementation of civil freedoms, the establishment of the state ruled by law, and in the field of military reforms. The failure of the Union to accomplish its goals in these areas was perceived by the Octobrists in terms of damaged national pride. Toward the end of the Third Duma, many Octobrists felt that despite five years of strenuous effort on their part the country was undergoing internal disintegration, and that the coveted state ruled by law was becoming a state ruled by "dark medieval forces"— in the center and in the provinces. At the same time Russia's relative military might had actually decreased, as Guchkov proved during the last month of the Third Duma.

The same forces that thwarted and politically destroyed Stolypin were responsible for the lack of internal security and the blocking of basic reforms in the army. It was not too difficult to realize that the cause for the "rule of arbitrariness" as well as the lack of substantial reforms that would have strengthened the army lay in the kind of regime that made it possible for "the irresponsible forces" to function undisturbed. During the fifth session, when nationalistic feelings reached new peaks, many Octobrists were becoming not only more oppositional in the tone of their remarks, but undoubtedly had second thoughts about the nature of the regime. When the Octobrists, or some of them, would decide that Nicholas's tsarism was incompatible with their national honor, the Union's preoccupation with military reforms and its connections with the military higher command during the Third Duma would be of the utmost importance.

The significance of the Octobrists' attempt to cooperate with tsarism goes beyond their failure to achieve certain goals during the period of the Third Duma. The Union's disillusionment proved once again the determining influence of political power in shaping the destiny of Russia, for it meant the loss of support for tsarism from an important sector of Russian society. Tsarism became increasingly isolated from the major social forces in the country, relying more and more on the most reactionary nobility. That Octobrism as a movement tried and failed to cooperate with tsarism bode ill for the future of the regime and proved that an unreformed tsarism had outlived itself and was incapable of adapting itself to the changing circumstances of twentieth-century Russia. Guchkov and others were arriving at the conclusion that autocracy could not meet the most elemental requirements of all governments—those of internal and external security and honor. Many Octobrists thought that Russia's big-power status could not be maintained with the existing regime in control. It was no accident that several prominent Octobrists were among the leaders of the February 1917 Revolution.

Notes

Chapter 1

1. The zemstvo, or territorial assembly, was a county and province self-governing institution with extensive autonomous powers established in 1864. The zemstvo was composed of elected representatives of all the estates: the towns, the peasant communes, and all individual landowners, including nonnobility. From the outset the nobility predominated in the zemstvo. The self-governing institution had partial or complete jurisdiction over several areas of local rural life, such as education, welfare, and administration. In 1890 the composition and functions of the zemstvo assemblies were changed slightly in an attempt to restrict their autonomy.

2. No exact date can be ascertained for the founding of the Union. It was rather a series of meetings between various groups that took place between October 17, 1905, and November 10, 1910, when the proclamation announcing the founding of a Union was published in Moscow. See *Novoe vremia*, Oct. 29—Nov. 11, 1905 (hereafter, *NV*).

3. E. D. Chermenskii, *Burzhuaziia i tsarizm v revoliutsii 1905—1907 gg.*, p. 192.

4. Ibid., p. 245.

5. See p. 6, this volume.

6. Quoted by P. N. Miliukov in *God Bor'by*, p. 155.

7. B. Veselovskii, "Dvizhenie zemledeltsev," in *Obshchestvennoe dvizhenie v Rossii v nachale 20 veka* (hereafter, *OD*), 1, pt. 2:16.

8. "Ustav Soiuza 17-go Oktiabria" in *Sbornik program politicheskikh partii v Rossii*, ed. V. V. Vodovozov, p. 58.

9. Ibid., p. 61.

10. *NV*, May 10, 1907.

11. Based on G. Fischer, *Russian Liberalism: From Gentry to Intelligentsia*, pp. 23—27.

12. D. W. Treadgold, *Lenin and His Rivals*, p. 135

13. D. N. Shipov, *Vospominaniia i dumy o perezhitom*, p. 419.

14. V. V. Vodovozov, *Sbornik program politicheskikh partii v Rossii*, p. 44.

15. From Guchkov's presidential acceptance address to the Third Duma, in *Gosudarstvennaia Duma. Stenograficheskie otchety, Sozyv III. Sess.* 3, vol. 3, col. 451. Translated by L. Menashe in his Ph.D. dissertation, "Alexander Guchkov and the Origins of the Octobrist Party: The Russian Bourgeoisie in Politics, 1905," p. 77.

16. Veselovskii, "Dvizhenie zemledeltsev," p. 18.

17. Shipov, *Vospominaniia i dumy* . . . , p. 413.

18. Ibid., p. 414, from Stakhovich's speech before the first party convention in February, 1906.

19. *Polnoe sobranie zakonov*, 3rd ser., vol. 25, sect. 1, no. 26805. Translation quoted from Sidney Harcave, *First Blood: The Russian Revolution of 1905*, pp. 195—96.

20. Vodovozov, *Sbornik program* . . . , pp. 43—57.

21. Ibid., pp. 50—51.

22. Ibid., p. 46.

23. Ibid., p. 51.

24. *NV*, May 10, 1907.

25. Ibid.

26. *NV*, May 8, 1907.

27. Ibid.

28. Shipov, *Vospominaniia i dumy* . . . , p. 421.

29. P. N. Miliukov, *Tri popytki*, p. 26 passim.

30. Shipov, *Vospominaniia i dumy* . . . , pp. 496—98.

31. Chermenskii, *Burzhuaziia i tsarizm* . . . , pp. 315—16.

32. F. Dan and A. Cherevanin, "Soiuz 17-go Oktiabria," *OD*, 2, pt. 2:204.

33. See Alfred Levin, "The Russian Voter in the Elections to the Third Duma," *Slavic Review* 21 (1962):660—77.

Chapter 2

1. D. W. Treadgold, *Lenin and His Rivals*, p. 19.

2. Golovin's testimony in *Padenie tsar'skogo rezhima*, 5:372. Golovin was president of the Second Duma.

3. "Perepiska N. A. Romanova i P. A. Stolypina," *Krasnyi arkhiv* 5:115. Letter dated Nov. 9, 1907.

4. V. A. Maklakov, *The First State Duma*, p. 119.

5. S. E. Kryzhanovskii, *Vospominaniia*, p. 123. In a letter to Stolypin on July 29, 1906, he made the remark that Guchkov and others "are not men of action, i.e., of statesmanlike behavior" (*Krasnyi arkhiv* 5:102).

6. V. I. Gurko, *Features and Figures of the Past*, p. 493.

7. Kryzhanovskii, *Vospominaniia*, pp. 127—41.

8. S. I. Shidlovskii, *Vospominaniia*, 1:185.

9. Gurko, *Features and Figures of the Past*, pp. 499—500.

10. P. B. Struve, "Prestuplenie i zhertva," *Russkaia mysl'*, Oct. 1910, p. 139.

11. *Novoe vremia*, Sept. 18, 1911 (hereafter, *NV*).

12. *NV*, Sept. 6, 1911.
13. Gurko, *Features and Figures of the Past*, p. 511.
14. P. G. Kurlov, *Gibel' imperatorskoi Rossii*, p. 101.
15. P. N. Miliukov, *Vospominaniia*, 1:429–31.
16. Kryzhanovskii's testimony in *Padenie tsar'skogo rezhima*, 5:381, 418.
17. A. V. Zen'kovskii, *Pravda o Stolypine*, pp. 134–37.
18. Kryzhanovskii, *Vospominaniia*, p. 214.
19. A. I. Guchkov, "Iz vospominanii A. I. Guchkova," *Posledniia novosti*, no. 5623.
20. Gurko, *Features and Figures of the Past*, p. 795.
21. Guchkov on Stolypin after his assassination (*NV*, Sept. 15, 1911).
22. C. J. Smith, "The Russian Third State Duma: An Analytical Profile," *Russian Review* 17:202.
23. Ibid., p. 204.
24. See *Gosudarstvennaia Duma. Ukazatel'k stenograficheskim otchetam, Sozyv III.* Sess. 1–5.
25. Ibid., sess. 1, pp. 13–18.
26. The Octobrists were aware of the constant Kadet criticism of their diluted constitutionalism and that the Constitutional Democrats (the Kadets) had a much broader mass appeal in the country than was reflected in the Duma.
27. The existence of the opposition, even in its underrepresented form, was of utmost importance to the value of the Duma as a representative institution. It prevented, to a large extent, the development of the representative chamber into just another branch of the bureaucratic structure. It served on many occasions as a legitimate tool for the expression of popular moods and demands and thus influenced both the Octobrists and the government.
28. Guchkov on Stolypin, *NV*, Sept. 15, 1911.
29. *Slovo*, Nov. 11, 1907.
30. N. E. Markov's testimony in *Padenie tsar'skogo rezhima*, 6:181.
31. Guchkov on Stolypin, *NV*, Sept. 15, 1911.
32. Shidlovskii, *Vospominaniia*, pp. 202–3.
33. *NV*, Nov. 17, 1907.
34. Shidlovskii, *Vospominaniia*, pp. 202–3.
35. Ibid.
36. Of the 125 Octobrists listed in *Gosudarstvennaia Duma: Spravochnik, 1910*, pp. 7–93, 102 were Russian; 11, German; 8, Ukrainian; 2, White Russian; 1, Greek; and 1, Crimean Tatar.
37. P. Gerasimov, "Lichnyi sostav Gosudarstvennoi Dumy," in *Ezhegodnik gazety Rech', na 1912 god*, p. 128.
38. Smith, "The Russian Third State Duma," p. 204.
39. A. Ia. Avrekh, "Stolypinskii bonapartizm i voprosy voennoi politiki v tret'ei Dume," *Voprosy istorii* 11:20.
40. *Golos Moskvy*, Dec. 30, 1908.
41. *Vestnik Evropy* (Feb. 1909), p. 897.
42. L. Nemanov, "Evoliutsiia partiinykh otnoshenii v tret'ei Gosudarstvennoi Dume," *Russkaia mysl'* (Aug. 1910), p. 158.

43. Ibid., pp. 158–59.
44. Shidlovskii, *Vospominaniia*, p. 204.
45. Ibid., pp. 204–5.
46. Guchkov's testimony in *Padenie tsar'skogo rezhima*, 6:249.
47. *NV*, Nov. 2, 1907.
48. *Slovo*, Oct. 30, 1907.

Chapter 3

1. A. I. Guchkov, "Iz vospominanii A. I. Guchkova," *Posledniia novosti*, no. 5623.
2. *Slovo*, Oct. 30, 1907; *Novoe vremia*, Oct. 31, 1907 (hereafter, *NV*).
3. *Slovo*, Nov. 10, 1907.
4. Ibid., Nov. 3, 1907.
5. *NV*, Nov. 6, 1907.
6. *Gosudarstvennaia Duma. Stenograficheskie otchety. Sozyv III.* Sess. 1, vol. 1, col. 8 (hereafter, *GD*).
7. *NV*, Nov. 14, 1907.
8. *GD*, sess. 1, vol. 1, col. 158.
9. Ibid., col. 204.
10. Ibid., col. 137.
11. Ibid., cols. 138–39.
12. Ibid., col. 139.
13. Ibid., cols. 168–69.
14. Ibid., col. 241.
15. Ibid., cols. 237–38.
16. Ibid., cols. 245–46.
17. Ibid., col. 136.
18. Ibid., cols. 307–8.
19. Ibid., col. 349.
20. Ibid., cols. 308–9.
21. Ibid., col. 309.
22. Ibid., col. 314.
23. Ibid., col. 316.
24. Ibid., col. 312.
25. Ibid., cols. 424, 425.
26. Ibid., col. 426.
27. Ibid., cols. 427–28.
28. Ibid., col. 445.
29. Ibid., cols. 440–41.
30. *NV*, Nov. 23, 1907.
31. *Slovo*, Nov. 25, 1907.
32. *Slovo*, Nov. 18, 1907.
33. P. N. Miliukov, *Vospominaniia*, 2:19.
34. *Slovo*, Jan. 30, 1908.
35. Ibid., Feb. 25, 1908.
36. *GD*, sess. 1, vol. 1, col. 1843.
37. Ibid., vol. 2. col. 1995.
38. Ibid., cols. 2006–7.

39. Ibid., col. 2010.
40. *NV*, Apr. 27, 1908.
41. S. Ia. Elpat'evskii, *Vospominaniia*, p. 358.
42. Ibid., p. 359.
43. I. Gessen, "Vnutrennaia Zhizn," in *Ezhegodnik gazety* Rech', *na 1912 god*, pp. 26–27.
44. *GD*, sess. 1, vol. 2, col. 2411.
45. Ibid., col. 2412.
46. Ibid., 2414.
47. Ibid., cols. 2519–26.
48. *NV*, Apr. 30, 1908.
49. *GD*, sess. 1, vol. 2, col. 2429.
50. Ibid., col. 2430.
51. Ibid.
52. Ibid., col. 2673.
53. Ibid., col. 2672.
54. Ibid., cols. 2621–32.
55. *Slovo*, Apr. 30, 1908.
56. *GD*, sess. 1, vol. 2, col. 2663.
57. Ibid., col. 2734.
58. F. Dan and A. Cherevanin, "Soiuz 17 Oktiabria," *Obshchestvennoe dvizhenie v Rossii*, 2:192.
59. "Peaceful renovation."
60. *Russkoe Slovo*, Nov. 24, 1906, quoted by E. D. Chermenskii, *Burzhuaziia i tsarizm v revoliutsii 1905–1907 gg.*, p. 319.
61. S. M. Dubrovskii, *Stolypinskaia zemel'naia reforma.*
62. D. W. Treadgold, *The Great Siberian Migration*, p. 155 passim.
63. G. L. Yaney, "The Concept of the Stolypin Land Reform," *Slavic Review* 23:275–93.
64. Dubrovskii, *Stolypinskaia zemel'naia reforma*, pp. 121–25.
65. Ibid.
66. Guchkov quoted in V. I. Gurko, *Features and Figures in the Past*, p. 721.
67. *GD*, sess. 2, vol. 1, col. 145.
68. Ibid., cols. 148–98.
69. Ibid., col. 196.
70. Ibid., col. 171.
71. Ibid.
72. Ibid., cols. 416–22.
73. Ibid., cols. 801–10.
74. Ibid., cols. 880–85.
75. Ibid., col. 883.
76. Ibid., cols. 869–76.
77. Ibid., cols. 1051–62.
78. Ibid., col. 1056.
79. Ibid., cols. 1255–57.
80. L. Nemanov, "Itogi deiatel'nosti tret'ei Gosudarstvennoi Dumy," *Ezhegodnik gazety* Rech', *na 1912 god*, p. 112.
81. *GD*, sess. 2, vol. 1, cols. 1531–33.

82. Ibid., col. 1532.
83. Ibid., cols. 1309—10.
84. Ibid., col. 1539.
85. Ibid., cols. 1259—60.
86. Ibid., col. 1317.
87. *NV*, Nov. 17, 1908.

Chapter 4

1. A. I. Guchkov, "Iz vospominanii A. I. Guchkova," *Posledniia novosti*, no. 5626.
2. Ibid.
3. N. V. Savich, "Tri vstrechi," *Arkhiv Russkoi revoliutsi*, 10:619.
4. Polivanov's testimony in *Padenie tsar'skogo rezhima*, 7:58. Polivanov was deputy war minister.
5. V. A. Sukhomlinov, *Vospominaniia*, p. 178.
6. Ibid., p. 179.
7. Ibid., p. 235.
8. Guchkov, "Iz vospominanii A. I. Guchkova."
9. *Gosudarstvennaia Duma. Stenograficheskie otchety. Sozyv III.* Sess. 1, vol. 1, col. 641 (hereafter, *GD*).
10. L. Nemanov, "Itogi deiatel'nosti tret'ei Gosudarstvennoi Dumy," *Ezhegodnik gazety Rech'*, *na 1912 god*, p. 113.
11. Guchkov's testimony in *Padenie tsar'skogo rezhima*, 6:250.
12. Ibid., p. 251.
13. Ibid., p. 281.
14. *GD*, sess. 1, vol. 3, cols. 1578—1600.
15. Guchkov, *Padenie tsar'skogo rezhima*, 6:250.
16. A. A. Polivanov, *Iz dnevnikov i vospominanii po dolzhnosti voennogo ministra i ego pomoshchnika, 1907—1916*, p. 46.
17. *GD*, sess. 1, vol. 3, cols. 1578—1600.
18. Ibid., col. 1578.
19. Ibid., cols. 1582—83.
20. Ibid., col. 1589.
21. Ibid., col. 1593.
22. Ibid., col. 1597.
23. Ibid., col. 1599.
24. Ibid., col. 1600.
25. *Slovo*, May 29, 1908.
26. *Novoe vremia*, May 28, 1908 (hereafter, *NV*).
27. *GD*, sess. 1, vol. 3, col. 1632.
28. Ibid., cols. 1611—21.
29. Guchkov, *Padenie tsar'skogo rezhima*, 6:250.
30. Polivanov, *Iz dnevnikov i vospominanii* . . . , p. 38.
31. V. A. Sukhomlinov, *Vospominaniia*, pp. 224—25.
32. Savich, *Tri vstrechi*, pp. 169—71.
33. *GD*, sess. 1, vol. 3, cols. 1190—1202.
34. *NV*, May 13, 21, 1908.

35. *GD*, sess. 1, vol. 3, cols. 1211—12.
36. *NV*, May 20, 1908.
37. *GD*, sess. 1, vol. 3, cols. 1213—33.
38. Ibid., col. 1228.
39. Ibid., cols. 1341—43.
40. Ibid., cols. 1377—85.
41. Ibid., cols. 1392—97.
42. Ibid., col. 1392.
43. Ibid., col. 1396.
44. Ibid., cols. 1397—1408.
45. Ibid., col. 1400.
46. Ibid., cols. 1415—17.
47. P. N. Miliukov, *Vospominaniia*, 2:84.
48. Ibid., pp. 84—85.
49. *Golos Moskvy*, June 21, 1908, quoted by A. Ia. Avrekh, "Stolypinskii bonapartizm i voprosy voennoi politiki v III Dume," *Voprosy istorii* 11:27.
50. V. I. Gurko, *Features and Figures of the Past*, pp. 513—14.
51. S. E. Kryzhanovskii, *Vospominaniia*, pp. 154—57.
52. M. P. Bok, *Vospominaniia o moem ottse P. A. Stolypine*, p. 302.
53. S. Iu. Witte, *Vospominaniia*, 2:503.
54. Ibid., p. 505.
55. A. Ia. Avrekh, "III Duma i nachalo krizisa tret'eiiunskoi sistemy (1908—1909 gg.)," *Istoricheskie zapiski* 53:60 passim.
56. *GD*, sess. 2, vol. 4, col. 763.
57. Polivanov, *Iz dnevnikov i vospominanii*, p. 69.
58. "Perepiska N. A. Romanova i P. A. Stolypina," *Krasnyi arkhiv* 5:120.
59. Returning from abroad a year before the "Young Turk" revolution, Guchkov maintained that there had been a great similarity between the Octobrists and the Young Turks. When the latter overthrew Abdul Hamid in April 1909, Guchkov's comparison was used against the Union. See Avrekh, "III Duma," p. 62.
60. *GD*, sess. 2, vol. 1, col. 2674.
61. Ibid.
62. *GD*, sess. 2, vol. 3, cols. 959—89.
63. Ibid., cols. 992—1002.
64. Sukhomlinov, *Vospominaniia*, p. 175.
65. Polivanov, *Iz dnevnikov i vospominanii*, p. 61.
66. Ibid.
67. *GD*, sess. 2, vol. 3, cols. 1221—23.
68. Ibid., col. 1223.
69. Ibid., cols. 1237—41.
70. Ibid., cols. 1269—77.
71. *NV*, Apr. 7, 1909.
72. Ibid., Apr. 12, 1909.
73. Ibid., Apr. 18, 1909.
74. Polivanov, *Iz dnevnikov i vospominanii*, pp. 67—68.

Chapter 5

1. *Rech'*, Oct. 26, 1908, cited by A. Ia. Avrekh, "III Duma i nachalo krizisa tret'eiiunskoi sistemy," p. 94.
2. *Novoe vremia*, Oct. 22, 1908 (hereafter, *NV*).
3. Quoted by Avrekh, "III Duma," p. 94, from archival material.
4. *Gosudarstvennaia Duma. Stenograficheskie otchety. Sozyv III.* Sess. 2, vol. 1, col. 2813 (hereafter, *GD*).
5. *GD*, sess. 2, vol. 2, col. 23.
6. Ibid., col. 24.
7. Ibid., col. 1158.
8. Ibid., cols. 1961–71.
9. Ibid., col. 1969.
10. Ibid., col. 2151.
11. Ibid., col. 2156.
12. Ibid., cols. 2218–30.
13. Ibid., cols. 2225, 2229.
14. Ibid., col. 2369.
15. Ibid., col. 2399.
16. *NV*, Apr. 9, 1909.
17. Ibid., Mar. 7, May 1, 1909.
18. *GD*, sess. 2, vol. 2, cols. 2466–69.
19. *NV*, Mar. 11, 1909.
20. Ibid., May 19, 1909.
21. The Old Believers, a sect originating in the 17th century protests against liturgical reforms, had members among the important industrial and commercial entrepreneurs in the 19th century. Guchkov, although baptized a Greek Orthodox, was the descendant of an Old Believer family.
22. *GD*, sess. 2, vol. 3, cols. 2167–81.
23. *GD*, sess. 2, vol. 4, cols. 787–91.
24. Ibid., col. 796.
25. Ibid., cols. 1006–7.
26. Ibid., cols. 1010–23.
27. Ibid., cols. 1023–29.
28. Ibid., col. 1029.
29. Ibid., col. 1041.
30. Ibid., cols. 1379–86.
31. Ibid., col. 1741.
32. Ibid., col. 1749.
33. Ibid., cols. 1753–64.
34. Ibid., col. 1763.
35. Ibid., col. 1764.
36. Ibid., cols. 1777–80.
37. *GD*, sess. 2, vol. 4, cols. 1261–70.
38. *GD*, sess. 2, vol. 4, col. 1926.
39. *NV*, May 25, 1909.
40. P. N. Miliukov, *Vospominaniia*, 2:70.
41. *NV*, May 12, 1909.

42. Ibid., May 16, 1909.
43. Ibid., May 18, 1909.
44. Ibid., May 17, 1909.
45. Ibid., May 24, 1909.
46. GD, sess. 2, vol. 4, cols. 2216–17.
47. NV, June 3, 1909.
48. Ibid., Oct. 7, 1909.
49. Ibid., Oct. 9, 1909.
50. Ibid., Oct. 17, 1909.
51. Ibid., Feb. 2, 1910.
52. Ibid., Oct. 21, 1909.
53. GD, ₁sess.₁3, vol. 1, cols. 169–71.
54. NV, Oct. 31, 1909.
55. GD, sess. 3, vol. 1, cols. 954–58.
56. Ibid., cols. 1005–10.
57. Ibid., cols. 1389–90.
58. *Russkaia mysl'*, Aug. 1910, p. 172.
59. GD, sess. 3, vol. 1, cols. 1059–74.
60. Ibid., cols. 1196–1201.
61. Ibid., cols. 1674–86.
62. *Russkaia mysl'*, Aug. 1910, pp. 172–73.
63. NV, Jan. 26, 1910.
64. GD, sess. 3, vol. 1, cols. 1946–53.
65. Ibid., col. 2207.
66. NV, Dec. 4, 1909.
67. GD, sess. 3, vol. 2. cols. 58–59, 61–63.
68. Ibid., col. 2902.
69. Ibid., cols. 1758–76.
70. Ibid., col. 1763.
71. Ibid., col. 1764.
72. Ibid., col. 1974.
73. Ibid., col. 1970.
74. Ibid., col. 1971.
75. Ibid., col. 2376.
76. Ibid.
77. P. B. Struve, "Tekushchie voprosy vnutrennei zhizni," *Russkaia mysl'*, Apr. 1910, p. 167.
78. NV, Dec. 5, 1908.
79. GD, sess. 3, vol. 1, col. 2846.
80. NV, Jan. 26, 1910.
81. GD, sess. 3, vol. 2, col. 2566.
82. *Krasnyi arkhiv* 28:206.
83. NV, Mar. 7, 1910.
84. Ibid., Mar. 9, 1910.
85. Ibid., Jan. 28, 1909.
86. Ibid., Mar. 11, 1910.
87. L. Nemanov, "Evoliutsia partiinykh otnoshenii," *Russkaia mysl'*, Aug. 1910, p. 174.

Chapter 6

1. S. I. Shidlovskii, *Vospominaniia*, 1:217–18.
2. Guchkov's testimony in *Padenie tsar'skogo rezhima*, 6:293.
3. Ibid.
4. A. V. Zenkovskii, *Pravda o Stolypine*, p. 61.
5. A. A. Polivanov, *Iz dnevnikov i vospominanii po dolzhnosti voennogo ministra i ego pomoshchnika, 1907–1916*, p. 99.
6. Shidlovskii, *Vospominaniia*, 1:218.
7. *Gosudarstvennaia Duma. Stenograficheskie otchety. Sozyv III.* Sess. 3, vol. 2, cols. 449–52 (hereafter, *GD*).
8. Ibid., col. 451.
9. Ibid.
10. A. A. Kizevetter, *Na rubezhe dvukh stoletii*, p. 503.
11. *GD*, sess. 3, vol. 3, col. 1553.
12. Ibid., cols. 1525–41.
13. *Novoe vremia*, Mar. 20, 1910 (hereafter, *NV*).
14. *GD*, sess. 3, vol. 3, cols. 1965–73.
15. Ibid., col. 1971.
16. Ibid., cols. 2521–30.
17. Ibid., col. 2524.
18. Ibid., cols. 3129–48.
19. *GD*, sess. 3, vol. 4, cols. 683–97 (note: cols. 1–1285 of vol. 4 are included with vol. 3).
20. Ibid., cols. 689–90.
21. Ibid., cols. 695–96.
22. Ibid., cols. 705–6.
23. Ibid., col. 706.
24. V. Sukhomlinov, *Vospominaniia*, p. 221.
25. P. N. Miliukov, *Vospominaniia*, 2:72.
26. A. Ia. Avrekh, "Vopros o zapadnom zemstve i bankropstvo Stolypina," *Istoricheskie zapiski* 70:65–66.
27. *GD*, sess. 2, vol. 4, cols. 2750–57.
28. The White, or Belorussians, as well as the Little Russians, or Ukrainians, considered themselves as distinct ethnic entities and not simply Russians, the name usually used for the *Veliko* (Great) Russian.
29. Ibid., cols. 2757–61.
30. Ibid., col. 2761.
31. Avrekh, "Vopros o zapadnom zemstve," pp. 68–70.
32. E. Chmielewski, "Stolypin's Last Crisis," *California Slavic Studies* 3:100–102.
33. *NV*, Mar. 21, 1910.
34. *GD*, sess. 3. vol. 4, cols. 774–91.
35. Ibid., col. 776.
36. Ibid., col. 791.
37. Ibid., cols. 791–97.
38. Ibid., col. 918.
39. Ibid., col. 1223–24.
40. Ibid., col. 807.

41. *NV*, Mar. 29, 1910.
42. Ibid., Apr. 2, 1910.
43. *Golos Moskvy*, Apr. 15, 1910.
44. *Russkaia mysl'*, Aug. 1910, p. 175.
45. *GD*, sess. 3, vol. 4, cols. 1135–40; 1206–12; 1021–27.
46. Ibid., cols. 1229–30.
47. Ibid., col. 1230.
48. *NV*, May 12, 1910.
49. Ibid., May 14, 1910.
50. *GD*, sess. 3, vol. 4, cols. 1363–67.
51. Ibid., cols. 1393–96.
52. Ibid., col. 1395.
53. Ibid., col. 1407.
54. Ibid., col. 1456.
55. Ibid., col. 1486.
56. Ibid., col. 1488. In a letter to *Novoe vremia* on May 19, Rodzianko refuted Iskritskii's claim. Rodzianko contended that the actual vote in the Duma proved that the majority of the faction supported the government's version.
57. *NV*, May 19, 1910.
58. *GD*, sess. 3, vol. 4, col. 2763.
59. Ibid., col. 2829.
60. *Slovo*, Mar. 26, 1908.
61. *GD*, sess. 1, vol. 2, cols. 2919–41.
62. Ibid., col. 2920.
63. Ibid., col. 2941.
64. *NV*, Mar. 17, 1910.
65. Ibid., Apr. 29, 1910.
66. Ibid., Apr. 30, 1910.
67. *Golos Moskvy*, May 24, 1910.
68. *GD*, sess. 3, vol. 4, col. 1958.
69. Ibid., cols. 1928–53.
70. Ibid., cols. 1936–37.
71. Ibid., cols. 2025–42.
72. Ibid., col. 2035.
73. Ibid., cols. 2155–62.
74. Ibid., cols. 1997–2006.
75. Ibid., col. 2003.
76. Ibid., col. 2242.
77. Ibid., cols. 2312–28.
78. Ibid., col. 2328.
79. Miliukov, *Vospominaniia*, 2:75.

Chapter 7

1. *Gosudarstvennaia Duma. Stenograficheskie otchety. Sozyv III.* Sess. 4, vol. 1, cols. 1–2 (hereafter, *GD*).
2. *Novoe vremia*, Oct. 16, 1910, (hereafter, *NV*) .
3. Ibid., Nov. 9, 1910.

212   *Notes, Chapter 7*

4. A. A. Bobrinskii, "Dnevnik A. A. Bobrinskogo (1910–1911 gg.),"
Krasnyi arkhiv 26:137.

5. *NV*, Nov. 24, 1910.

6. *GD*, sess. 3, vol. 2, col. 2902.

7. Ibid.

8. Ibid., cols. 2902–9.

9. Ibid., col. 2913.

10. *GD*, sess. 4, vol. 1, cols. 6–11.

11. Ibid., col. 7.

12. Ibid., col. 8.

13. Ibid., cols. 16–44.

14. Ibid., cols. 473–93.

15. Ibid., col. 492.

16. Ibid., cols. 164–82.

17. Ibid., cols. 319–23.

18. Ibid., cols. 209–10.

19. Ibid., col. 211.

20. Ibid., the speeches of Timarev, cols. 324–26; Kliuzhev, cols. 420–36.

21. Ibid., cols. 704–14.

22. Purishkevich shouted from the floor: "Chkheidze [a Social Democrat] you may rejoice, he has joined your camp" (ibid., col. 711).

23. Ibid., cols. 712–13.

24. Ibid., cols. 846–48.

25. Ibid., cols. 1244–45.

26. *NV*, May 19; Dec. 5, 1910. Reports on the reconcilable positions of the Council's and Duma's representatives in the "conciliation committees."

27. L. Nemanov, "Itogi deiatel'nosti Tret'ei Gosudarstvennoi Dume," *Ezhegodnik gazety* Rech', *na 1912 god*, p. 110

28. *GD*, sess. 4, vol. 2, cols. 502–7.

29. Ibid., cols. 507–14.

30. Ibid., col. 563.

31. Ibid., col. 1785.

32. Ibid., cols. 1791–92.

33. Ibid., cols. 1794–95.

34. *NV*, Feb. 28, 1910.

35. *GD*, sess. 4, vol. 1, cols. 2499–2501.

36. "Perepiska N. A. Romanova i P. A. Stolypina," *Krasnyi arkhiv* 5:122.

37. *GD*, sess. 4, vol. 2, cols. 43–46.

38. Ibid., col. 277.

39. Ibid., col. 778.

40. Ibid., col. 2800.

41. Ibid., cols. 2942–63.

42. Ibid., col. 2945.

43. Ibid., col. 2947.

44. Ibid., col. 2950.

45. Ibid., col. 2962.

46. *NV*, Dec. 21, 1910.

Chapter 8

1. V. M. Gessen, "Vnutrenniaia zhizn," *Ezhegodnik gazety* Rech', *na 1912 god*, pp. 22–23.

2. Guchkov's testimony in *Padenie tsar'skogo rezhima*, 6:252.

3. I. Idin, "Trudy Gosudarstvennogo soveta," *Ezhegodnik gazety* Rech', *na 1912 god*, pp. 132–41.

4. Ibid., p. 142.

5. Ibid., pp. 142–43.

6. *Russkaia mysl'*, Jan. 1910, p. 190.

7. A. A. Bobrinskii, "Dnevnik A. A. Bobrinskogo (1910–1911 gg.)," *Krasnyi arkhiv* 26:141.

8. V. N. Kokovtsov, *Iz moego proshlago*, 1:451.

9. A. Ia. Avrekh, "Vopros o zapadnom zemstve i bankroptstvo Stoly-pina," *Istoricheskiie zapiski* 70:91–101.

10. S. Iu. Witte, *Vospominaniia*, 3:547.

11. Kokovtsov, *Iz moego proshlago*, 1:452–53.

12. Avrekh, "Vopros o zapadnom zemstve . . . ," pp. 110–12.

13. Kokovtsov, *Iz moego proshlago*, p. 453.

14. *Novoe vremia*, Mar. 8, 1911 (hereafter, *NV*).

15. Ibid., Mar. 12, 1911.

16. Ibid., Mar. 13, 1911.

17. Ibid.

18. A. I. Guchkov, "Iz vospominanii A. I. Guchkova," *Poslednie novosti,* no. 5637.

19. Ibid.

20. Ibid.

21. Bobrinskii, "Dnevnik A. A. Bobrinskogo . . . ," p. 147.

22. *NV*, Mar. 15, 1911.

23. Ibid.

24. Ibid.

25. *Gosudarstvennaia Duma. Stenograficheskie otchety. Sozyv III.* Sess. 4. vol. 3, cols. 719–20 (hereafter, *GD*).

26. Ibid., cols. 728–29.

27. Ibid., cols. 730–39.

28. Ibid., cols. 735–36.

29. Ibid., col. 738.

30. *NV*, Mar, 20, 1911.

31. Ibid., Mar. 19, 1911.

32. Ibid., Mar. 22, 1911.

33. Ibid., Mar. 23, 1911.

34. A. A. Polivanov, *Iz dnevnikov i vospominanii po dolzhnosti voennogo ministra i ego pomoshchnika, 1907–1916*, p. 104. A recorded conversation with Guchkov on Mar. 23, 1911.

35. *NV*, Mar. 27, 1911.

36. P. B. Struve, "Eshche odin 'krizis' na politicheskoi stsene," *Russkaia mysl'*, Apr. 1911, p. 164.

37. *GD*, sess. 4, vol. 3, cols. 2850–63.

38. Ibid., col. 1863.

39. Ibid., cols. 2864–68.

40. Ibid., col. 2866.

41. Ibid., cols. 3005–16.

42. Ibid., cols. 2867–68.

43. Ibid., col. 3025.

44. M. Ganfman, "Zakonodatelstvo," *Ezhegodnik gazety* Rech', *na 1912 god*, p. 56.

45. Shingarev's testimony in *Padenie tsar'skogo rezhima*, 7:8–9.

46. S. N. Harper, "The Budget Rights of the Russian Duma," *Journal of Political Economy* 16 (1908):152–56.

47. Shingarev's testimony, *Padenie tsar'skogo rezhima*, 7:11.

48. Ibid., p. 10.

49. Ibid., p. 20.

50. A. Shingarev, "Gosudarstvennaia Rospis' 1912 Goda," *Ezhegodnik gazety* Rech', *na 1912 god*, pp. 150–51.

51. *GD*, sess. 1, vol. 1, col. 637.

52. *GD*, sess. 1, vol. 1, cols. 1179–89.

53. Ibid., cols. 1189–90.

54. *NV*, Dec. 9, 1909.

55. *GD*, sess. 4, vol. 3, cols. 3962–69.

56. Ibid., col. 3964.

57. Ibid., col. 3966.

58. Ibid., col. 3969.

59. Ibid., cols. 3971–86.

60. Ibid., col. 3971.

61. Ibid., col. 3986.

62. Ibid., col. 3987.

63. Ibid., col. 3989.

64. Shingarev's testimony in *Padenie tsar'skogo rezhima*, 7:20.

65. *NV*, Apr. 6, 1911.

Chapter 9

1. A. Petrishcheva, "Khronika vnutrennoi zhizni," *Russkoe bogatstvo* (St. Petersburg, May 1912), pp. 55–84. The author proves how the attitudes and mood of progovernment papers like the *Kievlianin*, *Zemshchina*, *Grazhdanin*, *Golos Moskvy*, and *Novoe vremia* underwent a perceptible change when Kokovtsov became prime minister. These papers frequently expressed a deepening feeling of dissatisfaction and even disaffection.

2. Guchkov's testimony in *Padenie tsar'skogo rezhima*, 6:253.

3. Ibid.

4. Ibid.

5. V. N. Kokovtsov, *Iz moego proshlago*, 2:8. Kokovtsov maintained that this quote of the tsarina's words is exact.

6. Ibid., pp. 7–8.

7. M. V. Rodzianko, *Gosudarstvennaia Duma: Fevral'skaia 1917 goda revoliutsiia*, p. 12.

8. Kokovtsov, *Iz moego proshlago*, 2:102.

9. Ibid., p. 7.

10. S. D. Sazonov, *Vospominaniia*, p. 345.

11. Guchkov, "Iz vospominanii A. I. Guchkova," *Posledniia novosti*, no. 5640.

12. *Novoe vremia*, Sept. 7, 1911 (hereafter, *NV*).

13. See the review of the "loyal" press in *Vestnik Evropy*, Oct. 1911, pp. 359–61.

14. *NV*, Oct. 18, 1911.

15. *NV*, Sept. 15, 16, 1911. Reports on the meeting between Rodzianko and Shcheglovitov.

16. *Gosudarstvennaia Duma. Stenograficheskie otchety. Sozyv III.* Sess. 5, vol. 1, cols. 25–26 (hereafter, *GD*).

17. Ibid., cols. 31–33.

18. Ibid., cols. 2056–66.

19. Ibid., cols. 2064–65.

20. Ibid., col. 2065.

21. Ibid., col. 2066.

22. Ibid.

23. Ibid., col. 2068.

24. Ibid., col. 3005.

25. Ibid., col. 3008.

26. P. G. Kurlov, *Gibel' imperatorskoi Rossii*, pp. 132–33.

27. V. M. Gessen, "Vnutrenniaia zhizn," *Ezhegodnik gazety* Rech', *na 1912 god*, p. 25.

28. Kokovtsov, *Iz moego proshlago*, 2:12–13.

29. *GD*, sess. 5, vol. 1, col. 690.

30. Ibid., cols. 690–701.

31. Ibid., cols. 692–93.

32. Ibid., col. 694. Kokovtsov's speech was interrupted at this point by a standing applause from the Union, Nationalists, and the Right.

33. Ibid., cols. 694–95.

34. *NV*, Oct. 29, 1911 .

35. *GD*, sess. 5, vol. 1, col. 756.

36. Ibid., col. 757.

37. Ibid., col. 750.

38. Ibid., col. 756.

39. Ibid., cols. 814–18.

40. Ibid., col. 814.

41. Ibid., cols. 920–29.

42. Ibid., cols. 949–58.

43. Ibid., col. 1065.

44. *NV*, Oct. 31, 1911.

45. Ibid., Dec. 9–13, 1911.

46. Guchkov, "Iz vospominanii A. I. Guchkova," no. 5623.

47. *GD*, sess. 4, vol. 2, cols. 1593–1607.

48. *GD*, sess. 4, vol. 3, col. 3112.
49. Ibid., col. 3127.
50. *GD*, sess. 5, vol. 1, col. 25.
51. Ibid., col. 59.
52. A. Ia. Avrekh, *Stolypin i tret'ia Duma*, pp. 108–24.
53. *GD*, sess. 5, vol. 1, cols. 2608–20.
54. *GD*, sess. 5, vol. 2, cols. 136–43.
55. Ibid., cols. 717–19.
56. Ibid., col. 719.
57. *NV*, Feb. 16, 1912.
58. *GD*, sess. 5, vol. 2, col. 2187.
59. *NV*, Feb. 16, 1912.
60. *GD*, sess. 5, vol. 3, cols. 3366–68.

Chapter 10

1. *Gosudarstvennaia Duma. Stenograficheskie otchety. Sozyv III.*
Sess. 5, vol. 1, cols. 125–26 (hereafter, *GD*).
2. Ibid., col. 136.
3. Ibid., cols. 136–37.
4. Ibid., col. 155.
5. Ibid., col. 2096.
6. Ibid., cols. 2100–2102.
7. Ibid., col. 2111.
8. *GD*, sess. 5, vol. 2, cols. 1743–44.
9. I. Idin, "Trudy Gosudarstvennogo Soveta," *Ezhegodnik gazety
Rech', na 1912 god*, pp. 131–33.
10. *Novoe vremia*, Dec. 4, 1911 (hereafter, *NV*).
11. Ibid., Nov. 15, 1911.
12. Ibid., May 21, 1912.
13. *GD*, sess. 5, vol. 3, cols. 911–22.
14. Ibid., col. 1401.
15. Ibid., col. 1413.
16. *NV*, Apr. 5–8, 1912.
17. V. N. Kokovtsov, *Iz moego proshlago*, 2:57.
18. *Russkoe bogatstvo*, May 1912, pp. 65–69.
19. Ibid., p. 67.
20. *NV*, Apr. 7, 1912.
21. *GD*, sess. 5, vol. 3, cols. 1664–65.
22. Ibid., cols. 1674–75.
23. Kokovtsov, *Iz moego proshlago*, 2:58.
24. *GD*, sess. 5, vol. 3, cols. 1953–63.
25. Ibid., cols. 1941–53.
26. Ibid., col. 1953.
27. *NV*, Apr. 14, 1912.
28. *GD*, sess. 5, vol. 3, cols. 3323–26.
29. Ibid., col. 3326.
30. Kokovtsov, *Iz moego proshlago*, 2:21.
31. M. Kilcoyne, in his Ph.D. dissertation. "The Political Influ-

ence of Rasputin," University of Washington, Seattle, 1961, strongly suggests that Rasputin's actual political influence was small.

32. P. G. Kurlov, *Gibel' imperatorskoi Rossii*, pp. 146–47.
33. M. P. Bok, *Vospominaniia o moem ottse P. A. Stolypine*, p. 331.
34. Kokovtsov, *Iz moego proshlago*, pp. 20–26.
35. *GD*, sess. 5, vol. 2, col. 1015.
36. A. I. Guchkov, "Iz vospominanii A. I. Guchkova," *Posledniia novosti*, no. 5640.
37. M. V. Rodzianko, *Krushenie imperii*, p. 38.
38. *GD*, sess. 5, vol. 2, cols. 1013–14.
39. Ibid., col. 1015.
40. Ibid., col. 1016.
41. Rodzianko, *Krushenie imperii*, p. 40.
42. Kokovtsov, *Iz moego proshlago*, 2:32–33.
43. Rodzianko, *Krushenie imperii*, pp. 46–48.
44. *GD*, sess. 5, vol. 3, cols. 582–85.
45. Ibid., col. 583.
46. Ibid., col. 585.
47. Ibid., col. 876.
48. Rodzianko, *Krushenie imperii*, p. 52.
49. Kokovtsov, *Iz moego proshlago*, 2:50.
50. Ibid., pp. 50–51.
51. Sukhomlinov, *Vospominaniia*, pp. 175–79; 222–23.
52. Ibid., p. 223.
53. Guchkov, "Iz vospominanii A. I. Guchkova," no. 5633; Guchkov's testimony in *Padenie tsar'skogo rezhima*, 6:291.
54. A. A. Polivanov, *Iz dnevnikov i vospominanii po dolzhnosti voennogo ministra i ego pomoshchnika, 1907–1916*, pp. 110–12.
55. Guchkov, "Iz vospominanii A. I. Guchkova," no. 5630.
56. *NV*, Apr. 17–23, 1912.
57. Kokovtsov, *Iz moego proshlago*, 2:59–60.
58. *NV*, Apr. 29, 1912. Interviews with Protopopov and Krupenskii.
59. *GD*, sess. 5, vol. 4, cols. 722–36.
60. Ibid., col. 735.
61. Ibid., col. 758.
62. Ibid., col. 736.
63. Ibid., cols. 762–63.
64. Kokovtsov, *Iz moego proshlago*, pp. 52–53.
65. Ibid., pp. 63, 71.
66. *NV*, May 27, 1912.
67. *GD*, sess. 5, vol. 4, cols. 3773–77.
68. *NV*, June 9, 1912.
69. Ibid., June 14, 1912.

Conclusion

1. The existence of an open forum using interpellation to voice popular criticism certainly had a restraining influence on the regime and an important impact on public opinion. Through the opposition, important

segments of Russian society were able to voice their discontent and aspirations. Many issues raised in the Duma were followed with great interest by the masses, thus slowly establishing the Duma as a means to improve their lot.

2. *Gosudarstvennaia Duma. Stenograficheskie otchety. Sozyv III.* Sess. 5, vol. 4, col. 624.

3. P. B. Struve, "Esche odin 'krizis' na politicheskoi stsene," *Russkaia mysl'*, Apr. 1911, p. 164.

Bibliography

Avrekh, A. Ia. *Stolypin i tret'ia Duma*. Moscow, 1968.
———. "Stolypinskii bonapartizm i voprosy voennoi politiki v III Dume." *Voprosy istorii*, vol. 11.
———. "III Duma i nachalo krizisa tret'eiiunskoi sistemy (1908–1909 gg.)." *Istoricheskie zapiski*, vol. 53.
———. *Tsarizm i tret'eiiunskaia sistema*. Moscow, 1966.
———. "Vopros o zapadnom zemstve i bankropstvo Stolypina." *Istoricheskie zapiski* 70 (1961):61–112.
Bakhirev, A. V. *Tret'ia Gosudarstvennaia Duma v kartogrammakh*. St. Petersburg, 1907.
Belonkonskii, I. P. *Zemskoe dvizhenie*. 2d ed. Moscow, 1914.
Bobrinskii, A. A. "Dnevnik A. A. Bobrinskogo (1910–1911 g.g.)." *Krasnyi arkhiv* 26 (1928):127–50.
Bok, M. P. *Vospominaniia o moem ottse P. A. Stolypine*. New York: Chekhov Publishing, 1953.
Budberg, R. Iv. "S'ezd zemskikh deiatelei 6–9 Noiabra 1904 g. v Peterburge." *Byloe*, March, 1907.
Buryshkin, P. A. *Moskva kupecheskaia*. New York: Chekhov Publishing, 1954.
Chermenskii, E. D. *Burzhuaziia i tsarizm v revoliutsii 1905–1907 gg*. Moscow, 1939.
Chistiakov, P. A. *Rechi oktiabrista 1905–7*. St. Petersburg, 1908.
Chmielewski, E. "Stolypin's Last Crisis." *California Slavic Studies* 3 (1964):95–126.
Chto sdelala Tret'ia Gosudarstvennaia Duma dlia gorodov. St. Petersburg, 1912.

Curtiss, J. S. *Church and State in Russia: The Last Years of the Empire, 1900–1917.* 1940. New York: Octagon Books, 1965.

Dan, F. "Ocherk politicheskoi evoliutsii burzhuaznykh elementov gorodskogo naseleniia." In *Obshchestvennoe dvizhenie v Rossii,* vol. 1, pt. 2.

Dan, F. and Cherevanin, A. "Soiuz 17 Oktiabria." In *Obshchestvennoe dvizhenie v Rossii,* vol. 2, pt. 2.

Dashkevich, L. *Agrarnyi perevorot.* Moscow, 1909.

Dolgorukov, P. "Pamiati gr. P. A. Geidena." *Byloe,* August, 1907.

———. *Avtobiografiia.* Sofia, 1921.

Dubrovskii, S. M. *Stolypinskaia zemel'naia reforma.* Moscow: Institute of History of the Academy of Sciences, 1963.

Elpatevskii, S. Ia. *Vospominaniia.* N.p., 1929.

Ermanskii, O. A. "Krupnaia burzhuaziia do 1905 goda." In *Obshchestvennoe dvizhenie v Rossii,* vol. 2, pt. 2.

Eropkin, A. *Chto delala i chto sdelala III Gosudarstvennaia Duma.* St. Petersburg, 1912.

Ezhegodnik gazety Rech', *na 1912 god.* St. Petersburg, 1912.

Fischer, George. *Russian Liberalism: From Gentry to Intelligentsia.* Cambridge, Mass.: Harvard University Press, 1958.

Gerschenkron, Alexander. *Economic Backwardness in Historical Perspective.* Cambridge, Mass.: Harvard University Press, 1962.

Gessen, V. M. *Na rubezhe, 1901–1905.* St. Petersburg, 1906.

Golos Moskvy. Moscow, 1907–12.

Gosudarstvennaia Duma. Prilozhenie k stenograficheskim otchetam. Tret'ii Sozyv. St. Petersburg, 1908–12.

———. *Stenograficheskie otchety. Tret'ii Sozyv.* St. Petersburg, 1908–12.

———. *Ukazatel' k stenograficheskim otchetam. Tret'ii Sozyv.* St. Petersburg, 1908–12.

Guchkov, A. I. "Iz vospominanii A. I. Guchkova." *Posledniia novosti* (Paris), nos. 5616–68, Aug. 9–Sept. 30, 1936.

———. *Rechi po voprosam gosudarstvennoi oborony i ob obshchei politike, 1908–1917.* Petrograd, 1917.

Gurko, V. I. *Features and Figures of the Past: Government and Opinion in the Reign of Nicholas II.* Edited by J. E. Wallace Sterling, Xenia Joukoff Eudin, H. H. Fisher; translated by Laura Matveev. Stanford: Stanford University Press, 1939.

Harcave, Sidney. *First Blood: The Russian Revolution of 1905.* New York: The Macmillan Co., 1964.

Harper, S. N. "The Budget Rights of the Russian Duma." *Journal of Political Economy* 16 (1908):152–56.

Hosking, Geoffrey A. *The Russian Constitutional Experiment: Government and Duma 1907–1914.* Cambridge: Cambridge University Press, 1973.

Kilcoyne, M. "The Political Influence of Rasputin." Ph.D. dissertation, University of Washington, Seattle, 1961.

Kizevetter, A. A. *Na rubezhe dvukh stoletii.* Prague, 1929.

Kliachko [L'vov], L. *Povesti proshlago.* Leningrad, 1929.

Kokovtsov, V. N. *Iz moego proshlago.* 2 vols. Paris, 1933.

Kryzhanovskii, S. E. *Vospominaniia.* Petropolis, n.d.

Kuchinskii, I. *Proekt vydeleniia kholmshchiny.* St. Petersburg, 1911.

Kurlov, P. G. *Gibel' imperatorskoi Rossii.* Berlin, 1923.

Laski, H. J. *The Rise of European Liberalism.* London: Allen, 1936.

Leontovitsch, V. *Geschichte des Liberalismus in Russland.* Frankfurt am Main: Vittorio Klostermann, 1957.

Levin, A. *The Second Duma: A Study of the Social-Democratic Party and the Russian Constitutional Experiment.* New Haven: Yale University Press, 1940.

―――. "The Russian Voter in the Elections to the Third Duma." *Slavic Review* 21 (1962):660–77.

Levitsky, S. L. "Legislative Initiative in the Russian Duma." *American Slavic and East European Review* 15 (1956):313–24.

Maevskii, V. L. *Borets za blago Rossii.* Madrid: Izd. Pochitatelei gosudarstvennoi deiatel'nosti P. A. Stolypina, 1962.

Maklakov, V. A. *Vlast' i obshchestvennost' na zakate staroi Rossii.* 1936. Paris, 1938.

―――. *Iz vospominanii.* New York: Chekhov Publishing, 1954.

―――. *The First State Duma.* Bloomington: Indiana University Press, 1964.

Materialy k voprosu ob obrazovanii kholmskoi gubernii. Warsaw, 1908–11.

Menashe, L. "Alexander Guchkov and the Origins of the Octobrist Party: The Russian Bourgeoisie in Politics, 1905." Ph.D. dissertation. New York University, 1966.

Miliukov, P. N. *God bor'by. Publitsisticheskaia khronika 1905–1906.* St. Petersburg, 1907.

―――. *Tri popytki.* Paris: Franko-russkaia Pechat, 1921.

Miliukov, P. N. *Russia and its Crisis.* 1905. New York: Collier Paperback, 1962.

———. *Vospominaniia (1859–1917).* 2 vols. New York: Chekhov Publishing, 1955.

Novoe vremia. St. Petersburg, 1907–12.

Obolenskoi, A. V. *Moi vospominaniia i razmyshleniia.* Stockholm: Podnye Perozvomy, 1961.

Obshchestvennoe dvizhenie v Rossii v nachale XX-go veka. Edited by L. Martov, P. Maslov, A. Potresov. 4 vols. in 6. St. Petersburg, 1909–14.

Obzor deiatel'nosti Gosudarstvennoi Dumy Tret'iago Sozyva, 1907–1912. St. Petersburg, 1912.

Padenie tsar'skogo rezhima. 7 vols. Moscow-Leningrad, 1924–27.

Pares, Bernard. *My Russian Memoirs.* 1931. London: J. Cape, 1935.

———. *The Fall of the Russian Monarchy: A Study of the Evidence.* 1939. New York: Vintage ed., 1961.

———. "Alexander Guchkov." *Slavonic and East European Review* 15 (July 1936):121–34.

Partiia mirnogo obnovleniia. St. Petersburg, 1907.

"Perepiska N. A. Romanova i P. A. Stolypina." *Krasnyi arkhiv,* vol. 5.

Petrunkevich, I. I. "Iz zapisok obshchestvennago deiatelia." *Archiv Russkoi revoliutsii* 21 (Berlin, 1934):336–37.

Plevako, F. N. *Rechi.* 2 vols. Moscow, 1912.

Polivanov, A. A. *Iz dnevnikov i vospominanii po dolzhnosti voennogo ministra i ego pomoshchnika 1907–1916.* Moscow, 1924.

Polnoe sobranie zakanov Rossiiskoi imperii. St. Petersburg, 1885–1916.

Rabota III Gosudarstvennoi Dumy po voprosam sudebno-pravovym. St. Petersburg, 1912.

Raeff, M. "Some Reflections on Russian Liberalism." *Russian Review* 18, no. 3 (1959):218–30.

Rodzianko, M. V. *Gosudarstvennaia Duma: Fevral'skaia 1917 goda revoliutsiia. Archiv Russkoi revoliutsii,* vol. 6. (Berlin, 1922).

———. *Krushenie imperii. Archiv Russkoi revoliutsii,* vol. 17. (Berlin, 1926).

Ruggiero, G. de. *The History of European Liberalism.* London: Oxford University Press, H. Milford, 1927.

Russkaia mysl'. Moscow, 1907–12.

Russkoe bogatstvo, St. Petersburg, 1907–12.

Savich, N. "Tri vstrechi." *Arkhiv Russkoi revoliutsii,* vol. 10 (1923).

Sazonov, S. D. *Vospominaniia,* Paris: Kn-vo E. Siialskoi, 1927.

Sbornik kluba Russkikh natsionalistov. Kiev, 1913.

Schaeffer, M. A. "The Political Policies of P. A. Stolypin." Ph.D. dissertation. University of Indiana, Bloomington, 1968.

Schapiro, J. S. *Liberalism, Its Meaning and History.* Princeton, N. J.: Van Nostrand, 1958.

Sef, S. E. *Burzhuaziia v 1905 godu.* Moscow and Leningrad: State Publishers, 1926.

Shakhovskoi, V. N. *Sic Transit Gloria Mundi (Tak prokhodit mirskaia slava), 1893–1917.* Paris, 1952.

Shidlovskii, S. I. *Vospominaniia.* 2 vols. Berlin: O. Kirchner, 1923.

Shipov, D. N. *Vospominaniia i dumy o perezhitom.* Moscow: Sabashnikovs, 1918.

Shulgin, V. V. *Dni.* Belgrade, 1925.

Sidel'nikov, S. M. *Obrazovanie i deiatel'nost' pervoi gosudarstvennoi Dumy.* Moscow: Izd-vo Moskovskogo universiteta, 1962.

Slovo. St. Petersburg, 1907–12.

Smith, C. J. "The Russian Third State Duma: An Analytical Profile." *Russian Review* 17 (July 1958):201–10.

"Soiuz 17 Oktiabria v 1906 g." *Krasnyi arkhiv,* vols. 35, 36.

Sukhomlinov, V. A. *Vospominaniia.* Berlin: Russkoe universalnoe izd-vo, 1924.

Szeftel, Marc. "The Form of Government of the Russian Empire Prior to the Constitutional Reforms of 1905–1906." In *Essays in Russian and Soviet History in Honor of Geroid T. Robinson,* pp. 105–19. Edited by J. S. Curtiss. New York: Columbia University Press, 1963.

Tagantsev, N. S. *Perezhitoe: Uchrezdenie Gosudarstvennoi Dumy v 1905–1906.* Petrograd, 1919.

Treadgold, D. W. *Lenin and His Rivals: The Struggle for Russia's Future, 1898–1906.* New York: Frederick A. Praeger, 1955.

——. *The Great Siberian Migration.* Princeton: Princeton University Press, 1957.

Trubetskoi, E. N. *Vospominaniia.* Sofia: Rossiisko-bolgar skoe knigoizdatelstvo, 1921.

"Tsarskosel'skiia soveshchannia (protokoly)." *Byloe,* August, 1917.

Tyrkova-Williams, Ariadna. *Na putiakh k svobode.* New York: Chekhov Publishing, 1952.

Vasilevskii, E. G. *Ideinaia bor'ba vokrug Stolypinskoi agrarnoi reformy.* Moscow, 1960.

Veselovskii, Boris. "Dvizhenie zemledeltsev." *Obshchestvennoe dvizhenie v Rossii,* vol. 1, pt. 2.

Vestnik Evropy. St. Petersburg, 1907–12.

Vodovozov, V. V., ed. *Sbornik program politicheskikh partii v Rossii.* St. Petersburg, 1906. .

Von Laue, Theodore H. "Count Witte and the Russian Revolution of 1905." *American Slavic and East European Review* 17 (1958):25–46.

Walsh, W. B. "Political Parties in the Russian Dumas." *The Journal of Modern History* 22(1950):144–50.

Witte, S. Iu. *Vospominaniia.* Edited by A. L. Sidorov. 3 vols. Moscow: Izd-vo sotsialno-ekonomicheskoi literatury, 1960.

Yaney, G. L. "The Concept of the Stolypin Land Reform." *Slavic Review* 23 (1964):275–93.

Zen'kovskii, A. V. *Pravda o Stolypine.* New York: Pan-Slav, 1956.

Index

Institute for Comparative and Foreign Area Studies Publications on Russia and Eastern Europe

1. Sugar, Peter F., and Ivo J. Lederer, eds. *Nationalism in Eastern Europe.* 1969. 478 pp., index.

2. Jackson, W. A. Douglas, ed. *Agrarian Policies and Problems in Communist and Non-Communist Countries.* 1971. 485 pp., maps, figures, tables, index.

3. Muller, Alexander V., trans. and ed. *The* Spiritual Regulation *of Peter the Great.* 1972. 150 pp., index.

4. Pinchuk, Ben-Cion. *The Octobrists in the Third Duma, 1907–1912.* 232 pp., index.

Institute for Comparative and Foreign Area Studies Publications on Russia and Eastern Europe was formerly Far Eastern and Russian Institute Publications on Russia and Eastern Europe.